Social Humanism

Routledge Studies in Ethics and Moral Theory

1 **The Contradictions of Modern Moral Philosophy**
Ethics after Wittgenstein
Paul Johnston

2 **Kant, Duty and Moral Worth**
Philip Stratton-Lake

3 **Justifying Emotions**
Pride and Jealousy
Kristján Kristjánsson

4 **Classical Utilitarianism from Hume to Mill**
Frederick Rosen

5 **The Self, the Soul and the Psychology of Good and Evil**
Ilham Dilman

6 **Moral Responsibility**
The Ways of Scepticism
Carlos J. Moya

7 **The Ethics of Confucius and Aristotle**
Mirrors of Virtue
Jiyuan Yu

8 **Caste Wars**
A Philosophy of Discrimination
David Edmonds

9 **Deprivation and Freedom**
A Philosophical Enquiry
Richard J. Hull

10 **Needs and Moral Necessity**
Soran Reader

11 **Reasons, Patterns, and Cooperation**
Christopher Woodard

12 **Challenging Moral Particularism**
Edited by Mark Norris Lance, Matjaž Potrč, and Vojko Strahovnik

13 **Rationality and Moral Theory**
How Intimacy Generates Reasons
Diane Jeske

14 **The Ethics of Forgiveness**
A Collection of Essays
Christel Fricke

15 **Moral Exemplars in the Analects**
The Good Person is That
Amy Olberding

16 **The Phenomenology of Moral Normativity**
William H. Smith

17 **The Second-Person Perspective in Aquinas's Ethics**
Virtues and Gifts
Andrew Pinsent

18 **Social Humanism**
A New Metaphysics
Brian Ellis

Social Humanism
A New Metaphysics

Brian Ellis

NEW YORK   LONDON

First published 2012
by Routledge
711 Third Avenue, New York, NY 10017

Simultaneously published in the UK
by Routledge
2 Park Square, Milton Park, Abingdon, Oxfordshire OX14 4RN

First issued in paperback 2014

*Routledge is an imprint of the Taylor and Francis Group,
an informa business*

© 2012 Taylor & Francis

The right of Brian Ellis to be identified as author of this work has been
asserted by him in accordance with sections 77 and 78 of the Copyright,
Designs and Patents Act 1988.

All rights reserved. No part of this book may be reprinted or reproduced or
utilised in any form or by any electronic, mechanical, or other means, now
known or hereafter invented, including photocopying and recording, or in
any information storage or retrieval system, without permission in writing
from the publishers.

Trademark Notice: Product or corporate names may be trademarks or
registered trademarks, and are used only for identification and explanation
without intent to infringe.

Library of Congress Cataloging-in-Publication Data
Social humanism : a new metaphysics / Brian Ellis.
    p. cm. — (Routledge studies in ethics and moral theory ; 18)
  Includes bibliographical references and index.
 1. Humanism.   2. Social service.   3. Public welfare.
4. Idealism.   I. Title.
  B821.E45 2012
  144—dc23
  2011052861

ISBN 978-0-415-53561-8 (hbk)
ISBN 978-1-138-92222-8 (pbk)
ISBN 978-0-203-11098-0 (ebk)

Typeset in Sabon
by IBT Global.

To Tony Judt
whose impassioned plea for a new way of understanding society, and the moral and political philosophy that must inform it, demands a considered response.

Contents

Preface	ix
Introduction	1

PART I
Social Humanism

	Introduction to Social Humanism	15
1	The Ideals of Social Humanism	21
2	The Humanistic Theory of Social Equality	39

PART II
Causal Realism

	Introduction to Causal Realism	61
3	The Metaphysics of Causal Realism	63

PART III
Social Idealism

	Introduction to Social Idealism	95
4	The Social Theory of Morality	101
5	Individualism	127

viii *Contents*

6   Theory and Method   152

PART IV
Global Humanism

Introduction to Global Humanism   177

7   A Global Social Contract   179

Conclusion   201

Notes   209
References   217
Index   221

Preface

In 2005, I wrote a draft of the present book, in which I argued that the foundation for the theory of the welfare state must be a kind of social humanism. But I was not then able to develop the theory of social humanism to my own satisfaction. It needed to be a theory that could reasonably be seen as a rival to the classical theories of socialism and neo-liberalism—not as a compromise between them. But the task proved to be much more difficult than I had imagined, and I have been struggling with these issues ever since.

To complete this task to my own satisfaction, I have had to go back to basics and develop a new metaphysics of moral and political theory, which I call social idealism. This new metaphysics changes nearly everything. Most importantly, the concept of a social agent that is required for the theory is not one that is restricted only to individuals. All individuals and organisations that are capable of making and implementing decisions are social agents of one kind or another. The normal class, viz. that of socially responsible people in a given society, is just one class of social agents among many. Hence, the new metaphysics of morals grounds a much broader range of moral imperatives. It includes not only the moral imperatives of normal individuals. It also includes the moral imperatives of governments, industrial corporations, universities, media and internet companies, police forces, churches, and all of the other really important social agents in our society. Consequently, the scope of moral theory is enormously increased, and we are now able to deal adequately with a much wider range of social moral issues within the same moral framework. We are, for example, able to discuss rationally which political philosophies go with which moral ones and which are in conflict with one another. I will argue that in fact there are no defensible moral theories that have the same moral foundations as either capitalism or communism. Indeed, the only political philosophy of which I am aware that has the same moral foundations as a decent moral philosophy is social humanism, which is the philosophical grounding for a welfare state of some kind. And this, I will argue, is why the welfare state is a productive and highly successful political system.

x *Preface*

The new metaphysical foundation for morals also requires a distinction between two kinds of moral principles, primitive ones that are well justifiable, independently of the nature of the society in which one lives, and social ones that may well turn out to be culturally relative. It is therefore possible to make a principled distinction between kinds of moral principles that will enable a limited form of cultural relativism to be defended. And this fact is very important if we are serious about trying to develop a globally acceptable social contract. The new theory also requires changes to both the methodology and epistemology of morals. Traditionally, morals have been thought to be discoverable *a priori*, i.e. just by thinking carefully about various possible situations and listening to your conscience to determine what is morally right or wrong. Accordingly, the normal methodology of moral inquiry is said to be that of reflection, or of Socratic dialogue, in which moral propositions are proposed and tested in discussion. But one cannot determine the moral responsibilities of corporations or governments in this manner. Nor can this methodology be expected to cope with cross-cultural disagreements about morals. What is required is a far more pragmatic approach. In practice, the social moral principles we now accept depend mainly on what social decisions were actually made in the past, what we now feel comfortable with, and what we would like to see preserved in future. That is, morality must be seen as being an evolving system—evolving as societies shift their policies to adapt to environmental or technological changes.

Obviously, the theory to be presented here is not a discussion of contemporary moral or political issues, or even a continuation of the conversations on ethics, politics, or morality that have occurred in the philosophical journals. Nor is the welfare state, or welfarism, seriously discussed. When I speak of the welfare state, the social systems that I have in mind are just those of Sweden, Norway, Finland, Denmark, and the Netherlands, which, as Tony Judt argues, are certainly among the most successful states, socially and economically, that have ever existed. Social idealism, which is the underlying metaphysics of morals and politics, is a new theory that is capable of replacing the original Kantian one, and four of the seven chapters of this book are taken up with its development. I did not write this book as an answer to Judt's (2010) impassioned plea for someone to provide a coherent metaphysics of social policy. But I hope that this book is relevant to the task of answering it.

I wish to thank La Trobe University for a grant for research assistance; William Hebblewhite and Vincent Galante for the excellent assistance they provided; Richard Ashcroft, Elaine Miller, Graham Nerlich, Robert Young, and Greg Bailey, who read drafts of this book and made many helpful comments and suggestions for improvements; Norva Lo, whose critiques of papers by Christine Korsgaard and Michael Smith initially stimulated my interest in the principles of humanism; Behan McCullagh for his encouragement to pursue this project; staff members of the Philosophy Program at

La Trobe University, who pointed out some of my more serious errors; and members of the Humanist Society of Victoria and of the Eltham philosophy group, especially Chris Peters and Lyn Hatherly, for their stimulating discussions. Finally, I wish to thank Jenny, who has put up with me spending far too much time in my study and helped me time and again with her insightful and commonsense approach to social issues.

Brian Ellis
*Professor Emeritus of La Trobe
University, and Professorial Fellow,
Department of Philosophy,
University of Melbourne*
November 2011

Introduction

Social humanism is both a moral and a political philosophy. As a political philosophy, it requires the establishment and development of a kind of welfare state, and it proposes a framework for a series of agreements between states on global social and moral issues. As a moral philosophy, it provides a theory for the development of charters of human rights, which could reasonably be expected, over time, to command something approaching universal assent. To develop this moral and political theory, it has been necessary to revisit some basic questions concerning the metaphysics of morals, and to construct a new basic theory. This new theory is one of social idealism, which is like Kant's rational idealism in some ways, but it is metaphysically realistic and based on the social ideals of ordinary, rather than perfectly rational, individuals. It is argued that there are two sorts of social ideals relevant to moral and political philosophy, ideals of character and ideals of society, corresponding roughly to the distinction between morals and politics. But the two are not really distinct, and it is a serious mistake to try to develop either one without an adequate theory of the other. An ideal society needs good people who are motivated and able to service and develop its institutions, and good people need a good society in which to live and work—one that will encourage them to express their natural virtues and to develop their natural talents for the good of all.

Tony Judt's book, *Ill Fares the Land*, is one of the more important books of our time. It describes the attack on the welfare state that began in earnest with the elections of Ronald Reagan and Margaret Thatcher and spread rapidly around the world. What surprised him was how quickly support for the welfare state collapsed under this attack, even though it had been enormously successful, both economically and socially. Also, it remains very successful to this day in the countries of Scandinavia and northern Europe for reasons yet to be fully explained. Judt traces the causes of this sudden collapse back to the fear of socialism in all of its forms, the individualist philosophers of the Austrian School (Von Mises, Popper, and Hayek), who laid the philosophical foundations for modern capitalism; the monetarist economic philosophy of the Chicago School, which developed its economic basis; and the rampant anti-authoritarianism of the cultural revolution of

2 *Social Humanism*

the 1960s. The left wings of politics in the 1940s were all strongly anti-capitalist, particularly so following the catastrophic event of the Great Depression. But it was harder to identify what the 'left wing' was really in favour of after the war. The welfare state had never been championed by the left and was in fact the product of social liberalism in the UK,[1] and of social distress elsewhere. Thus, it appears to be just the force of moral persuasion that created the welfare states in Australia, New Zealand, Canada, and the Scandinavian countries. But social liberalism was never a clearly articulated doctrine, and moral persuasion could only be a powerful social force in (a) a capitalist world in which there were great and prevalent social injustices within the jurisdictions of nation states, or (b) a world (such as that exemplified by the countries of Scandinavia), in which morality was not considered to be just a matter for individual conscience.

By the 1970s, the widespread suffering that led to the creation of welfare states was no longer so evident, and was either unknown, or had been forgotten, almost everywhere except in the Lutheran states of northern Europe.[2] Moreover, there was no general theory to justify the welfare state, and it was very widely regarded as just a wishy-washy mixture of capitalism and socialism. Defenders of the welfare state were spoken of as 'pinkos' or 'wets' and thought of as people whose views on social theory were hardly worth considering. It is no wonder, then, that the welfare state was left undefended, when the neo-liberal onslaught on it began. Its defenders, such as they were, had no ideology to fall back on. Mostly, they too thought of it as a compromise, and that the only real choices, ultimately, were between *laissez faire* capitalism and socialism, more or less as these concepts had been understood originally by Karl Marx. 'Given that we already had a welfare state, which was half way there', most members of the left would have said, 'there would be no need for a communist revolution'. Most of the defenders of the welfare state simply thought that one could be a democratic socialist and just take the state in the direction of socialism—a bit at a time.

But I am convinced, and so is Tony Judt, that the welfare state has much more to be said for it than this. It is a very successful political philosophy, overwhelmingly so in many ways, and the evidence of northern Europe is that it would be fundamentally stable in any society in which people are encouraged to develop and maintain a social humanist conscience. It is the so-called 'pure' positions that are essentially unstable. And these positions are unstable, I shall argue, because they are either grossly immoral or totally unrealistic. Laissez faire capitalism would be stable only if social morality were independent of the nature of the society (as it would be, if morality were *a priori*), and so could survive in a society in which people did not recognise any social obligations that were neither enforced by law nor subsidised by financial rewards; and socialism would be stable only if morals were arbitrary social constructs, and people could be changed morally to work for the state according to their capacities while being paid only according to their needs.

Introduction 3

The welfare state is the stable system, or so I shall argue, because it, or something very like it, is the only truly moral state. It is founded on (a) a metaphysics of causal realism, (b) a kind of social idealism that is compatible with a realistic view of human nature and its limitations, and (c) ideals of the state[3] and of human goodness that are very attractive and compatible with all of these realistic presuppositions.

I shall proceed in Chapters 1 and 2 to develop the theory of social humanism. In these two chapters, I will focus on elaborating the fundamental principles of humanism, and of social humanism in particular. The characteristic theses of social humanism include:

(a) *a version of social contractual utilitarianism,*
(b) *social contractual egalitarianism*, and
(c) *real equality of opportunity.*

Social contractual utilitarianism is based on the idea that every society that is governed by consent has a real social contract of some kind. You may think of this contract as a complete and true anthropological description of the society, what its institutions are, what people's understandings are of their rights, obligations, and responsibilities, what its values, laws, and customs are, and everything else that is relevant to understanding how the society works. Presumably, from the point of view of its members, the best society must be the one with the best social contract. It is reasonable, therefore, for the members of any society to seek to improve their society's social contract. Therefore, those who think that this should be the primary aim of moral or political philosophers may reasonably be described as 'social contractual utilitarians' of some kind. The question then is: What kind? I will argue that a social humanist should aim to promote a good that is a 'whole-of-life' and 'whole-of-society' kind of good, because I do not believe that either aim can be pursued successfully independently of the other. For example, if good people are ones who are generally compassionate towards other sentient creatures, and honest and fair in their dealings with other human beings, then a good society must also have such attitudes towards its members and to the animals in their care. At the very least, we should aim to construct a good society with good people. Therefore, whatever our social ideals may be, they should at least be ones that cohere with our character ideals.

Our basic character ideals of compassion, honesty, and fairness are primitive and appear to be almost universal. There is, however, some dispute about what constitutes fairness. In some societies, what would be widely regarded as fair would, in other societies, be regarded as unfair. However, there is a humanistic principle of social equality that seems likely to become much more widely accepted than it is today, as the social world shrinks and communication between cultures increases. This is the principle of social contractual egalitarianism. I contend, therefore, that, with an eye to the future, a social humanist should aim to construct a society that:

4   Social Humanism

   (a) is compatible with the basic human values of compassion and hon-
        esty, and with the projected post-cultural value of social equality, and
   (b) provides, within this framework, real opportunities for all of its
        members to flourish as individuals as well as they are able.

I make no apology for the complexity of this aim, because the basic task
of trying to realize our complex social ideals requires such a complex good
as the object of our social contractual utilitarian theory. All that matters is
that we have a basic good that is not plausibly a good that is required for
the realization of any greater good.

Social contractual egalitarianism is the comprehensive principle that
underlies all non-discriminatory policies and is the foundation of most
human rights legislation. It is the thesis that all competent members of
society should be equal in and before the society's social contract, whatever
their ethnic origin, religion, gender, or sexual preference. The social contract must, of course, include the law. Therefore, social contractual egalitarianism entails the familiar principles of equality in and before the law.
But the social mores or customs of society are seldom legislated. Therefore,
the principle of equality in and before the society's social contract is a much
stronger principle.

Real equality of opportunity requires that individuals should have not
only the liberty, but also the practical liberty, to access the relevant programs. It is therefore considerably stronger than the usual principles of
equality of opportunity. Nevertheless, it is one that was developed and pursued in some of the earliest kinds of welfare states, because it, or something
like it, is required in any state in which there is entrenched poverty or disadvantage. Social contractual egalitarianism might be able to sustain a high
degree of social equality once gross inequalities have been eliminated. But
in many societies, other measures will probably be required initially.

In the final chapter of this book, I will argue that social humanism also
serves to found the theory of human rights. With very few exceptions, accepted
human rights are among the moral rights that social humanists would instantly
recognise, because they are natural consequences of the social humanistic
point of view. No one could say the same of the theory of metaphysical individualism, which is the underlying theory of the minimal state advocated by
the Austrian school. Nor could anyone reasonably say that Marx, Lenin, or
Mao provided the world with a sound basis for a theory of human rights.
Social humanism and the welfare state are, therefore, uniquely positioned,
both morally and globally. Therefore, it is appropriate that I should devote the
last section of this book to a consideration of the global issues that we face.
Is there, or could there be, an acceptable global social contract? If so, what
must be included in it, what might not be, and what form might it take? These
questions will be discussed briefly in Part IV of this book.

To justify my moral position, I have had to reconstruct the theory of
morality, because any adequate theory of morality must be able to provide an

Introduction 5

adequate account of moral obligations, rights, and responsibilities, not only of individuals, but also of governments, corporations, and a wide range of other varieties of collective and specialised agents. The reason is straightforward: if people have human rights, and these rights are moral rights, then the governments of human societies have moral obligations, viz. to ensure that these rights are upheld. Similarly, if workers in factories have moral rights, qua employees, then employers have moral obligations to observe them; and, if people have moral rights to privacy, then newspaper and other media proprietors have moral obligations to respect these rights. On the other hand, if citizens have moral rights to physical security, liberty, or property, then governments have moral duties to provide these things. And, if governments have moral duties, then citizens must have moral duties to provide their governments with the revenues they need, e.g. by paying their taxes, to exercise their moral duties. But, traditionally, the class of moral agents in any given society has been considered to be restricted to just that of socially responsible individuals. Moreover, the moral principles that should guide individual behaviour have been thought to be discoverable *a priori* or, if assistance should be needed, then by a process of Socratic dialogue. Hence, the very idea that governments, or other collective social agents, should have moral rights, obligations, or responsibilities is commonly rejected out of hand by moral theorists. Governments, according to the prevailing metaphysics of individualism, are nothing over and above the individuals who run them. Therefore, the so-called rights, obligations, and responsibilities of governments must ultimately be just those of the people in power.

The task of reconstructing the metaphysics of morality to accommodate the theory of social humanism is taken up in Parts II and III of this book. Part II is concerned with the metaphysics of realism, which informs the whole of this work. But even this is non-standard, since the metaphysical position from which I write is one of causal power realism. It is necessary, therefore, that I should say something about it. According to David Hume, who was the towering figure of the Scottish Enlightenment, there are no causal powers in nature; there are just regularities. If things seem to be regulated by forces or causal powers, then this is just an illusion. Nature itself, he says, is essentially passive; it does not cause anything to happen. Consistently with this position, Hume argued that this is true even of human beings; if we seem to have free will, and hence the power of agency, then this too is an illusion. A causal power realist rejects Hume's position and argues that there are real causal powers in nature. Indeed, causal power realists believe that every object in the universe has causal powers of one kind or another. They have, among other things, the power to affect us and so make their existence known. In a sense, causal power realists believe that every physical thing is an agent. Of course, there are very few agents with anything like the causal powers of normal human beings, and, according to Aristotle, what is distinctive about us is precisely that we are the only *rational* agents in nature.

6 Social Humanism

Hume's view of the nature of reality, and of causation, was widely accepted in Europe in the late eighteenth century. But apart from the Calvinists, who believed in predestination, few European philosophers accepted his view that human agency was an illusion. Most of them thought it was obvious that they were free to choose and to act according to the choices they made. But they were not so inclined to think that anything else had genuine causal powers. On the contrary, they thought that they alone in the world had genuine causal powers; everything else was governed by God's laws. So, they accepted Hume's theory of causation for the rest of nature, but not for themselves. It made sense for them to do so, because, if mankind could be distinguished in this way from the rest of nature, then (a) the idea that mankind is the unique god-like creation of God could be maintained, (b) it would make human beings alone in the universe morally responsible for their own free choices, and (c) it would allow for the possibility of miracles, because, if the regularities in nature were all sustained by God, rather than by the causal powers of things, then God could easily change what happened in the world, just by an act of his own free will—he would not have to change the natures of the things he originally created.

Kant's rational idealism, which is the only existing metaphysics of morals I know of that has much plausibility, was based on this marriage of theology and philosophy. But it is hardly the sort of conception of human existence on which to base a modern metaphysics of morals. A sound, scientifically realistic metaphysics of human nature must be causally realistic. Kant's theory is not. But, if this were the only objection to Kantianism, it would not, in the end, prove to be a very serious one. For, what Kant really needs for his theory is a metaphysics of human nature that is adequate to explain the possibility of our choosing rationally. And, given his conception of the human will as an instrument for translating thought into action, he has a possible mechanism. If mental events can cause non-mental ones (through the action of 'the will'), as Kant believed, and, conversely, non-mental events can cause mental ones (through perception), as everyone believes, then Kant has all he needs—a rationally controlled will. The main objection to Kantianism is that rationality is simply not enough to establish a moral theory (H. Smith, 1991). It explains the structure of moral theories well enough, because the conception of morality as a rationally ideal legal framework allows us to define moral rights, obligations, and responsibilities, just as we would define the corresponding legal ones. But, as I will argue, a moral theory must be humanistic, i.e. it must, perhaps among other things, be essentially concerned with promoting human wellbeing. I believe that Kant himself ultimately came to believe something like this— when he spoke of human beings as 'ends in themselves'.

In Part III of this book, I will argue that morals are social ideals. But they are constructed from the social ideals of ordinary human beings, not of ideally rational ones, as Kant tried to. They are the standards, erected on this more mundane basis to which we appeal when we engage in social

Introduction 7

or legal criticism. They are socially idealized, quasi-legal principles, just as they are assumed to be in Kantian theory, but they have been constructed rather differently from the way that Kant believed they would have to be. I start by distinguishing two importantly different kinds of ideals of social behaviour. There are our primitive ideals of moral character based on our innate values of compassion, honesty, and fairness, and the ideals social behaviour that we require for the maintenance of a good society. For a person who lives in a society of individuals with a normal distribution of physical, mental, and emotional qualities, our basic moral character ideals are our answers to the following question: What kinds of social character traits would you ideally wish nearly everyone in your society to have, whatever their accomplishments? You could not reasonably expect everyone to be strong, brave, highly intelligent, or calm and collected, because this would be to wish to live in a different kind of society—one not made up of ordinary people. However, one could reasonably wish to live in a society of ordinary people who, whatever their accomplishments, are kind, generous, helpful, considerate, fair-minded, honest, and trustworthy. These are all basic moral character traits that ordinary people could have, regardless of their cognitive or physical abilities.

Our ideals of society must proceed from a somewhat different base of normality. To arrive at these ideals, we must realistically accept that we live in a society in which there are some good people, many who are, from time to time, disposed to tell lies or act selfishly, greedily, inconsiderately, unfairly, or dishonestly, and some who are capable of great cruelty, brutality, or bigotry. Therefore, our ideals of society must be constructed on the assumption that our ideals of character have not been fully realized. We must now, and for the foreseeable future, assume a more or less normal distribution of admirable character traits and failings. We might want people to have better characters, and we may, indeed, have some success in promoting this aim. But it would be a mistake to focus all of our attention on trying to achieve this aim without also attending to the problem of how to create and maintain a better society. The two problems are interconnected. The promotion of our character ideals would require the implementation of social strategies, which, in turn, would require a social system within which such strategies could be implemented. An ideal society of the kind that I would envisage must therefore be one that is not unlike our own in many ways.[4] It must be able to cope with saints, but also with criminals, social deviants, hooligans, misfits, and people who, from time to time, are tempted to do what they know they ought not to do, and yield to this temptation. It is a society that must legislate, or otherwise reach an accord, to uphold the values that are inherent in our primitive judgements of moral goodness.

In his famous essay, 'My Station and its Duties', F. H. Bradley (1876/1959: 188) argued many years ago that the social ideals of character and of society are strongly interconnected:

8 *Social Humanism*

> the best communities are those that have the best men for their members, and the best men are the members of the best communities. Circle as this is, it is not a vicious circle. The two problems of the best men and best state are two sides, two distinguishable aspects of the one problem, how to realize in human nature the perfect unity of homogeneity and specification; and when we see that each of these without the other is unreal, then we see that (speaking in general) the welfare of the state and the welfare of its individuals are questions which it is mistaken and ruinous to separate. Personal morality and political and social institutions can not (sic.) exist apart, and (in general) the better the one the better the other.

Bradley argued that our belief and value systems, and our characters and attitudes, are, and always have been, mainly shaped by other people, and by the institutions and cultural events occurring in our surroundings. This is the common experience of our upbringing, and we cannot reasonably deny that it is true. But our rational actions necessarily depend on our socially acquired beliefs and values, and therefore on our education and upbringing. Therefore, he concluded, our rational choices and actions are necessarily affected by our culture, and it would be a mistake to think of a society as just a collection of individuals acting for their own independent reasons. A society is more like an organism, he thought. I agree with Bradley about this, but not necessarily with all he has to say about it.[5] In a human community, as well as in any other organic system, the health of the whole depends on the health of its parts, *and* conversely.

In every society that is governed by consent, there exists a kind of social contract, which effectively defines the social structure of the society and how it is regulated.[6] Specifically, the members of a consensual society must all have some kind of place or role in that society, know what it is, and have some idea of what their rights, obligations, responsibilities, and powers are as individuals having these places or social roles. So, it is probably best to think of a society as a social organism that is loosely structured by a social contract into place/role-defined classes of social agents, who are bound by the laws or conventions that define their rights, obligations, responsibilities, and formal powers. Consequently, the members of a society should have much more in common than just their shared humanity and everything that follows from that. They are members of the same social structure, with the same institutions; they are bound by the same laws (both criminal and civil), as they have come to be interpreted, and they are bound socially by the same conventions concerning the ways in which people are normally expected to behave towards each other.[7] They also have the same government (a federal one in my case) and the same economic system, and they enjoy much the same health, welfare, and social service provisions.

In a fully articulated social contract, these facts about our common heritage would all be described. But the social contract of a society should also describe the society's *moral* system, i.e. its agreed system of *moral* rights, obligations, responsibilities, and formal powers. So, the question arises: What is the relationship between a society's social conventions and its moral ones? According to social idealism, the moral conventions of a society are just the social conventions that a substantial and seemingly permanent majority of people would like to see become entrenched in the social system. If this is right, then the social and moral principles should both be listed in the society's social contract, even if they are in many cases the same. The great advantage of this conception is that it defines the structure of a moral system and explains immediately how and why morality can have the role it has as a tool of social criticism. The theory of social idealism, which I propose as the new metaphysics of morals required to replace rational idealism, will be developed in Chapter 4. It is, of course, only a meta-theory for a moral theory, not itself a moral theory. The moral theory for which it is intended is social humanism.

The struggle between capitalism and communism in the twentieth century had two major dimensions. One of these was economic; the other was moral and political. My focus in this book will be on the moral and political dimensions. The theory of political individualism, which is the dominant political theory of our age, has played a major role in the overthrow of social moral theory. But political individualism is based on an underlying metaphysics of individualism, which denies that there are any social forces to which human beings are subject. All so-called 'social forces', these metaphysicians say, are ultimately reducible to the influences other individuals and should not, therefore, be considered explanatory. The state, therefore, has no moral rights, duties, or responsibilities; it is only the politicians that have these. Strictly speaking, this pernicious doctrine implies that there are no such things as human rights, and that the state has no moral responsibility to provide for or even acknowledge them. The rebuttal of this socially irresponsible doctrine will be the work of Chapter 5.

Yet, neo-liberalism has glorified political individualism to the point where it has become socially debilitating. It has resulted in the triumph of individual concerns over social ones and, consequently, over the social foundations of morality. Morality has, consequently, limped along under the banner of neo-liberalism since this revolution began. But, by being disabled, it has become more and more focused on personal moral character development, and thus restricted in its scope to issues, such as those concerned with sex, sexual preferences, situation ethics, feminism, and so on, that can be seen as being independent of social welfare policy. The positive rights of humankind[g] have consequently been neglected nearly everywhere in the neo-liberal world, and the welfare state has been seriously undermined, even in societies in which neo-liberalism is not the dominant political philosophy.

I am sure it was not the intention of the neo-liberal revolutionaries to undermine morality in this way. But this is effectively what they have done.

10   *Social Humanism*

For, the only sufficiently comprehensive, but metaphysically plausible, theory of the nature of morality is that morals are social ideals. A moral person must therefore stand on the left social leg of morality as well as on its right individualistic one (whose strength derives directly from the natural human virtues of honesty, compassion, and fairness) if he or she is not to lose balance. That is, moral people must have views about how people and other decision-makers should ideally behave in a society that is, for example, geared towards maximizing human and animal wellbeing and work to develop social policies that will contribute to this end. To do this, I will argue, they must work towards, and actively support, the creation and maintenance of some kind of welfare state. That is, they must not be just liberal humanists who are concerned mainly about human freedoms; they must be social humanists who are as concerned about the positive rights of people as they are about their liberties.[9]

Moral theorists have themselves contributed to the downgrading, and consequent neglect, of social moral concerns. For, the methodology they have developed over the years is geared towards the assumption that morals are discoverable *a priori*. Basically, it had been assumed that the methodology of moral inquiry is that of Socratic dialogue, and that the aim of this inquiry is ultimately to find out what we should believe about moral issues. This will be achieved, it is commonly supposed, when we finally reach a stage of broad reflective equilibrium in our inquiries and all of the issues are effectively settled. However, if social idealism is accepted as one's meta-theory, then the only moral judgements that can be made *a priori* are those concerning the kinds of behaviour that we could reasonably argue for as morally required in a Hobbesian state of nature (Hobbes, 1651/1914). For the rest, we need to be relieved of our veil of ignorance and introduced to the real world in which we live. In this real world, most decisions about what kinds of actions are right or wrong must ultimately be taken by the whole community, not by individuals.

It is important, therefore, that I should include a chapter here (Chapter 6) discussing the methodology and theoretical development of morality. By itself, social idealism is not a moral theory; it is a meta-theory. Therefore, if a system of morality is to be developed on the basis of this meta-theory, an epistemology of morals, and a methodology of its theoretical development, is required. Firstly, it will be argued that the methodology of Socratic dialogue must be assigned only a subsidiary role in moral theory development. For there is no reason to believe that we could do anything more than consolidate and unify the moral beliefs of our own culture in this way. Secondly, since the definitions of the basic concepts of moral theory given in Chapter 4 all allow for the possibility of socially or culturally relative differences between moral systems, the objectivist meta-theories that have been proposed are all likely to prove unsatisfactory in one way or another—as I think most moral philosophers would now concede. Nevertheless, many moral philosophers continue to assume an objectivist position, because subjectivism is

Introduction 11

seen as being too destructive of morality and of the discipline to which they have devoted their lives. For, there does not seem to be a principled way for them to distinguish between moral principles that we should insist on and ones on which differences of opinion are tolerable. Specifically, they accept objectivism as a working hypothesis and argue that: (a) the methodology of morals is that of Socratic dialogue; (b) the aim of such discourse is to reach a position of broad reflective equilibrium on the moral issues that are being discussed; and (c) this process is capable of overcoming whatever differences people may have in their social or cultural outlooks. Chapter 6 challenges this working hypothesis. It denies that there is a unique methodology of moral theory development. It argues that (a) Socratic dialogue has a role to play in developing a coherent moral philosophy for a given society, but (b) some moral issues require, or have arisen from, political solutions to social problems, rather than as a result of Socratic dialogue, and (c) some social moral issues are not resolvable by Socratic dialogue, because they reflect fundamentally different social attitudes that have developed, and gained widespread acceptance, in different cultures.

In Part IV of this book, I consider the possibility of developing a global social contract, in which any agreements on human rights that have already been reached, and any global agreements on moral toleration and other social moral issues, can be embedded. For, globalization is here to stay, and global solutions to social, economic, financial, and environmental issues will become more and more urgent as the years go by. Specifically, I consider the possibility of reaching a global moral accommodation and a global agreement on corporate regulation. The first of these two issues arises directly out of the main focus of this book on morality. The second arises out of the meta-theory developed in Chapter 4, because one thing that is clearly established, there is a theory of collective moral responsibility applicable directly to the boards of directors of corporations—a fact that makes it right and proper for societies to demand that these people sign off on appropriate international charters of corporate responsibilities and be held *personally* liable for upholding this charter in their own corporations.

Part I
Social Humanism

Introduction to Social Humanism

Humanism is the principle of unconditional equality of concern for the dignity and wellbeing of all people, independently of their natural characteristics and their social, cultural, and religious backgrounds. Liberal humanism is a moral and political philosophy that seeks to promote the dignity and wellbeing of people everywhere, which is called 'liberal' to stress its commitment to secular liberal democratic values. Morally, liberal humanism requires us to behave with honesty, compassion, and fairness towards others and to respect their rights to liberty. Politically, it requires the development and maintenance of a secular liberal democratic state. Social humanism is also both a moral and a political philosophy. Like liberal humanism, it requires the development and maintenance of a secular liberal democratic state. But it also accepts the existence of a number of positive human rights[1] and answers the question of what the society owes to its members, above and beyond the liberal conservative agenda of protection from threats to life, limb, and property. In answering this question, social humanism is fit to serve not only as the theoretical foundation for a liberal democratic state, but also for the existence and nature of the whole spread of human rights.

As a moral philosophy, I will argue that social humanism is founded on social idealism and seeks to answer the question of what the members of the various classes of individual social agents owe to each other and to the society, and conversely, what society owes to them. To do this, it is necessary to consider two kinds of social ideals: ideals of society, and ideals of social behaviour. My ideal of society would be something like this: A good society is one that is populated by healthy, well-educated, productive, and basically moral and competent people, with well-developed individual and social consciences, whose overall quality of life is as good as it can be, given the society's resources and international obligations. The political question, then, must be how best to build such a society and a population that has all of the required qualities and attitudes. The moral question is this: What qualities and attitudes would you require of people in your ideal society? Are they anything more than those moral qualities and attitudes that we are able to discover in ourselves just by introspection? If not, then

16   *Social Humanism*

our moral theory is independent of our political theory, unless our political theory actually requires us to act immorally. But my answer is yes. I think there are social requirements on morality as well as intuitive individualistic ones. The additional moral question must therefore be asked: What do we, given our respective social roles, owe to other social agents and to the society as a whole? Accordingly, I shall have quite a lot to say about what I call 'social moral principles', i.e. moral principles that are socially derived.

Politically, social humanism is the philosophy of the welfare state. It legitimizes welfare-statism in the way that political individualism sought to legitimize *laissez faire* capitalism. But social humanism differs from the liberal humanist tradition in both its theoretical structure and its development of the idea that morals are fundamentally concerned with what we should wish to see included in the society's social contract. Liberal humanism is the form of humanistic thought that emerged and gained wide currency in the Enlightenment. Thomas Paine's *Rights of Man* was probably the most influential humanist manifesto of the time. But Enlightenment political philosophy was fundamentally liberationist. The American settlers sought liberation from Britain. The French revolutionaries sought liberation from their aristocratic rulers. So freedom and autonomy were among the dominant values of the era, and these values were naturally incorporated into Thomas Paine's writings and into the constitutions of these newly emerging societies. These aims are certainly compatible with social humanism. But social humanism is also fundamentally concerned with the promotion of social equality and human and animal wellbeing. It does not see itself as just a liberation philosophy; it is much more constructive than that. The role for government that is envisaged by social humanists is not only to protect the society and its institutions from corruption, but also to ensure that adequate provision is made for the safety, shelter, health, welfare, and education of its citizens, in so far as this is possible.

Chapter 1 begins with an analysis of moral principles. For, these are the principles of social behaviour that we must seek to establish in the social contracts of our own societies. What most people understand by 'moral' principles is that they are principles of social behaviour to which all responsible human beings should adhere. 'Responsible' human beings are traditionally considered to be people who are mature enough to 'know the difference between right and wrong' and are free to choose between them. That is, they are supposed to know roughly what things, according to the laws and customs of their society, they are allowed to do and are free to choose whether to do them. So defined, the class of responsible human beings is a very broad one that includes most adult citizens in most modern societies. I see no good reason to change this definition; it is readily understood and normally presupposed by writers in the field. The accepted moral principles of a society must therefore be just the laws or customs that most adult citizens of that society believe they should ideally act on or be bound by.

Introduction to Social Humanism 17

There are two kinds of moral principles that may be included in a society's social contract. Firstly, there are individualistic moral principles, the justifications for which are not culturally dependent, and, secondly, there are the 'social moral principles' required for the maintenance of a good society. The individualistic principles are all concerned with our natural human virtues and vices. They are prima facie moral obligations to act on these virtues wherever we can and to refrain from acting contrary to them. The natural human virtues include those of honesty, compassion, and fair-mindedness. We are all well aware of what is involved in being virtuous in these ways, and, normally, we are able to recognize such actions when they occur. We act honestly when we tell the truth and are true to our word. We act compassionately when we come to the aid of someone in distress, show sympathy for them, or offer to help them in whatever ways we can. We act fairly when we distribute goods intended for a group equally, where there is no good case for doing otherwise, or according to need or desert, where there is. Or, we share the blame for that which we are all equally guilty. But difficulties arise in at least two kinds of cases: (a) when the requirement that we should act virtuously with respect to one group or people requires that we should cause harm to another, or (b) where it is unclear who is deserving of equal/proportionate consideration and therefore of equal/proportionate treatment.

Difficulties of the first of these two kinds may not have any obvious solutions, because there is no clear way of measuring goods and harms on the same scale. Where there is no wrongdoing or threat of wrongdoing, the rule of thumb is that we should minimize harm. But it is easy enough to think of plausible exceptions to this rule, e.g. where there is wrongdoing on all sides, or the wrongdoing fairly trivial, or the good very great. These are among the well-known difficulties that must be faced by those who wish to defend any form of act-utilitarianism. However, these difficulties do not impugn the most elementary principles of greatest good or least harm. These are sub-act-utilitarian principles. They aim simply to increase good in the world and reduce harm. But, unlike the principle of act-utilitarianism, they are not intended to apply in conflict cases. They are important principles, because they are (a) the ones to which we naturally appeal in our treatment of animals, and (b) the principles that carry no cultural baggage and should, in principle, be defensible in any society. We will discuss them further in Chapter 1. The form of utilitarianism defended in this book does not require that these problems of act-utilitarianism be resolvable analytically. Indeed, it is my belief that they cannot be, and that conflict cases normally require social or political resolution. The second difficulty, viz. that involving the question of which classes of people are deserving of equal consideration, is not so intractable. On the contrary, the issue is one on which considerable progress can be made. For, there is a sound trans-cultural argument from a basically humanistic perspective for a way of defining the relevant equivalence classes. This principle, which I call that of 'social contractual egalitarianism', will be argued for in Chapter 2.

18 *Social Humanism*

Humanism proves to be a powerful position from which to develop a moral theory. Firstly, the theory of social idealism (see Chapter 4) demands some form of social contractual utilitarianism for the development of a moral theory. The required theories could differ from one another in the identities of the goods that are to be maximized. But almost every plausible candidate for such a good is one that is basically compatible with the theory of humanism. My preferred candidate would be to aim to maximize human wellbeing and to increase animal wellbeing as much as possible compatibly with this aim. Secondly, the prima facie moral principles of greatest good and least harm, which are pre-cultural in nature and directly relevant to our treatment of animals, are clearly compatible with this aim. Thirdly, the principle of social contractual egalitarianism provides a sound basis for a theory of social equality, and hence for determining the relevant classes of individuals, who are prima facie deserving of equal consideration.

However, the provision of social equality evidently requires more than just adherence to the principle of social contractual egalitarianism. What seems to be needed is a program that aims to provide not only formal, but also practical, equality of opportunity. The theory of social humanism provides a sound basis for the development of such a program. But the precise form that it should take is fairly clearly one that will require a social solution. Hence, the principle of equality of opportunity must be considered to be fundamentally a social principle. And, if it should become entrenched in a given society and elevated to the status of a social ideal, then it would become a social moral principle of that society. Social issues of this kind probably cannot be settled rationally. If there is a way of doing this, then I am certainly not alone in not knowing what it is. Normally, disputes arising from conflicting basic values ultimately have to be resolved by the slow processes of historical settlement. A parliament, president, judge, or someone else in a position of authority has to make a decision to the best of his or her ability, trying to balance goods against harms, and wait to see how it works out. If it is successful, then opposition to it will gradually diminish, and public opinion will settle down in its favour. If the times suit the settlement that has been reached, then the resolution of the dispute may come to be seen as definitive, and public opinion in favour of the resolution may harden to the point that opposition to it becomes difficult or even unthinkable. At this point, the position taken becomes accepted with all of the force of a deeply held moral conviction. Indeed, I believe that many of the moral principles of our own society have this kind of origin. They are what I call 'social moral principles'. I do not decry them for this reason. They are accepted as moral principles, they function as moral principles, and the issues they resolved needed to be settled for the good of the society, and hence for the good of its members.

The concepts of freedom of speech, freedom of expression, and of the right to property are considered by a great many people in America (and elsewhere) to be primary moral values, capable of outweighing any

Introduction to Social Humanism 19

considerations of compassion or justice. The trade-off favouring the concept of negative liberty over that of social egalitarianism was, at the time of the American War of Independence, utterly irresistible, and in the minds of many people it remains so today. It was irresistible at the time, because those most disadvantaged were the slaves, the Native Americans, and the landless poor, who had no significant voice. The settlers, who had made their homes in this incredibly wealthy land, and the newly arrived immigrants, who hoped to be able to profit from all this bounty in the same way, were naturally strongly in favour of this stance. But the concepts of freedom and property that prevailed in the eighteenth century are not as favourable to Americans today as they were to the settler society of that earlier time. And the concepts that have to some extent replaced the original ones (viz. those of the Murdoch press and the Republican Party) are, at the time of writing, proving to be highly destructive of America's own economic and social systems.

Social moral systems, and the values to which they give rise, must therefore be treated with caution. They need, from time to time, to be re-examined. The same holds for the social moral principles and values of other countries. The American social moral framework is not an ancient one; at least it belongs to the current era. But the social moral frameworks of many other cultures belong to much earlier, and frequently much more violent, times. My strategy for dealing with this problem is to focus on, and give priority to, the core humanistic moral principles that should theoretically be binding on all human beings, and thus rule out the most brutal and immoral of the practices that disgrace humankind. But thereafter we must be tolerant of differences. The social moral principles of different societies are bound to reflect different social and cultural histories, and, if we haven't thoroughly re-examined our own, we have no good reason to think that our own are immune from criticism.

In Chapter 2, I develop the theories of liberty and equality for social humanists. Specifically, I argue for an ideal form of social equality, which, though unachievable, is certainly a worthy goal. If we can come anywhere near to achieving this goal, then that will be very worthwhile. As a social humanist would define it, social equality requires equality of respect for everyone. It does not require equality of wealth, income, or social status. It demands only that everyone should have attitudes of equal and unconditional concern for the wellbeing and dignity of all others, i.e. a concern for others that does not depend on whether they deserve it. For many societies, the difficulties in the way of building a socially egalitarian society would be very great, and such societies would need to prepare the ground to make this possible. Specifically, they would need at least: (a) an education system that is geared towards giving all children the best opportunity possible to develop and exploit their natural talents, and to make the best lives for themselves that they are capable of; and (b) a health and social welfare system that would increase the range of social choices that socially

20 *Social Humanism*

disadvantaged people are practically able to make. For, without these two conditions being satisfied, a state in which a high degree of social equality exists probably cannot be achieved.

But, let us suppose that the amount of social inequality that exists in a given society is not so crippling that socially biased attitudes could not possibly be tackled effectively. In such a society, there is an obvious and plausibly viable strategy for rooting out these socially biased attitudes and thereafter maintaining a high degree of social equality. Everyone is familiar with the conception of equality *before* the law, and most advanced countries pride themselves on having such procedures firmly entrenched in their statutes. Most philosophers are also familiar with the conception of equality *in* the law, which is having laws that do not discriminate between people on the basis of gender, sexual preference, race, ethnic origin, and so on. But even if we have equality both in and before the law, this may still not be enough to guarantee social equality. For, many of the most discriminatory practices may not be illegal. These discriminatory practices may well be just the remnants of traditional or tribal practices that no one has had the courage to tackle legally. So, what is needed is something stronger than equality in and before the law. What is required, ultimately, is equality in and before the social contract. This is the aim of social contractual egalitarianism. However, traditional cultures do not die overnight. Nor can they be effectively suppressed. They just have to wither away.

The theory of social contractual egalitarianism has obvious implications for the theory of cosmopolitanism. If every society in the world were socially contractually egalitarian, it would, by most definitions, be a cosmopolitan world. The theory of social contractual egalitarianism thus provides a series of stepping stones to cosmopolitanism. We do not have to try to defend or embrace cosmopolitan principles of human kindness or fair-mindedness in our daily lives. Without a global social structure to allocate moral responsibilities, that would, in any case, be impossible.[2] What we can do, and what we should do, is adopt measures that would result in the principle of social contractual egalitarianism being established in our own social contract, and then work towards creating the conditions that would make it possible for other societies to do likewise.

In the final chapter of this book (in Part IV), I consider some of the global moral issues of social humanism. It is convenient to delay these considerations until then, however, because of the strong relevance of social idealism to what I have to say. The theory of social idealism will be developed in Part III.

1 The Ideals of Social Humanism

1.1 INTRODUCTION

Humanists have an unconditional concern for the wellbeing and dignity of humankind. They are fundamentally concerned with increasing the overall quality of people's lives, regardless of their behaviour, and to treat people with respect. They seek to do so by promoting the development of people's natural talents and inculcating attitudes of mutual respect and tolerance. Their central idea is that every person should be treated with equal concern for their good.

There are two main sources of these humanistic attitudes. The first of these is that human beings are compassionate beings. That is, they have the compassionate virtues of love, friendship, empathy, kindness, and generosity. These are recognised and widely appreciated virtues that we are all capable of expressing. The second source is one that philosophers have been aware of for centuries. Moral philosophers from Kant onwards have spoken of human beings as ends-in-themselves. Writers and poets have spoken of the 'the brotherhood of man', where the concern is clearly for all humanity. 'The dignity of man' is a relatively new concept, which belongs to the same family as these others. It is a kind of concern for others that has long existed, but that acquired new strength and significance in the thinking of moral theorists as a result of the Holocaust. When the Holocaust was brought to the attention of the world with the release of films of these terrible events just after the Second World War, the contrasts between decency and indecency, and humanity and inhumanity, acquired a whole new depth of meaning. This was not treating men and women as human beings: It was treating them as vermin. It was not only mass murder; it was a display of the utmost contempt and disrespect for those who were murdered. It was not just a crime against them, the world thought; it was a crime against humanity.

It is no accident, therefore, that the *Universal Declaration of Human Rights* (United Nations, 1948), which spoke of the dignity of man, was passed shortly after these dreadful events became widely known. And the term 'humanism', which refers to our natural concern for the wellbeing and dignity of all humanity, has likewise taken on a new significance.

22   *Social Humanism*

The *Universal Declaration of Human Rights* and subsequent declarations, such as our own *Charter of Human Rights and Responsibilities Act* (Victorian Government, 2006) are strikingly different from those of the eighteenth century. The modern declarations all arise from concerns for the dignity or wellbeing of humankind, and therefore with the kinds of human activities that must be required, permitted, or outlawed. But the purpose of the eighteenth century declarations was to protect citizens from the arbitrary use of state power, and the principles enunciated were intended to outlaw government interference with the fundamental and inalienable rights of individuals.

The *Declaration of the Rights of Man and of Citizens* endorsed by the National Assembly of France at the time of the French Revolution stated that:

> The end of all political associations is the preservation of the natural and imprescriptible rights of man; and these rights are Liberty, Property, Security and Resistance of Oppression. (Thomas Paine, 1791–1792/1996: 72)

These rights, as they are defined in the Declaration, are all pretty minimal, reflecting a defensive theory of the state.

Social humanists see a much larger role for the state. They believe that the government must actively participate in constructing the social contract of the society they govern. Some people in government call it 'nation building'. They believe that the state must act positively to promote the good of humankind, not just protect their liberty, their persons, or their property. They could, for example, legislate to guarantee the positive human rights of citizens in their own societies, as many societies did after the Second World War. Also, social humanism is not indifferent to the wellbeing of animals. For, our compassionate virtues have natural applications to our treatment of them. This point is worth making, since the name 'humanism' may suggest to some people that it is concerned solely with the wellbeing and dignity of human beings. But all things that are capable of pain, suffering, pleasure, and happiness are fitting objects for our compassionate virtues. Nor is humanism indifferent to the environment, since a good, healthy environment is necessary for both human and animal wellbeing.

I begin the discussion of social humanism by distinguishing two kinds of moral principles: *individualistic principles* that derive straightforwardly from the basic tenets of humanism, and *social moral principles* that reflect the entrenched social mores that have evolved in the societies in which they feature. The individualistic principles simply require us to act honestly and compassionately, unless there are compelling reasons not to do so. They do not involve any significant trade-offs between goods and harms as all social moral principles do; and they are universally valid, because these principles could only be rejected within a society that was prepared to deny

The Ideals of Social Humanism   23

our greatest moral virtues their proper expression. Some of the social moral principles that we accept may not be universally valid. As principles, they are bound to reflect the particular religious, historical, or cultural histories of the societies in which they have become accepted and may have no claim to be accepted universally.

There is, however, at least one moral principle that is arguably universal, which is neither individualistic nor social in origin, viz. that of social contractual egalitarianism. This prima facie moral principle is one that any humanist must regard as universally valid, since it is just the default position of the humanistic moral stance. It is not straightforwardly a demand that a natural human value (such as fairness) should not be denied expression, because it is clear that the members of different cultures have very different concepts of fairness. So, its origin is not so plausibly pre-cultural, as the sub-act-utilitarian principles of greatest good and least harm are. Rather, the argument for social contractual egalitarianism seems to depend heavily on the argument for adopting the humanistic moral stance. In my view, the increasing connectedness of human beings everywhere makes any nationalistic, sub-nationalistic, ethnic, or gender-specific perspective on the social organism that morality is concerned with increasingly anachronistic. Therefore, it should be abandoned. The case for accepting this principle as universally valid is therefore trans-cultural, not pre-cultural.

1.2   MORAL PRINCIPLES

I understand moral principles to be statements that, like the criminal laws of most countries, encode both the rules of conduct and punishments for misconduct, which have both simple statements in black and white law and complex but sophisticated and evolving interpretations in case law. For, this is what the thesis of social idealism implies. It does so, because the thesis identifies our moral principles as the laws or social conventions that we should ideally like to see become entrenched in the society's social contract. But, because we are already aware of many of the complexities and sophisticated interpretations of the social laws of our present society, we can hardly make our idealistic projections from the black and white laws alone. The society's present social contract must already include these interpretations. But, if it does, then its idealisation must not only refer to what we should ideally like to see included in this black and white description of our laws and social customs, but also what interpretations we should like to see changed, added, or preserved. The study of morality must therefore be a very complex one, which no individual, or society even, could possibly complete. Moralities cannot, therefore, be written down in black and white. The best that we can possibly do here is to enunciate some principles of black and white moral law, or their conventional equivalents, which may provide some guidance to the preferred direction of moral development.

24 *Social Humanism*

1.3 TWO KINDS OF MORAL PRINCIPLES

There are two basic kinds of moral principles: individualistic and social. The individualistic moral principles are concerned primarily with nurturing the good in humankind. They have an important social role. But this social role is not what is of overriding importance. What is most important is that individuals should be encouraged as much as possible to give expression to their natural virtues and to avoid vicious behaviour. They must be encouraged to act compassionately, justly, and honestly, wherever they can, and to avoid acting cruelly, callously, and so on. Every moral principle of a society must feature, in one way or another, in the current social contract of that society, and where it is normal for people to behave compassionately, fairly, and honestly, these facts about normal behaviour would have to be recorded. There may be nothing prescribed, or fixed in law, that they should behave in these ways. Indeed, it would undermine these principles of moral behaviour and destroy their value to the individual to attempt to legislate for them. It would do so, because it would put people who are behaving well because they want to on an equal footing with those who are behaving well only because they are required to do so, and so discourage the practice.

The individualistic moral principles requiring good behaviour all have this property: They require no legislation, and no legislation is desirable. They are like this, I suggest, because the actions in question are so obviously virtuous, and the principles of these actions are so clearly acceptable that one would expect them to be internalised. For this very reason, the individualistic moral principles are certainly among those that should ideally be accepted in every society. They have the advantage over all other moral principles that they do not go significantly beyond being simple injunctions to exercise our basic human virtues. They are, indeed, principles of moral behaviour that could be persuasively argued for even in a Hobbesian state of nature, and therefore independently of the cultural history of one's own society. Of course, our natural virtues of compassion, honesty, and fair-mindedness are suppressed in some societies. But, in the absence of a very good reason why not, the presumption must always be that this is wrong.

There are at least three kinds of universal moral principles accepted by social humanists—those requiring us to exercise our compassionate virtues, those requiring that we act fairly or equitably, and those requiring that we act honestly. The compassionate moral principles of social humanism are those individualistic principles that are grounded in our feelings for other people and for animals. The principles of this kind that social humanists would accept include those of greatest good and least harm. These specific principles are, by definition, ones whose observance would normally require little or no self-sacrifice. On the contrary, their observance would often involve doing things from which we might reasonably expect to derive some pleasure. They can be stated as follows:

1. The *principle of greatest good*: Where there are no conflicting interests, one has a moral obligation to choose the action that does the most good.
2. The *principle of least harm*: Where there are no conflicting interests, one has a moral obligation to choose the action that will do as little harm as possible.

These principles are among the first that every child should learn. For, they are the ultimate bases of many of our social concerns. They also provide the foundations for every decent theory of animal welfare. Therefore, the principles of greatest good and least harm must be counted among the basic principles of any acceptable moral theory. There cannot be much argument about them, although there might be some argument about their interpretation.

These two compassionate principles are straightforwardly invocations to show love, generosity, friendship, welcome, consideration, kindness, or compassion in our actions whenever we reasonably can. And, as such, they are certainly universal. However, they are not to be confused with the principle of utility discussed by utilitarians. For, they are neither separately nor together equivalent to it. Except in extreme cases, there is no obvious way of comparing the good that might be done for one person, or one group of people, with the harm that might have to be done to another person, or another group of people, in order to do this good.

The requirement that we should act fairly or equitably is likewise primitive. It involves a natural presumption in favour of equality of treatment within what we conceive to be our community. The question then is: What is the extent of our community? In ancient times, it was very small and extended no further than the tribe. In classical Athens, the community would have been thought to include all morally responsible adult male citizens, but not women or slaves. In more modern times, the communities vary in size and composition, from small groups of tribesmen to all of the morally responsible citizens of a nation state. There are also sub-communities, groups like dining clubs, sports clubs, book groups, and so on, each with its own rules and practices. And, more recently still, there is a growing movement, known as cosmopolitanism, to include all morally responsible people in a global community, and to think of the principles of fairness as applying to all morally competent people everywhere. Social humanists, likewise, would have this as an ultimate goal, as would all objectivist moral philosophers.

Equality of treatment within a community involves at least the idea that everyone should be subject to the same laws, and that these laws should not be discriminatory in nature. That is, the laws should not distinguish people of different ethnic, racial, or religious backgrounds. Nor should they discriminate arbitrarily between people of different genders, sexual orientation, or other characteristics with which members of the

26 *Social Humanism*

community are born. In other words, the members of any given community must all be equal both in and before the law. But, in the view that is to be defended here, even this is not enough. In many communities, there are remnants of earlier discriminatory practices that have never been outlawed. These too need to be addressed. The position of social humanism requires not only equality in and before the *law*; it requires equality in and before the *social contract*.

The duty of honesty is likewise primitive. It may be stated as follows:

> The *duty of honesty*: Where there are no conflicting interests, we all have a primitive duty to be honest in our dealings with others and true to our word.

Like the other primitive duties, there is no compulsion about this duty. But to arbitrarily cheat or lie to someone is to harm them. It gives them false expectations or false beliefs or it reinforces such expectations or beliefs. Therefore, by the principle of least harm, it is always to be avoided unless there are compelling reasons not to do so. This duty is worthy of special mention, because lying, cheating, and bearing false witness are normally harmful or destructive acts that do not involve the infliction of pain. We are sophisticated and emotional beings, whose welfare depends in all sorts of ways, not only on our ability to avoid pain, but also on our complex systems of beliefs, desires, and attitudes. Therefore, we should always aim to improve such systems, not to harm them.

The principles involving substantial trade-offs between goods and harms that have come to be generally accepted as just or fair belong to a different category of morals. They are not, as the principles of social equity are, grounded in human nature. They are accepted as social ideals, because they work and satisfy most people's demands for fairness in the community. Principles of crime and just punishment, for example, are principles of this kind. Those of punishment are not based on the principle of respect for persons, although some kinds of punishments (such as hangings and stonings) would be excluded for these reasons. They are socially established principles that require the doing of harm to convicted individuals for the greater good of society as a whole. Thus, they are principles that can easily be seen to be actions taken for the greater good of everyone but the criminal. But the criminal and civil laws of different societies are significantly different from one another, as are the punishments and amounts of compensation that are considered to be just. Yet there is no doubt in the minds of most people that the principles of right social behaviour must be enforced, and that the actions taken by the state in enforcing its laws are mostly morally justified. Therefore, there are, fairly obviously, different social moral principles of crime, punishment, professional negligence, and compensation involved in the legal practices of different countries. Not all of these principles would be considered to be moral principles, but many of them would be. And the principles of justice that have the standing of moral principles are among those that I would call 'social moral principles'.

1.4 HUMANIST PRINCIPLES OF SOCIAL JUSTICE

The individualistic moral principles of social humanism concerned with social justice are those grounded in human nature. They are based on the following two premises:

(a) The principle of *no unjustified disadvantage*. No people should be arbitrarily prevented, hindered, or otherwise disadvantaged in their quest to live as well as they can in the society in which they live.
(b) The principle of *no unjustified advantage*. No people should be arbitrarily advantaged in their quest to live as well as they can in the society in which they live.

What is entailed can then be deduced from a knowledge of what it is for anyone to live well as a human being, and what kinds of actions or obstacles would make this goal easier or more difficult to achieve. All of the principles of non-discrimination, including those of discrimination by gender, sexual preference, race, ethnic origin, and religion, are essentially humanistic. For, from a humanistic point of view, all such discrimination must be arbitrary. It is arbitrary, because there could be no good humanistic reason for having it, and there are no good social reasons for having it that could possibly hold in every society. The moral principles forbidding actions that involve treating others with disrespect, or subjecting them to indignity, are likewise simple and humanistic, as are the principles of equality and equal treatment before the law, of equality in conditions of employment, and so on. These and all other humanistic moral principles are universal, because they are all ultimately independent of the nature of the societies in which people currently live.

But not all moral principles can be deduced from these two premises. There are, for example, many moral principles concerning the provision of opportunities through education, training, work, travel, and so on, which do not depend only on such considerations. The statements of human rights in the Universal Declaration (1948) and the Victorian Charter (2006) provide other examples of putative moral principles of this social nature. These statements are about defining the laws and constitutions of states that are supposedly ideally adapted to promoting human wellbeing—about defining the limits of tolerable behaviour, law enforcement and due process, the provision of basic levels of services, support for families, freedom to travel, property rights, and so on. But many of these statements represent just possible solutions to the general problem of how best to organise and regulate societies for the wellbeing of their members. They were presumably chosen

28 *Social Humanism*

because they appealed to the foundation members of the UN shortly after World War II or to the Victorian government in 2006. But it cannot reasonably be said that they are all universal. Consider Article 13 of the Universal Declaration:

(1) Everyone has the right to freedom of movement and residence within the borders of each state.
(2) Everyone has the right to leave any country, including his own, and to return to his own country.

The ideals here are clearly social ideals. For, if the implied freedoms of movement and settlement were human rights, then it would have to be necessarily wrong to restrict freedom of movement and settlement within the borders of any state. But the borders of states are not fixed by nature; they are fixed by force or agreement. No doubt, it would often be bad policy for a government to restrict the rights of travel within its territory. But it is hard to see how it could possibly be necessarily wrong to do it. For, not allowing any exceptions to this general rule does not appear to have any possible justification. Would you agree, for example, that the Han Chinese have the natural human right to travel to and set up residence in Tibet Province? I do not think that many native-born Tibetans would think this, even though Tibet is legally part of China.

Unfortunately, the simple humanistic moral principles are not universally observed. Indeed, they are systematically violated in most societies. They are violated, for example, in every society in which there are native classes of people who enjoy social rights at the expense of others. By 'native classes', I mean classes into which people are born or otherwise have no choice whether they wish to belong. Thus, they are violated in India, where the caste system still operates to the advantage of some people but at the expense of others; they are violated in all racially divided countries, where those of some racial groups have the right to exercise power over the members of the other groups; they are violated in all states in which the social rights of women are significantly different from those of men; they are violated in states in which homosexuals and other minorities are discriminated against; and they are violated in every state in which it makes a significant difference to one's prospects in life into which religion one is born. Moreover, in every such society, acts of love, generosity, friendship, welcome, and so on, across any one or more of the social divides are not universally approved. On the contrary, they are acts that may well be regarded as betrayals or impertinences by those who enjoy the privileges of being on the dominant side of the divide, or as supine, or breaches of solidarity, by those who are disadvantaged by it.

In some countries in which such violations of basic human respect occur, they do so despite the law, because, often, the violations reflect age-old prejudices that have since been officially rejected. But, in many countries, these old prejudices are actually reinforced by the laws of the land or by religious edicts. And where this occurs, there is an obvious clash between the social laws of the society and humanism, i.e. the simple humanistic moral laws that have their grounding in human nature. In my view, humanism should normally prevail wherever there is such a conflict. For, the simple humanistic principles requiring us to express our natural virtues have clear and immutable foundations in human nature, whereas the social moral principles that have evolved to counter the natural rights of disadvantaged peoples are mostly remnants of archaic social practices based on very different conceptions of community from the present one.

1.5 SOCIAL MORAL PRINCIPLES

The distinguishing feature of individualistic moral principles is that their justification derives directly from what adds to or detracts less from human wellbeing. It may be necessary to decide what one's best option may be, if one's aim is to please, or to relieve someone from pain or suffering. But there is no significant balancing of goods against harms required to make this decision. Therefore, one does not need to make any complicated utilitarian calculations, or appeal to the laws or collective wisdom of the society, to know what is for the best. Nor are these principles grounded in the laws or customs of the society, as the social moral principles are. So one does not need to know what is legally required, or customary, to know what one ought morally to do.

There are two classes of social moral principles. Firstly, there are some that serve to define the generally preferred limits of socially acceptable behaviour, and to protect the members of society, and its established social structure, from those who would exceed these limits. The social or legal principles on which such judgements are made are mostly defined in black and white law, and refined by amendments or case law. The laws include, for example, those against rape, murder, theft, arson, fraud, and assault. These laws all offer definitions of the prescribed limits, and all of them have been extensively tested in the courts. In each of these cases, the alleged criminal offence involves a significant harm being done, and the questions to be settled by the courts include (a) whether a harm of the alleged kind occurred, and (b) whether the harm was done by the accused acting alone. If so, then the court must further decide (c) whether the accused was responsible for his or her actions in doing this harm, and if so to what extent; (d) whether there were any extenuating or mitigating circumstances to be considered; and, if so, (e) what they were, and how they are relevant to the case; and (f) what sentence would be appropriate. Naturally, decisions of this nature concerning similar offences are made in courts around the world. But the black and white laws concerning these offences were not the same to begin with, and, even if they were, the case laws concerning

30 Social Humanism

them would be unlikely to have followed the same trajectories in different countries. Therefore, the social prohibitions of different societies concerning such offences would be unlikely to be the same. Rape does not mean the same thing in England as in Saudi Arabia. Hence, the social principles banning rape in these two countries cannot be the same.

But, if the laws and their case law trajectories are not the same in different jurisdictions, it must be very unlikely that the social moral principles derived from them, which are the principles of crime and punishment about which the vast majority of people in these jurisdictions would agree, would be the same. There is, therefore, likely to be a very high degree of cultural relativism concerning the social moral principles of crime and punishment. And the same is probably true of all social moral principles. They all involve significant trade-offs between goods and harms. And these trade-offs are normally of a kind that individuals are rarely in a position to make. Except in some extreme cases, individuals cannot presume to speak on behalf of everyone who might be affected. Sometimes, it might be obvious enough how these trade-offs should be made, where, for example, the good is very great and the harm quite insignificant, or conversely. But normally it is not obvious how they should be made, and there is no systematic way of deciding. What price does one put on freedom or on providing an education for the nation's children? Some would say that it is better that many of the nation's children should go uneducated than that I, or anyone else, should have to support a public education system. In the end, it will be argued, if a decision must be made, that it is one that should be made collectively, by the political processes involved in achieving social agreement. For no other processes are, or can be seen to be, fair and binding.

Typical of the social moral principles involving both goods and harms are the 'Robin Hood' ones,[1] which involve taking money from the rich to give to the poor, taking privileges from the privileged to make opportunities for the underprivileged, taking land from the landed to give land to the landless, and requiring people to make sacrifices now for the sake of a better future or for the sake of future generations or for the environment. These principles are likely to evolve in different ways in different societies, depending on their political and cultural histories, on their economic needs, the threats they face, and the common perceptions of these threats. Of course, the trade-offs do not need to be one to one. Any of a very wide range of sacrifices may be made or required to allow for the provision of any of an equally wide range of goods or services. Nor need the sacrifices involve any real harms. The rich or privileged can just be denied some of the benefits that others will receive. The variations on this theme are almost endless, and there are no obvious formulae for deciding what trade-offs would be best. Therefore, the chances of any two societies evolving independently in the same way, or towards a common set of social goals, would appear to be almost zero.

The Ideals of Social Humanism   31

We may conclude, therefore, that the social moral principles of different societies are likely to be significantly different from one another. One of the virtues of social idealism (see Part III) is that it recognises this reality. Plausibly, the social contract of any given society that is ruled by consent seems likely in the long run to evolve in ways that will accommodate the most profound social wishes of its members. But there is no good reason to think that the most profound wishes of the members of consensual societies will converge quickly or converge to the same ordered list. On the contrary, many societies around the world that are said to be ruled by consent have been systematically abandoning their socially progressive programs in favour of highly regressive ones. In these societies, the rich are getting richer, the poor are staying more or less where they are or getting poorer, saving for the future is being discouraged, and the environment is being allowed to deteriorate, possibly beyond repair. Free market fundamentalism has probably set back the cause of moral progress on a global scale by several generations, because it tends to regard all social programs, which are not directly concerned with national defence, personal safety, or the protection of private property, as limiting people's freedoms and creating free market distortions—considerations that are given an extraordinary degree of prominence in modern political debate.

Given the uneven development of our own society's social programs, it seems arrogant to regard our own social moral preferences (such as the strong social preferences we have for the kinds of provisions we make for health, education, or welfare services) as universal, i.e. as social preferences that should exist in the social contracts of every decent society. But if we are social relativists about such issues, then we cannot, at the same time, insist that our own social moral stance is the right one, or that the different moral stances taken by the members of other societies are therefore wrong. That is, we shall have to abandon what I have called 'the dominance principle'.

1.6   FORMS OF UTILITARIANISM

We began this chapter by defining two sub-utilitarian theses: the principle of greatest good, and the principle of least harm. These principles are both entailed by the principle of utility, where the utility of an action is understood to be the difference between the amount of good it does and the amount of harm it produces. It is hard to think of any serious objections to either of these principles, since both are grounded directly on our compassionate virtues. The principle of greatest good naturally encourages us to act in ways that others will appreciate, such as being kind, generous, helpful, welcoming, and so on. In our kind of society, there is no harm done by such acts, and obviously they make people feel better. Normally, the person who acts in such a way also feels good about it. So, the net

32 Social Humanism

result is good all around. The principle of least harm, in contrast, discourages people from hurting others unnecessarily or more than is necessary. And, if one must hurt someone, e.g. to extract a tooth, then one should try to minimise the hurt as much as one can. These principles are not controversial, and I think that most of us would wish to see them firmly established and retained in the cultural traditions of every society. Therefore, if this were all there was to morality, the moral problem would be very simple. Also, the dominance principle would be almost self-evidently true. For, in our society, if there were any pieces of legislation or any social customs that were inconsistent with either of these sub-utilitarian principles, then that would be a very good reason to oppose them. Would we really want to live in a society where such good-intentioned behaviour was not socially approved?

But utilitarian theory requires that these two sub-principles be replaced by a more general principle—one that would also apply to actions, rules, or policies involving substantial trade-offs between goods and harms. Thus, the utility of an action is usually defined as the measure of the amount of good it does less the amount of harm that it produces. Jeremy Bentham identified utility with pleasure and disutility with pain. John Stuart Mill identified it with happiness and disutility with unhappiness. Mill (1861/1971) thought that making people happy, or at least happier than they would otherwise be, is what morality is really all about. My inclination would be to follow Mill, because happiness is a possible outcome of various activities, situations, or states of mind, whereas pleasure seems to have a narrower, more sensual, focus. Hence, the promotion of happiness is more plausible as a moral objective than pleasure.

Happiness can, in principle, be achieved in many different ways. But happiness of any kind would appear to be good as an end in itself, i.e. a good that can be given no further justification. One does not seek happiness for the sake of anything else. One does things of one's own free will mainly because one just wants to do them. And what you want to do is normally what you believe would make you happier. But happiness itself is an amorphous, somewhat negative, concept. Roughly, one is happy if one is not suffering, lonely, anxious, depressed, or bored. Or, to define it more positively, to be happy is to be free of suffering, not unduly worried by things, cheerful, to have friends or loved ones around, and be generally interested in, or satisfied by, what one is doing. Therefore, equally roughly, to create happiness, one must reduce suffering, remove anxiety, reduce depression, make or see friends, and encourage others to do what they really want to do.

The aims of utilitarianism are certainly laudable, if they are understood in this way. When the concept of happiness is expanded to cover the full range of ways of achieving it (which I have not attempted here), it is a concept that can be seen to have the sort of breadth that one would wish for in a moral objective. Certainly, it is well able to justify

The Ideals of Social Humanism 33

the two sub-utilitarian principles: that of the greatest good, and that of least harm. But these two principles could, in principle, operate among a group of well brought-up strangers washed ashore on a desert island. One does not need a society, a social contract, or any social structure at all for these two principles to be effective in bringing peace and harmony to a group of people. But, for these very reasons, these sub-principles do not constitute an adequate moral system. For what is characteristic of any society is that it has a social contract that allows some trade-off between doing good and doing harm. The same basic sub-utilitarian principles apply, but the goods and harms must now be summed, so that it is overall good that the social contract is seeking to maximise, and the overall harm that it is seeking to minimise—at least that is what the social contract of any ideal society should aim to do.

The difficulty is that no one knows how to sum the goods and harms (long-term and short-term) that might be done across all of the members of a given society, taking due account of any uncertainties about the possible outcomes, and about their respective utilities. If we imagine an action (such as raising taxes), which will do harm to some (e.g. the individuals or collective agents who have to pay the taxes), and good to others (e.g. those who will be in receipt of some possibly much needed social services), the problem of measuring the utility of this action is evidently not just a technical one. For the technical problem is how to measure the probable accumulated good that the action will achieve, and the probable accumulated harm that it will do, on a common additive scale. And, to solve this problem, we would need to have a way of calculating the probable utility of what would have happened if the action had not been taken or if some other action had been taken instead. The trouble is that no one knows how to do any of this convincingly. There is not even much agreement about what exactly we should be trying to measure. If we are talking about a new law that will restrict the liberty of certain classes of people or businesses, in order to improve the safety of workers in certain industries, then presumably we should be evaluating restrictions and safety measures. That is, what would be required in these cases are rule-utilitarian measures and calculations. But if we are talking about a one-off action that is designed to rob Peter to pay Paul, so to speak, then what would be required must be act-utilitarian measures and calculations. Therefore, any adequate utilitarian theory must allow for both kinds of measures and calculations, and the common argument that rule-utilitarianism reduces to act-utilitarianism is untenable. You might arrive at such a conclusion, if you were a metaphysical individualist, and thought that the only important questions for a utilitarian to ask were ones about the rightness or wrongness of particular acts, and that these questions were to be asked in the imagined circumstances in which there is no society and no social contract. However, this form of individualistic act-utilitarianism is demonstrably incoherent.

34 *Social Humanism*

1.7 THE INCOHERENCE OF INDIVIDUALISTIC ACT-UTILITARIANISM

By individualistic act-utilitarianism, I mean the doctrine that every responsible social agent is individually morally responsible for deciding how best to maximise utility for all concerned and for acting accordingly. For, it is demonstrable that even under the best imaginable conditions, if two people, X and Y, act independently of each other concerning an outcome that they are both in a position to influence, then the results could be much worse than they would otherwise be. This could happen, even though they are both perfectly well informed about the probabilities and respective values of the various possible actions and outcomes of X's doing A (or ~A) and Y's doing B (or ~B)[2].

Smart and Williams (1973: 12) argue that everyone has a moral obligation to act in such a way as to maximise probable benefit. For, they think, this would be the way to maximise probable benefit overall, provided that everyone was sufficiently well informed and mathematically competent and always had enough time to do the detailed calculations. In practice, they say, we are limited by our knowledge and abilities, and also by the time we have at our disposal. So, to that extent, they think that our moral obligations are unknown, or even unknowable, and we just have to rely on some not always very reliable rules of thumb to guide us. But ideally, they think we should treat each case on its merits, and if we had enough information and enough time to do the relevant calculations, then we should make these calculations and do whatever act has the greatest prospective utility. This, as I understand it, is the position known as 'act-utilitarianism'.

I interpret Smart and William's term 'the probable benefit of doing A' to mean what I mean by 'the prospective utility of doing A' (Ellis, 1981), which is a function of the range of possible consequences of doing A and their values. Suppose, for simplicity, that there are just two such mutually exclusive and jointly exhaustive consequences, C and ~C, and let V (C) and V (~C) be their respective values. Then,

$$U (A) = V (C) \times P (C/A) + V(\sim C) \times P (\sim C/A).$$

That is, the prospective utility of doing A is the sum of the values of the possible consequences of doing A, weighted according to the probabilities of their occurring, given that A is done.

But act-utilitarianism, thus defined, is incoherent, because it is readily demonstrable that if anyone were serious about trying to maximise utility in society as a whole, he or she would have to collaborate with like-minded people to distribute responsibilities for deciding what to do for the best and be prepared to stick to this contractual arrangement. For prospective utility would not necessarily be maximised otherwise. It is

The Ideals of Social Humanism 35

not hard to demonstrate that there are clear cases in which, according to this individualistic act-utilitarian theory, X ought to do A and Y ought to do B, even though they place exactly the same values on all of the possible outcomes, have exactly the same information about the situation and what the possible outcomes are, and evaluate the probabilities of these outcomes in exactly the same way. Using this information correctly, they are able to calculate all of the relevant prospective utilities. But what they may find instead is that the prospective utility of the joint action, consisting of X doing A and Y doing B, is the worst of all combinations. Hence, the theory would make it right for X and Y, as individuals, to do what, as a pair, they ought not, *and know they ought not*, to do. In these cases, the only way of dealing satisfactorily with the problem, from a utilitarian point of view, is for them to get together and decide what to do and stick to this agreement. So, if your aim is to maximise utility, the prospective utilities of such contractual arrangements must be allowed to override the prospective utilities of individual choices. This is the only rational thing to do.

Consider two independently performable actions A and B of no intrinsic value, either of which could have the very good consequence C (e.g. a global catastrophe is avoided).

1. Let the value of C, $V(C) = 100$ and the value of $\sim C$, $V(\sim C) = -100$.
2. Let A be the event of America's delegate X to an international conference on the issue voting for a proposed resolution that would be binding, but probably ineffective in avoiding the catastrophe, and also seriously restrictive of American freedoms.
3. Let B be the event of the Chinese delegate Y voting for this same resolution, knowing that it would probably be insufficient to avoid the catastrophe, humiliating to the Chinese government, and be an outcome that would seriously hamper China's efforts to modernise.
4. Assume that X and Y both act independently as agents with complete authority, and that the only options open to them are to vote either for or against the resolution. That is, assume that

$$P(AB) = P(A) \times P(B),$$
$$P(A) + P(\sim A) = 1,$$
$$P(B) + P(\sim B) = 1.$$

Consistently with this assumption, let us also assume that

$$P(A) = 0.11, \text{ and}$$
$$P(B) = 0.11.$$

That is, it is *a priori* very unlikely that either delegate will vote for the resolution. (Nothing much hinges on the fact that this assumption makes the prior probabilities (PA) and P(B) the same.)

36 *Social Humanism*

Plausibly, if both America and China were to vote against the resolution, it would very likely be defeated, and the probability of avoiding the global catastrophe would be seriously reduced. However, if both delegates were to vote in favour of the resolution, the two superpowers would then both be committed to arguing that the inadequate measures they have taken were really adequate. Consequently, the chances of avoiding the global tragedy would still be very low. So, given these assumptions, the best result might well be a tied vote; for this would, at least, give the world some breathing space and allow the delegates to try again to avoid the global catastrophe they all fear. The following table of probability assignments and values is one that is demonstrably consistent with all of these assumptions, but the prior probabilities of C, AC, BC, and ABC are all chosen more or less arbitrarily, although consistently with the priors for A, B and AB, and with the independence of A and B.[3]

Table 1.1   Proof of the Incoherence of Individualistic Act-utilitarianism

Actions	*(a) Prior Probabilities*	*(b) Values*
A	.11	0
B	.11	0
AB	.012	0
Actions and outcomes		
C	.311	100
AC	.051	100
BC	.051	100
ABC	.001	100
(c) Derived probabilities of C/x, i.e. of C, given action x	(d) Derived probabilities of ~C/x	(e) Utilities of actions x $U(x) = 100\{P(C/x) - P(\sim C/x)\}$
$P(C/A) = .464$	$P(\sim C/A) = .536$	$U(A) = -7.2$
$P(C/B) = .464$	$P(\sim C/B) = .536$	$U(B) = -7.2$
$P(C/AB) = .083$	$P(\sim C/AB) = .917$	$U(AB) = -83.4$
$P(C/\sim AB) = .51$	$P(\sim C/\sim AB) = .49$	$U(\sim AB) = 2$
$P(C/A\sim B) = .51$	$P(\sim C/A\sim B) = .49$	$U(A\sim B) = 2$
$P(C/\sim A\sim B) = .265$	$P(\sim C/\sim A\sim B) = .735$	$U(\sim A\sim B) = -47$
$P(C/\sim A) = .29$	$P(\sim C/\sim A) = .71$	$U(\sim A) = -42$
$P(C/\sim B) = .29$	$P(\sim C/\sim B) = .71$	$U(\sim B) = -42$

The Ideals of Social Humanism 37

There are several things to note about this table. Firstly, the derived probabilities and utilities really are derived from the assumptions (a) and (b)[4] Therefore, given these assumptions, it follows that:

1. The utilities of A and B, i.e. U(A) and U(B), are both very much greater than the utilities of ~A and ~B. Therefore, if X and Y are rational agents, then X will do A and Y will do B. But if X does A and Y does B, then the utility of their joint action will be 83.4, which is the worst of all possible outcomes.
2. However, if it were rational for X to expect that Y will do B, and so decide to do ~A, then it would also be rational for Y to expect that X will do A, and so decide to do ~B. But if X were to do ~A and Y were to do ~B, then the utility of their joint action would be −47, which is the second worst of all of the possible outcomes.
3. The only acceptable outcome would result from X and Y doing the opposite, since ~AB and A~B are the only joint actions with positive utility. But there is no way of achieving this result rationally if they continue to act as individuals. One or other of the two delegates, but not both, would have to behave irrationally.
4. Rationally, the only solution is for X and Y to get together to decide who is to do what and stick to it. And both delegates must know this.

The necessary conclusion is that if X and Y both wish to maximize utility, they must consult, decide together what to do, and act accordingly.

It is crucial to this argument that what the agents are hoping to achieve should be something that is, in itself, worthwhile, but which would require cooperation that is unlikely to be realized by chance. What has been demonstrated is that act-utilitarians, however well intentioned, cannot reasonably hope to avoid disasters in such circumstances, or even achieve what they, and everyone else knows, is by far the best possible outcome for everyone. In general, cooperation, and hence some kind of social contract, is required in such circumstances. It is irrelevant to the case that the probabilities or values should be precisely as they are supposed to be in the above example. They are not arbitrary. But they are just one of infinitely many sets of probabilities and values that would yield the same result for two independent agents X and Y. It is also irrelevant that only two agents are involved. Indeed, as Feldman (1974) argues, the more agents there are making decisions, the more unlikely it is that their actions will be coordinated in the required ways by chance. Think of all the ways in which rational people of good will can find themselves acting at cross purposes, when, instead of a global catastrophe, they have only a flood, a bushfire, or an ailing economy to deal with.

It is important to understand that this point is not just a puzzle for theorists of the kind that the Prisoner's Dilemma might be thought to be. It is a

38   *Social Humanism*

problem for any utilitarian who wishes to promote social values. The example clearly demonstrates that such problems cannot be addressed satisfactorily by individualistic act-utilitarians acting alone. In general, they need to collaborate with each other, draw up plans of action, distribute responsibilities, or, in the cases of emergency, establish command centres and other monitoring and control mechanisms. In short, they need to establish a social contract for the purposes of those engaged in trying to solve these problems. But such social contracts are required not only in emergencies or dealing with specific social problems. They are required even where we are concerned only with the everyday affairs of state. A socio-legal contract that is binding on its members in all but very exceptional circumstances is required by any sensible utilitarian theory. Even if it were not clear precisely what should be done in a given situation, it would almost certainly be better that all members of society should collaborate on an announced plan of action developed for the purpose than that everyone should go it alone. The chance of serendipitous coordination by independent people deciding for themselves what is for the best for everyone rapidly approaches zero as the number of independent decision-makers increases.

1.8   SOCIAL CONTRACTUAL UTILITARIANISM

For these reasons, the version of utilitarianism that I favour is the social contractual one, and the conception of ultimate goodness that I favour is something like Aristotle's whole-of-life kind of happiness, which he called '*eudaimonia*'.[5] In other words, I assume that the task of moral/political philosophy is to create a society with a social contract that defines a social structure, and a system of laws and customs, that will prove to be ideal for people wishing to live morally good and productive lives. It may be objected that this is a political aim, not a moral one. But, like Aristotle, I believe that the moral and the political are rationally and conceptually bound together and cannot be wholly separated from one another. I do not assume that there is only one such structure or that there is only one set of laws and customs that are ideal for this purpose. On the contrary, I assume that there are likely to be very many of them. Nor do I assume that we should be trying to second-guess the kind of social contract that will be required. Social contracts profoundly affect people's lives and have to evolve gradually if they are to be accepted. Experiences in France in the eighteenth century, and in Russia and China in the twentieth, have amply demonstrated that one cannot foist a new social contract on to an existing society without enormous social costs—and even then it is unlikely to be enduring or acceptable to the majority of the people.

2 The Humanistic Theory of Social Equality

2.1 INTRODUCTION

Social humanism could equally well be described as 'social liberal humanism'. But social liberalism is not well understood these days, and, since I wish to distinguish social humanism from liberal humanism, it will be as well to stay with the present terminology. The theory of social humanism is, of course, humanistic in the sense described in Chapter 1. But there is more to social humanism than the standard humanistic moral principles. For, social humanists, like all other moral philosophers, have social moral principles that are at least as concerned with the development and maintenance of a just and humane society, which is not and cannot be any individual's responsibility. They include, for example, a principle of social equality and one of equality of opportunity. The aim of this chapter is to elaborate these social moral principles of humanism.

Most progressive societies pride themselves on having egalitarian legal systems, i.e. systems in which those charged with crimes are given fair trials, whatever their gender, race, ethnic background, sexual preference, or any of the other characteristics that commonly provide grounds for unfair discrimination. Societies that have such legal systems may reasonably be said to provide equality before the law. But equality of respect requires more than just equality before the law, because the law itself may be discriminatory. At the very least, there have to be fair and equitable laws, i.e. laws that are not discriminatory. The question, then, is how to define discriminatory laws. Here is what seems to be required: The laws must not be such as to advantage or disadvantage any group that anyone may belong to unavoidably (e.g. by the accidents of their birth, upbringing, or social history), unless this is to compensate for previous injustices or to achieve some public good. But even this may not be enough to guarantee equality before customary practices. For, in many societies, discrimination occurs extra-legally. It occurs in all sorts of cultural traditions. It occurs in various religious practices, in dress requirements, and in social restrictions on movement or communication. In many ways, these informal discriminatory practices often prove to be the real barriers to egalitarianism, because the extra-legal

40 *Social Humanism*

practices of discrimination cannot always be brought before the courts for trial. To guard against these discriminatory practices, what is needed is not just legal egalitarianism but social contractual egalitarianism.

Social contractual egalitarianism builds the attitudes required for social equality into the social contract of the society. For, if a society had an egalitarian social contract, members of the society would not be able to discriminate between people on any basis that would show disrespect for them as persons. Social contractual egalitarianism does not imply that they would actually respect them as persons, for the implied concern might not be there. Nevertheless, social contractual egalitarianism would clearly be a step in the right direction if one were aiming to establish a socially more equal society. In this chapter, I will discuss what more might be required to establish such a society and how we might go about it.

2.2 SOCIAL CONTRACTUAL EGALITARIANISM

Social contractual egalitarianism is not to be confused with social contractual utilitarianism. They are distinct theses, although the utilitarian thesis should embrace the egalitarian one. For this to be so, I would suppose that the kind of social contract that would maximise human wellbeing would in fact have to be an egalitarian one. I have no proof that this is so. But it does seem to me to be highly probable. Firstly, human wellbeing requires at least our having the freedom to choose a satisfying kind of life, from within the range of possibilities permitted by our physical, mental, and economic capacities. No doubt, it needs more than this. But the more that one's options are limited by formal or informal social constraints, the smaller the range of choices available. Therefore, the chances of our being able to lead satisfying and flourishing lives in a world in which our choices are artificially limited by social constraints must be less than they would otherwise be. Of course, there will always be some people who are so mentally or physically disabled that they cannot lead flourishing lives or so poor that they cannot afford to train for such a life.[1] But to have strong social constraints added to this mix must inevitably close off some of the options that would otherwise be viable.

Secondly, even if a choice of career or way of life remains technically open to a person from a disadvantaged group, the existence of social barriers of various kinds may make it almost impossible for that person to succeed. Hence, being a member of a socially disadvantaged group may not only block some career paths or life-style choices, it may make it much harder for one to pursue one's chosen path. Hence, having social equality, and being free to develop and pursue one's own goals in life on more or less the same terms as other people, are plausibly enabling conditions for human wellbeing. But, I do not know that this is so. If it were, then social contractual egalitarianism would be a simple humanistic

The Humanistic Theory of Social Equality   41

moral principle, and therefore one that should be accepted in every society for this reason alone.

But, I do not rest my case for social contractual egalitarianism only on this argument. There is another argument that some will find much more persuasive, viz. the argument from political individualism. Historically, arguments of this kind have been major influences in movements to eliminate arbitrary discrimination against women, gays, religious minorities, and other groups that have been the victims of such discrimination. Indeed, the rights of affected people have all been championed as claims to freedoms of one kind or another. But I do not present this argument because I am myself a political individualist, as this position is normally understood. I present it in acknowledgement of the positive contribution that political individualism has made to the cause of creating a higher degree of social equality in societies around the world. But, at the same time, I wish to distance myself from the negative concept of liberty that political individualists have normally presupposed, and I argue for an enabling concept of positive liberty. An argument based on the tenets of liberal humanism is better than no argument at all. But one that is based on the premises of social humanism is better. For, it requires that appropriate measures should be taken to provide practically available opportunities for people to develop their own lives as they would wish. A right to social equality is not much good to anyone in a poverty trap who has no means of escape.

A third argument is this: With the technological shrinking of the world due to the revolutions currently under way in communications and transport, and the trends toward multiculturalism in societies everywhere, people are now able, as they have not been before, to see and appreciate how people of different cultures can live together. For some, this will cause alarm, because it will be seen as threatening to some traditional ways of life. But, for many, multiculturalism will be a cause for celebration, because, where it is successful, it may, and often does, create a vibrant cosmopolitan society, which may serve as a model for societies everywhere. Such societies, as I understand them, are necessarily ones in which people of different cultural heritages are all accorded the same birthrights. There is no necessity that the birthrights of people in different multicultural societies will all converge to the same ideal. But it seems inevitable that there will be a high degree of such convergence. It is plausible, therefore, to think of this principle, at least, as a post-cultural ideal, and universal for this very reason. The principle of social contractual egalitarianism includes the principle of sameness of birthrights. For, the culture into which someone is born is one of that person's native characteristics, and the principle of social contractual egalitarianism applies to all people, independently of their native characteristics. Therefore, people with equality in and before the social contract of a society are, necessarily, people with the same birthrights in that society. Therefore, the principle of social contractual egalitarianism is

42   *Social Humanism*

a simple and plausible extension to the principle of sameness of birthrights characteristic of all multicultural societies.

2.3   COSMOPOLITANISM

The principle of social contractual egalitarianism is a restricted form of the moral thesis of cosmopolitanism. It is restricted because its scope is limited to societies that have social contracts. To obtain the global equivalent of the moral thesis of cosmopolitanism, one would need a global social contract in which social egalitarianism was almost universally accepted (as explained in Chapter 7). But, in my view, the aim of achieving such a social contract is complicated by cultural diversity and may require a staged strategy. I do, of course, have aims that are similar to those of moral cosmopolitans. But to achieve the global ambitions of cosmopolitanism, it would be necessary, I believe, to act locally and work independently on a strategy to develop the required global social contract.[2] I would advocate such a strategy, because, as I will argue in the final chapter, the establishment of a global social contract will require a principle of toleration, i.e. an international agreement on how the moral principles of different societies may be accommodated within a single system. The key to establishing such an agreement must, I believe, lie in the distinction made in Chapter 1 between essentially universal moral principles, which are grounded in human nature, and which could exist independently of a society's social structure, and the social moral principles that have evolved in various societies as solutions to social problems that may require (a) culturally specific social structures, or (b) trade-offs between goods and harms. At least, this is the only plausible basis that I can discover for making a principled distinction of the kind required. It is, as I have argued, a plausible basis for a viable distinction between locally and globally valid moral principles. Nevertheless, I would stress that social contractual egalitarianism is not a social moral principle: Its primary aim is to create attitudes of mutual tolerance and mutual concern and respect for other people. It is, therefore, a moral principle that is based firmly on the principles of humanism, and its acceptance involves no trade-offs between goods and harms, except for those enjoyed or suffered as a result of unfair distributions of social rights or opportunities.

In his book, Stan Van Hooft (2009: 4–5) claims that:

> cosmopolitanism is not just another name for egalitarianism or liberal humanism. What it targets are forms of discrimination that arise from the victim's being of a different nationality, ethnicity, religion, language, or any other form of identity that is used to classify people into discrete groups.

In explaining the theory, Van Hooft quotes Thomas Pogge (1992) with evident approval:

Three elements are shared by all cosmopolitan positions. First, *individualism*: the ultimate units of concern are *human beings*, or *persons*—rather than, say, family lines, tribes, ethnic, cultural, or religious communities, nations or states. The latter may be units of concern only indirectly, in virtue of their individual members or citizens. Second, *universality*: the status of ultimate unit of concern attaches to *every* living human being *equally*—not merely to some sub-set, such as men, aristocrats, Aryans, whites or Muslims. Third, *generality*: this special status has global force. Persons are ultimate units of concern for *everyone*—not only for their compatriots, fellow religionists, or such like.

I am happy enough to accept this characterisation of cosmopolitanism. However, I am not sure that this is how Van Hooft understands it. For his position appears to be individualistic in the stronger methodological sense. Pogge's claim is that the units of concern to cosmopolitans are individuals, just as they are in social contractual egalitarianism. But there is a difference between the ultimate units of concern in cosmopolitanism and what would be required for such a principle to be accepted and acted on. According to Van Hooft, cosmopolitanism requires neither world government nor even a global social contract for it to be accepted. It requires only that individuals should become convinced of the moral rectitude of such a position and act accordingly. Consequently, he argues that cosmopolitanism is a principle of social justice that deserves to be recognised and acted on by everyone. I would agree with this aim. However, there is no conceivable form of cosmopolitan world that could exist without a global social contract. For such a world would have to have a social structure with global reach—one that adequately defined how labour, resources, and responsibilities should be divided among individuals to serve the needs and interests of people everywhere. But this would require a degree of social organisation for which no individual could possibly be responsible. The principle that everyone should be responsible for everyone else is clearly nonsense. Therefore, to achieve a cosmopolitan world in which people were treated with equal concern for their wellbeing and dignity, one would require a global social contract that at least dealt meaningfully with the question: Who should be socially responsible for what?

I have no such objections to Pogge's conception of cosmopolitanism. For, if the global population existed as members of a global society, it would be socially contractually egalitarian if and only if all three of Pogge's conditions were satisfied. Therefore, the aims of cosmopolitanism would be achieved if either every society were socially contractually egalitarian or if this requirement were built into a global social contract. I differ from Pogge only in wishing to separate the two aims. The local benefits of social contractual egalitarianism are so great that it needs to be advocated locally as well as globally, and globalised as soon as favourable international agreements allow.

44 *Social Humanism*

In recent books, Tim Flannery (2010) and Kwame Anthony Appiah (2006) defend the development of other forms of cosmopolitanism. Flannery argues that, with globalisation occurring on so many different fronts, we are going to have to learn to live together and be able to cooperate with each other as human beings, which, he thinks, must lead to the development of cosmopolitan attitudes. Appiah thinks that cultural differences, while they will continue to exist, are bound to become less and less important, as global ties and connections become more dominant, and more advanced education levels in all societies overcome the folk theories and traditional beliefs that underpin most cultures. The strategy that he advocates for dealing with this trend is one of universal dialogue, which he thinks is the only realistic way of achieving the kind of mutual understanding between peoples that will be needed for cosmopolitan tolerance to become a reality. He argues that this dialogue must proceed from our acceptance of the premise that 'every human being has obligations to every other. Everybody matters: that is our central idea. And it sharply limits the scope of our tolerance.'

He then says that:

> To say what, in principle, distinguishes the cosmopolitan from the counter-cosmopolitan, we plainly need to go beyond talk of truth and tolerance. One distinctively cosmopolitan commitment is to *pluralism*. Cosmopolitans think that there are many values worth living by and that you cannot live by all of them. So we hope and expect that different people and different societies will embody different values. (But they have to be values *worth* living by.) Another aspect of cosmopolitanism is what philosophers call *fallibilism*—the sense that our knowledge is imperfect, provisional, subject to revision in the face of new evidence. (Appiah 2006: 144; italics original)

This is not far from the position that I wish to argue for here. We must all agree to a point of view that is essentially humanistic. But there is no good reason to think that we must all agree on every social moral principle.

2.4 SOCIAL EGALITARIANISM

If social equality depended only on people having basic attitudes of concern for one another's wellbeing, then social egalitarianism would be just the commitment to work towards the establishment of such attitudes. A first step might be for governments to show as much social concern for the wellbeing and dignity of all of those within their territory as their electorates will allow them to, given the costs that will inevitably be incurred. I put it in this qualified way, because trade-offs are necessarily involved, for which there can be no pre-set formulae. The costs may come in the form of taxing people in various ways to fund programs to provide educational,

The Humanistic Theory of Social Equality   45

housing, and cultural opportunities to those most in need of these things. Or, they may come in any number of other ways. The immediate benefits will come with the improved living conditions and opportunities in life that these measures will provide. But, plausibly, the social benefits that will arise from the development of socially more egalitarian attitudes could ultimately outweigh any costs that may be involved. The more that people have such attitudes, the more everyone should feel valued, and so the better the society will be.

It is implausible that the attitudes of humanism could flourish in a society in which there are gross inequalities of wealth, income, or realistic opportunities in life. For, humanism requires a measure of equality of wealth or income that is not so great that it is embarrassing. The poor must at least be able to participate in the life of the community and contribute to it in meaningful ways, according to their abilities. For example, the rich and the poor should be equally capable of participating in intellectual pursuits with their intellectual equals and of gaining the respect of all for their achievements. Wealth should not be a factor in such pursuits. The same is true of many other kinds of activities and many other social divisions. Men and women should be capable of participating as equals in the parliaments of the nation and of gaining the respect of all for what they do, given their natural physical and mental capacities. Muslims and Jews of equal musical talent should be equally able to participate in orchestras and recognised for their playing, without regard to their ethnic or religious backgrounds.

Social equality, as I have defined it, requires both equality of opportunity and equality of respect. What follows from equality of respect are just the simple humanistic principles of social contractual egalitarianism. But what are required for social equality are some social moral principles as well—ones that provide realistically for equality of opportunity. Plausibly, the moral attitudes required to sustain these principles cannot often exist in a very unequal society, i.e. one in which the social differences between peoples are very great. Therefore, the kinds of redistribution of wealth and income that must accompany any successful bid to promote social equality should help to sustain it. But I fear that it would be more likely to produce a backlash from those who must inevitably lose wealth and power relative to the rest of the community. In an adversarial democracy of the kind that exists in many Western societies, the goal of achieving significantly greater equality than is to be found at present is probably unachievable. For, in modern financial and industrial societies, those with the greatest capacity to influence voters through negative advertising and propaganda campaigns are precisely those who have most to lose in the process, and it is most unlikely that they would do nothing about it. Therefore, to bring about social reform of the kind required, it may be necessary to change the kind of democracy that operates in Western societies and introduce a collaborative model, e.g. of the kind that now exists in the Netherlands. As we shall see in the next chapter,

46 Social Humanism

the problem of political reform must be on the agenda in any case. For, the global moral project will require social reform almost everywhere, not just in the adversarial democracies.

However, the degrees of inequality of wealth and income that are compatible with high levels of social egalitarianism would appear to be high. Very considerable differences of wealth and income exist now in the Nordic countries, where social equality is largely realised. Similar income and wealth differences also existed in the white male communities of Australia and New Zealand in the 1950s and 1960s, among whom the attitudes of social egalitarianism also prevailed. So the reform program that is required need not be one that greatly reduces the power or influence of the very wealthy in advanced Western societies. Those who were rich and powerful before the era of the welfare state (1935–1975), which was also motivated by humanism, mostly maintained their social and economic dominance in their societies throughout this period. Nevertheless, I fear that the program of social reform that would be required to create or re-establish humanistic foundations for societies everywhere would be strongly opposed by vested interests—especially in the adversarial democracies, where irrational fear of social change has recently had a paralysing effect on government programs.

There is one small change that could be implemented almost immediately at any level of government or management that would take the society a considerable way towards the goal of social equalitarianism: viz. to employ non-discriminatory strategies in all selection processes, whether they are for making appointments, promotions, or admissions to programs. For, the key to defining social equality in the work-place, or in places where skills are being honed or developed, must be to distinguish between the qualities that are relevant and irrelevant to this area. Those that are relevant belong to the 'qualifications and experience profiles' of the candidates. Those that are irrelevant belong to what might be called the 'social profiles' for this area. Then, we may say quite generally that social equality can prevail at the local level if and only if the qualifications and experience profiles of individuals come to dominate over their social profiles.

The theory of equality to be developed here is one of social equality generally. It will be argued that the principle of social contractual egalitarianism would be an excellent one for maintaining social equality generally, once a satisfactory level of equality has been established. But it is not a transformative principle. If major inequalities exist in a society, observance of the principle of social contractual egalitarianism cannot reasonably be expected to change this situation radically. It could, perhaps, be expected to do so gradually. But the problems created by past injustices, poverty, ignorance, illiteracy, and linguistic impoverishment may be too great, and much too urgent, to be just put aside. They will require other, more constructive, strategies.

2.5 THEORY OF EQUALITY OF OPPORTUNITY

Equality of opportunity was the distinctive thesis of the social liberals of the early twentieth century.[3] It was also one defended by the democratic socialists of this period. What distinguished the social liberals from those of other kinds of liberals was mainly their commitment to overcoming the social, cultural, and economic barriers to social advancement. They argued for personal freedom and social democracy, as all liberals do. But they also held that people's opportunities in life should not be limited by the accidents of their birth, the quality of their education, or their lack of resources. Their success or failure in life, they argued, should depend primarily on their natural talents and their own efforts, not on their social class, educational opportunities, or parental wealth.

Social liberalism was highly influential in the 1930s and 1940s, leading to the establishment of welfare states in Great Britain and throughout the British Commonwealth. In New Zealand, Michael Savage, whose government created the welfare state of that country, defended the principle of equality of opportunity as that of 'equality at the starting line' (Salmond, 1996). In Great Britain, the welfare state was argued for on social liberal principles, and the national education programme was specifically designed to increase equality of opportunity. Arguably, some of the equalising policies of the 1930s and 1940s were expressions of democratic socialism, just as much as they were of social liberalism, but the demand for equality of opportunity had very little to do with any of the wider socialist objectives. It expressed the common demand, which was very strong in the Depression years, for greater social justice. At this time, the demand for greater social justice cut right across political boundaries.

To judge from some recent writings on the subject, it seems that the common understanding of equality of opportunity has changed considerably since these early days. Apparently, it is now interpreted, not as a demand for social reform designed to increase the competitiveness of socially disadvantaged people, but simply as a demand to create equal employment opportunities, with or without any increase in the competitiveness of the socially disadvantaged. According to Matt Cavanagh (2002), equality of opportunity is not an idealistic program to make people more able to compete for jobs or promotion on an equal basis. Rather, it is just a petulant demand that people should be given equality of opportunity, whatever their natural abilities, education, or training. Therefore, he argues, equality of opportunity would unjustly impose duties on employers to be socially even-handed and give everyone a more or less equal chance of being appointed to a given position, or of gaining promotion, whatever their qualifications. To my knowledge, no social liberal ever argued for such a bizarre program or believed in its justice. Plausibly, the new understanding of the demand for equality of opportunity reflects the mood of the Civil Rights and Feminist Movements of the 1960s and 1970s, where radical changes in employment

48 *Social Humanism*

policies were demanded in order to make amends for past injustices. But this new understanding of the demand for equality of opportunity is very different from the old one, and, as Cavanagh rightly argues, it is philosophically indefensible as a principle of social justice.

The principle of equality of opportunity depends crucially on a concept of useful or practical liberty. By 'a practical liberty' of a person at a time in a given society, I mean any legitimate liberty that that person is then capable or exercising. By a 'legitimate liberty' I mean any liberty to which a person is legally or morally entitled (according to the legal and moral systems of the society in question). Thus, to be practically free to act in a certain way, it is not enough that one should be legally and morally free to do so. What is also required is that one should be *capable* of exercising this freedom. Thus, practical liberty stands to liberty roughly as disposable income stands to income.[4] If one's disposable income is what remains of one's income after taxes and necessary transfers have been deducted, one's practical liberty is what remains of one's legitimate liberty after all of those liberties that we are incapable of exercising are imagined as taken away. The concept of practical liberty, thus defined, is derivative, just as the concept of disposable income is derivative. But these concepts are nevertheless important to their disciplines. If our disposable income determines our spending power, our practical liberty defines the area within which our legitimate opportunities arise. For, a legitimate opportunity is simply a chance to do something that is both legally and morally permitted. The concept of practical liberty is thus a fundamental one in the theory of legitimate opportunity.

Yet the concept of practical liberty, which is required for any serious discussion of the social liberal principle of equality of opportunity, has never, to my knowledge, been clearly articulated in the literature.[5] My principal aim here, and in the next few sections, is to elaborate this concept, to explain how it is relevant to the theory of liberalism, and to show how this concept can be used to develop a much more defensible theory of equality of opportunity than that attacked by Cavanagh.

2.6 FORMS OF LIBERALISM

There are many kinds of liberals. All are committed to establishing and maintaining a society in which individual and political liberties are promoted as the primary values of government. Following Hobhouse (1911), we may distinguish a number of different kinds of liberties that liberals would wish to defend—civil, fiscal, personal, social, economic, domestic, political, and so on. For the purposes of this chapter, I focus on Hobhouse's concept of social liberty,[6] because the salient distinction between the kinds of liberalism that are currently being advocated is that between social liberalism and neo-liberalism. Formally, social liberty requires the abolition

The Humanistic Theory of Social Equality   49

of any socially based restrictions on the kinds of lives that people may lead. Such restrictions are evident in the caste system of India. And any liberal government of that country, of whatever kind, would have to seek to abolish it. At the time he wrote, Hobhouse was concerned with the less restrictive, but no less real, class system in Britain, and he argued for its abolition. Practically, social liberty also requires that people should have equal opportunity to live the kinds of lives they would prefer. Even in those days, the 'lower' classes were not formally barred from access to the good things in life, as the Dalits were in India. But they were effectively excluded by their circumstances, and by their lack of decent education or training, from moving up the social scale.

On these issues, social liberals and neo-liberals part company. Social liberals tend to see the informal restraints on the kinds of lives that people can effectively choose as limitations of their freedoms. Neo-liberals do not. They think that what matters is that people should have the same legal rights; it does not matter that some may lack the education, skills, or resources to exercise them effectively. They sometimes go so far as to say that those who are disadvantaged by their circumstances are likely to be strongly motivated to overcome their lack of education, training, or whatever it is that is holding them back, and work all the harder to build decent lives for themselves. But social liberals are unimpressed by this rationalisation. Most people, they argue, need help to overcome serious disadvantage. Legal guarantees of freedom do not create the kind of equality of opportunity that social liberty requires. It requires, not just that we should all have the statutory right to live well according to our own lights and abilities, but also the practical liberty, i.e. the genuine capacity, to do so. Hobhouse's concept of social liberty, which highlighted this problem, was especially important in its day, because of the class structure that existed in England at that time. It remains an important and influential conception of liberty today among the so-called 'Small "l" liberals', as they are called in Australia, and the adherents of Britain's 'New Labour'. For, equality of opportunity is not adequately realised anywhere in the Western World, and in many countries this form of equality is diminishing (Argy, 2006).

In today's world, the primary division in liberal circles is due to differences of emphasis concerning the recognised forms of liberalism. Social liberals emphasise social liberty. Neo-liberals emphasise economic liberty and downplay the importance of social liberal concerns. Thus, the difference is not, as you might expect, between the holders of different theories of liberty. Rather, it is a difference due to different liberal objectives.

It is true that there are some correlations between preferred theories of liberty and the emphasis that is put on the various forms of liberty. Those who hold a negative theory of individual liberty, i.e. the view that liberty is fundamentally just freedom from coercion or restraint, are likely to be unimpressed by the demands of social liberals. Overwhelmingly, they are likely to favour the neo-liberal emphasis on economic liberty. For neo-liberals,

50 Social Humanism

the free market, with its individualism and private enterprise, is the essence of liberalism. The social liberals, in contrast, think that this is a distorted view of liberal philosophy. Liberalism requires social justice, they would say, and they would argue in favour of whatever limitations on economic freedom are necessary to establish and maintain adequate public education, health, and welfare services.

Social liberals are much more likely to endorse some form of positive liberty, either because they believe that social liberalism requires such a theory of liberty or, more likely, because they think that acceptance of the negative liberal ideal would commit them to a neo-liberal world view. But, as we shall see, there is no reason why a negative liberal theorist should not be just as deeply concerned about the informal constraints on people's choices and actions as any positive liberal theorist. Nor is there any good reason why positive liberal theorists should not accept the primacy of economic liberal considerations, if that is their inclination. For, the dispute between positive and negative liberalism is about the ideal of liberty, not about the relative importance of the different strands of liberalism that are justified with reference to this ideal.

People are said to be free, on the standard negative theory of liberty, just to the extent that they are able to choose to do or be whatever they might want without interference. A view of this kind was developed by Friedrich Hayek (1960). Positive liberty, as defined by Isiah Berlin (1969), is said to involve the self in a special kind of way. To be positively free in one's choices or actions, one must not only be free in the negative sense, one must also be the real author of one's choices or actions. One must own them, as it were, not just do them out of habit, or because it is customary, or for reasons that are not really one's own. But Berlin was not a positive liberal as many people would understand this conception. The best defence of positive liberalism that I know is due to Joseph Raz (1986), who develops a social, as opposed to a metaphysical, theory of autonomy. Raz argues that people are free to the extent that they are socially autonomous agents.[7] And, people are socially autonomous agents, he says, to the extent that they are able to shape and direct their own lives in the kind of society in which they live. That is, they are in a position to make significant choices affecting their future place and role in that society. To do this, he argues, people must be provided with genuine and realisable opportunities for making such choices. Therefore, Raz argues, positive liberty requires a positive programme of creating opportunities for people—specifically, the kinds of opportunities that they would need to shape and direct their lives in significant ways.

It is hard for a social liberal to disagree with Raz's conclusions. Nevertheless, I can understand that many would feel that Raz's social conception of autonomy is a good deal more than just an ideal of freedom. For any society that actively promotes this ideal of positive freedom must seek to provide opportunities for people to develop good lives for themselves

The Humanistic Theory of Social Equality   51

within the context of the society in which they live. It must act to provide or ensure education and training of the kinds that would allow people to make sound choices about their futures. It must give special attention to severely disadvantaged groups to improve their prospects in life—at least as much as budget considerations will allow. It must provide shelter and adequate health care for everyone, or at least ensure that these things are adequately provided for in other ways. One cannot make meaningful choices about one's future, Raz argues, if one is too ill or too impoverished to do so.

Nevertheless, I have strong reservations about Raz's conceptualisation of the issue. For, we expect our ideal of liberty to reflect our intuitions about responsibility. But the class of responsible agents is clearly wider than that of autonomous individuals. It includes, for example, such corporate entities as governments and universities. Therefore, we must be able to count such entities as being free in the relevant sense of 'freedom' to do various things, even if they are not socially autonomous. The problem is that the ideal of social autonomy is not just an ideal of liberty, but one that incorporates an important principle of social justice, viz. equality of opportunity. There is nothing particularly wrong with a mixed theory, if you do not mind restricting your theory of liberty to individuals. It is just that many who have other ideals of liberty may feel that they have to refute Raz's position before they can expound and defend their own. But, in fact, they do not need to do this. For, on almost any ideal of liberty, the important principle of equality of opportunity can be recast as a thesis within the theory of practical liberty that arises from that ideal.

Philip Pettit's (1997, 2001) republican theory of liberty is one that has the required breadth of application and also succeeds in linking liberty directly with responsibility. Basically, his theory is: (a) an action is free if and only if it is one for which the agent is fit to be held responsible; and (b) an agent is fit to be held responsible for an action if and only if the agent is in discursive control of the action and not acting under duress or threat of interference by any other agent or agents.

Pettit derives his theory of freedom from his theory of responsibility, which is a general theory that is just as readily applicable to organizations as it is to individuals. But Pettit's theory, like its earlier counterparts, defines only an ideal of liberty. It does not determine what attitudes republican liberals should take to social questions concerning the exercise of republican liberties. In principle, a person could be free in the republican sense of being in discursive control of his or her actions but have very little room to manoeuvre. For, like other theories of liberty, it allows for the possibility of one being free in theory but constrained in practice. So, one could easily imagine a political party made up entirely of republican liberals who were deeply divided among themselves on this issue. The social liberals among them would be demanding equality of opportunity and the institution of programmes designed to provide adequate opportunities for all. The neo-liberals among them would say it is up to individuals to determine what use

52 *Social Humanism*

they make of their state-sanctioned republican freedoms. The state's job, they would say, is just to ensure that people are in a position to exercise discursive control over what they do, not to enable them to do anything.

2.7 PRACTICAL LIBERTY

Each distinct ideal of liberty, which defines what one legally and morally has a right to do, carries its own conception of practical liberty. For what one is practically at liberty to do is limited to what one is capable of doing, from within the range of things that one is legally and morally at liberty to do. Naturally, the wider the theoretical range of legitimate freedom, the wider the corresponding practical one. Those with greatest power and wealth will benefit most from concepts that place very few restrictions on what people are legally and morally at liberty to do. Those with the least power or fewest resources will benefit the least. And they will have very little practical liberty, however liberty may be conceived.

The practical liberties that we have in any given society are limited in at least four kinds of ways: (a) by the social and legal restrictions on freedom of choice imposed by society; (b) by various informal social barriers to freedom of choice, thought, or action; (c) by restrictive or impoverished circumstances; and (d) by personal frailties or incapacities. The social and legal restrictions derive from the social contract of the society in which we live. The informal social barriers to freedom of choice may arise, either because people's rights are not recognised, or if they are recognised, then not respected. We may think of the situation in the US in the 1960s. The rights of blacks to participate fully in the American dream were widely resisted, and indeed they are still being resisted in some quarters. Some of this informal resistance was built into law. But even with the abolition of discriminatory laws, much resistance remained. We may think also of feminist demands for equality of opportunity in the workplace. The problem was not solved just by making gender discrimination in matters of employment illegal. Informal social restrictions concerning appointments and promotions remained in place long after the required anti-discrimination laws were passed. No doubt they still do.

In any society in which there are large differences of wealth or income, there are bound to be some deeply felt limitations on freedom of choice due to restricted or impoverished circumstances. If you cannot afford to send your child on a school excursion, if you have to rent substandard accommodation in a run-down area of the city, if you cannot get a job and have to live on hand-outs, or if you have ugly rotting teeth but cannot afford to get them fixed, then you are severely lacking in practical liberty. For, you cannot choose to do what you really need to do to live in an acceptable way in the community. You cannot participate fully as a member of that community. By world standards you might be quite wealthy. But if, as I

The Humanistic Theory of Social Equality   53

am imagining, you are a member of an economically First World society, then the poverty stricken people of the Third World are not a relevant comparison. Your neighbours down the street, or in the next suburb, are much more relevant.

Finally, there are many sorts of personal frailties or incapacities that may limit freedom of choice. Those who cannot read are naturally very limited in the kinds of choices they can effectively make. Those who are poorly educated, lack training, or are badly co-ordinated likewise have more limited opportunities in life. The same goes for those who are frail, sickly, grossly deformed, or intellectually disabled. These people all have few or highly restricted opportunities. In some cases, their plight is due to their own failings or incapacities, rather than to social ostracism or neglect. But their lack of practical liberty is no less real. And those who argue for equality of opportunity know that there will always be hard cases like these, where the failings are great and the prospects for significant personal improvement are slim.

These are some but not the only ways in which our practical freedoms may be limited. The informal threats of various rogue elements in society, such as gangs, hoodlums, terrorists, vigilantes, bullies, and thought police, are real and certainly restrictive of our freedom. For, they may well affect our willingness to travel alone, walk in the park, associate with strangers, tell ethnic jokes, or criticise Israel. But they do not fit neatly into any of the other categories. The same is true of social regulations designed to both empower and restrict the powers of organizations and people in various social roles. These regulations may or may not have the force of law, but they can certainly reduce people's practical freedoms. However, my aim is not to provide an exhaustive list of the kinds of limitations that exist to our practical freedoms. It is just to explain what it is, or is not, to be practically free to do something, and to contrast this with the more common notion of being socially and legally free to do it.

The domain of a person's practical freedom may be conceived as being a logical choice space that is hedged in by legal, social, and other kinds of barriers to freedom of choice, and by personal restraints on that individual's choice behaviour. Plausibly, the objects within the choice spaces of individuals should not be just individual choices, but rather choice sets. For the choices we make all have costs, and sometimes the making of one choice will preclude another, even if either would be viable by itself. So, following Sen, we should, perhaps, think of the logical choice spaces that confront people as being populated not by individual choices, but by choice sets. There is a case also for including long-term commitments in our logical choice spaces. For, the really significant choices that people have to make in life nearly always involve commitments to programs that will inevitably limit their future choices in unforeseeable ways. Consequently, the domain of practical freedom that confronts any individual might better be seen as populated by choices between ongoing commitments.

54 *Social Humanism*

2.8 PRACTICAL LIBERTY AND OPPORTUNITY

Social liberals are not bound to accept any particular theory of liberty. But they are bound to insist that members of society should normally be able to make good use of their liberties. For this to be the norm, several conditions must be satisfied. Firstly, the society needs to be competitively open. That is, it needs to be one in which people are normally accepted, appointed, or promoted to positions strictly on the basis of their qualifications, experience, and suitability, not on any other basis, such as class, ethnicity, gender, or sexual orientation. But competitive openness cannot easily be mandated, since it requires general acceptance. If people have the opportunity of doing something, then their right to do it must be widely respected. Therefore, for a practical freedom to exist, it is not enough that people should just be capable of doing what they have a right to do. The opportunity of doing it cannot, systematically, be being denied to them. If it is being denied, e.g. because their right to do it is either not recognised or not respected, then they are not practically free to do it. Practical freedom requires practical rights, i.e. rights that people are in practice able to act on.[8] The general acceptance condition is necessary because many of the social barriers to freedom of choice arise from entrenched attitudes, rather than from legal strictures. And often the barriers that are erected are just informal ones that reflect traditional beliefs and attitudes, such as fears of falling property values or unjustified fears of terrorism. But they are real barriers, nevertheless, and they can greatly diminish a person's practical liberty.

But the barriers to freedom of choice that are most relevant to the doctrine of equality of opportunity are those that depend on our personal capacities, straitened circumstances, or histories. Social liberals believe that these barriers should be lowered, where possible, to increase practical freedom. To some extent, this can be done after the event, when the personal limitations on a person's capacity to act as he or she would wish have become obvious. But social liberals generally believe that it is much better to act early to try to counter some of the negative influences of poor circumstances or education on people's lives and to build up their knowledge and understanding of the world, and their skills in dealing with it, while they are still young, so that they will be in a better position as adults to choose for themselves the kinds of lives that they really want to live. For example, Savage's 'starting line' was not set at birth, but at graduation into adulthood. It was set at the point at which young men or women might be starting to build lives for themselves—when they have finished with secondary or university education or learned a trade or are wanting to get married and start a family. Savage's idea was to ensure that from this point onwards, people of equal intelligence, industry, and perseverance should be able to compete with each other as equals, whatever their social or economic backgrounds.

There is undoubtedly a close link between practical liberty and opportunity. For, one could not be said to have the opportunity of doing a thing

The Humanistic Theory of Social Equality   55

if one is incapable of doing it. Opportunity therefore implies capacity. But more than that, it implies the existence of appropriate circumstances for the exercise of that capacity. Specifically, one has the opportunity of doing a thing if one is both able and in a position to do it. Thus, the vicar had the opportunity of committing the murder if he was both able to do the deed and present at the time, so that he could have chosen to do it if he had wanted to. But practical liberty is both more and less restrictive than opportunity. It is more restrictive, because the question of whether an opportunity existed to do a particular deed is independent of its nature. But what we are practically at liberty to do must be something that we have a perfect right to do: Otherwise we would not be free to do it. It cannot, for example, be a crime, such as the committing of a murder. The vicar may have had the opportunity to commit the crime. But he was not practically free to do it, because he was constrained in other ways. Practical liberty is also less restrictive than opportunity, because one can be practically free to do something that one never gets the opportunity of doing. John may be practically free to marry Mary, the person of his dreams. But if Mary refuses, he may never get the opportunity of doing so. Thus, the concept of practical liberty cuts across that of opportunity in two important ways.

Nevertheless, the concepts of practical liberty and opportunity are more in tune with each other than this analysis might suggest. For social liberals, who seek to increase the range and quality of the opportunities available to people, have no interest in creating opportunities to do things that, according to their own theory, they have no right to do. Their focus is on providing opportunities in life that are lawful, responsible, and moral, not ones that would involve breaking the law or acting irresponsibly or immorally. Specifically, they aim to increase the practical freedoms of the socially more disadvantaged people in society by seeking to overcome their sources of disadvantage and providing them with appropriate opportunities for exercising their newly acquired practical freedoms.

2.9   REAL EQUALITY OF OPPORTUNITY

There is no obvious way of quantifying opportunity, and therefore no easily characterizable state of affairs that can be said to be one of equal opportunity. According to Argy (2006), equality of opportunity can reasonably be measured by social mobility. Plausibly, intra-generational upward social mobility measures the degree of opportunity that individuals have to increase their social standing in the community in the course of their lifetimes. Also, inter-generational upward social mobility measures the degree of opportunity that people have to increase their social standing *vis-à-vis* their parents. But there is no clear rationale for taking social mobility, as opposed to upward social mobility, as measuring equality of opportunity. Presumably, if there were no social mobility, i.e. if people who are born

56 Social Humanism

into underprivileged households were destined to remain underprivileged, while those who are born into privileged households were sure to remain privileged, then the opportunities of the underprivileged would have to be very much less than those of the privileged. So the measure is plausible at this extreme. But if social mobility is high, then it is not so clear that this must be due to the opportunities of people with very different social backgrounds being more or less equal. The poorest blacks might be destined to remain poor, even though the poorest whites have quite high social mobility or conversely.

Nevertheless, we are all able to recognise gross inequalities of opportunity when we see them, and say which parties have, or lack, adequate opportunities in life. The phrase 'opportunities in life' is itself not clear. But those social liberals who spoke originally of equality of opportunity often used this, or some similar phrase, to imply that the judgement was concerned with the degree to which one's long-term prospects in life were (a) independent of one's personal circumstances, and (b) independent of one's class, ethnic group, or social background. A person's long-term prospects could be dependent on his or her talents, industry, or luck. But, they argued, it ought not to depend on family background, inherited wealth, class, or class connections. A boy from the wrong side of the tracks is inevitably disadvantaged by the circumstances of his early life. But if the school he attends is a good one, and the boy makes the most of his education, then a number of career options may be expected to open up to him. And, if the society in which he lives is competitively open, so that he can be selected, appointed, or promoted on his merits in his chosen career, then it is reasonable to say that that society has provided him with adequate opportunities in life.

I interpret the principle of equality of opportunity as the demand for (a) continuing adequate practical liberty to live well, and participate as fully as one is able, in the life of the community; (b) full recognition and acceptance of all people's rights and responsibilities; (c) all appointments and promotions to be based solely on merit, where the opportunities are competitive; and (d) all procedures for determining who should benefit from opportunities that are not competitive to be fair and impartially administered. Of these, the demand for continuing adequate practical liberty is the substantive part of the demand for equality of opportunity.[9] It is stronger than Savage's 'equality at the starting line', since it recognises the continuing need for improving, expanding, and updating our practical liberties. But it is less than some might wish for, since it does not include equality of income, wealth, or access to resources. However, these are utopian ideals of doubtful worth. An essentially egalitarian society can tolerate—even appreciate—quite large differences in these respects. Large discrepancies in wealth or income are not incompatible with all people living well and participating as fully as they are able in the life of the community. Nor is the elimination of such discrepancies anything that is required for a good society. Indeed, a good, vibrant, and interesting society may not be possible

The Humanistic Theory of Social Equality   57

without them. What is certainly required for a good society is that people should have adequate practical liberty for them to be able to flourish in their chosen lives.

The background condition (b), requiring the full recognition of all people's rights and responsibilities, is crucial to the viability of any programme for implementing equality of opportunity. For, if this condition were not satisfied, the society would almost certainly not be competitively open. Most societies harbour influential groups that are deeply prejudiced and, consequently, strongly resistant to selecting, appointing, or promoting people entirely on their merits. So, even with good will, governments that seek to overcome the personal disadvantages of poverty, poor education, or inadequate access to resources may fail badly. If there is insufficient willingness in the community to accept the newly liberated classes of people into positions of greater influence in society, then the efforts of governments to liberate them are likely to be thwarted, and it will be very difficult for any government to get its way. If the governments are too heavy-handed, they are likely to create a backlash that will set back the cause for which they are fighting. So, regrettably, governments have to tread very carefully in making social reforms designed to liberate oppressed peoples.

Nevertheless, the effort to carry out the required social reforms must be made by anyone who believes in the principles of social liberalism. For, the rights that are guaranteed in a liberal society do not, by themselves, guarantee social justice. As far as possible, the rights that are guaranteed need to be up to date and practical, i.e. ones that can be exercised by every competent citizen (other than, perhaps, those in prison), not just rights that exist only in theory. To ensure that our rights are practical—or at least as practical as we can make them—we need to (a) work towards a competitively open society, in which all people's rights are widely accepted and respected; (b) develop and update people's capacities to overcome the limitations of their social and cultural backgrounds; and (c) provide people with plenty of opportunity to make use of their natural talents and interests to construct the best lives for themselves of which they are capable.

Whatever one might make of the principle of equality of opportunity that Cavanagh finds in the recent literature (and quite rightly rejects), the original principle of the social liberals elaborated early in the twentieth century remains an important principle of social justice, which needs to be reinstated in liberal theory.

2.10   EQUALITY OF OPPORTUNITY AND SOCIAL HUMANISM

I began the discussion of social humanism by saying that it might equally well be called 'social liberal humanism'. For, social humanism is a somewhat less confusing name than anything with 'social liberal' in it. Nevertheless, I have chosen to discuss the theory of equality of opportunity as

58   *Social Humanism*

an issue in the theory of liberalism, because this is where it was originally developed. But equality of opportunity, as it is here interpreted, is certainly as much a part of the theory of social humanism as it is of social liberalism. For, the principle of equality of opportunity is clearly a humanistic social moral principle. It is a social moral principle, because, unlike the principles of non-discrimination derivable from social contractual egalitarianism, it is not a direct consequence of equality of respect for persons. Different societies are therefore likely to come up with different solutions to the problem of how to provide equality of opportunity for all.

This is an important conclusion. For, it shows that there are some humanistic principles other than the simple individualistic ones of non-discrimination, and that social equality is a much more demanding social ideal than social contractual egalitarianism. The principle of equality of opportunity is a complex principle that requires the adoption of substantial social policies, which inevitably must involve weighing goods against harms. Basically, this is why the concept of practical liberty is so important. Almost certainly, the practical liberties of those who are most disadvantaged in society can only be increased by adopting policies that will decrease the economic liberties of others. Moreover, it will almost certainly mean that some people will have to compete for good jobs much more than they have had to in the past. And all such political decisions are bound to be controversial.

Part II
Causal Realism

Introduction to Causal Realism

The basic metaphysical stance of this book is one of causal power realism. According to most philosophers of the Enlightenment period (Hume excepted),[1] the only free and socially responsible agents in nature are mature individuals. They and they alone, it was said, have the power of agency. But causal realism implies that collectives, such as governments, social organizations, and business corporations, are also capable of acting freely and responsibly. And, since these are unquestionably society's most powerful social agents, they, rather than individuals, should be a primary focus of moral theory.

To argue for this conclusion, it is necessary to develop the metaphysics of causal realism sufficiently to (a) distinguish it from the metaphysics of the Enlightenment; (b) explain how responsible human agency, autonomy, and freedom of choice are possible in a world of physical things that are related to each other by physical causal processes; (c) counter the kind of rational idealism that was developed by Kant in the eighteenth century to explain the nature of morals; and (d) prepare the ground for the new metaphysics of morality that is to be developed in Part III. It is important that we should prepare the ground in this way, because Kant's rational idealism not only defined the nature of morality better than any other theory had ever done, it has in fact shaped the thinking of moral philosophers ever since. With few exceptions,[2] the most widely accepted metaphysics of morals today are all forms of rational idealism. They are, as Kant's original theory was, individually focussed, and they all derive, more or less directly, from Kant's original theory. But, a system of morality should not be founded, as Kant's theory was, only on how we think it would be ideally rational for individuals to behave. Morality requires a social foundation, as well as an individual one and, as will be argued in the following chapters, cannot be an adequate if it lacks such a foundation.

3 The Metaphysics of Causal Realism

3.1 INTRODUCTION

The ideas that most people in Western societies now have about human freedom and deliberate action appear to derive from a seventeenth century mechanism and Kant's theory of the rational will. It is important, therefore, that we should say something about this background if we are to develop a realistic theory of morals. The metaphysics of scientific realism, which is now emerging as the dominant replacement for mechanism, would, at first sight, appear to be antithetical to the ideas that most people have about human freedom and deliberate action. But it turns out to be surprisingly sympathetic to them. The view of the nature of reality that scientific realists are now beginning to adopt is in fact much more sympathetic to current ideas of human freedom and deliberation than mechanism was. According to current theory, the deliberate actions of human beings are the displays of the causal powers they naturally acquire when they are deliberating. The story that scientific realists now tell is very different from the one that is traditionally told. But in several important respects it is the same. This thesis will be developed in Sections 3.2 to 3.5.

According to Kant (originally Aristotle), human beings are rational animals and are obliged by their nature to act rationally. But their duty is not just to act rationally to achieve their own ends, because their own ends might not be good in themselves. What they must try to do is act in intrinsically rational ways to achieve rationally good ends. That is, Kant's (1785/1946) theory is one of rational idealism. Indeed, he initially envisaged a society of ideally rational beings and considered how such beings would naturally seek to organise their own society. What are the principles of social behaviour or interaction that they would endorse? There are difficulties with Kant's strategy, as Kant himself realised. But this was the pure form of rational idealism with which he began. In Section 3.6, I will consider briefly some of the varieties of rational idealism that have been defended in the literature, including the positions of David Gauthier (1986, 1991), John Rawls (1971, 1993/1996), Thomas Scanlon (1982, 1988), and Derek Parfit (2011). However, I do so, not in order to engage with them, but

64 Social Humanism

to make some global objections to this whole tradition—the one that stems from Kant's pure rational idealism.

Philosophically, Kant was a Newtonian about causation, and my main objections to rational idealism stem from this fact. As a Newtonian, Kant believed that human beings have causal powers, but he did not believe that any other observable things have such powers. The non-human world simply responds to what we do as individuals or to what God commands. Moreover, on Kant's theory, societies must be built wholly by individuals, not, fundamentally, by governments, corporations, or other collective agents, because collectives cannot act with the required metaphysical freedom. Democratic governments might sometimes appear to be morally responsible for what they do. But, if Kant is right, they cannot be, because they are just tools in the hands of the individuals who run them. They cannot themselves act with the kind of metaphysical freedom required for moral responsibility. So, Kant's theory leads naturally to a distinction between pure and applied ethics. According to Kant, the pure theory is the one that applies to most people in society, specifically to the group of all socially responsible individuals, while the theory that applies to governments, corporations, or to those, e.g. surgeons or children, who are more or less responsible than the normal group, must be derivative—a distinction that has been rigorously maintained to this day. It also leads to a dominance principle, i.e. to the idea that our knowledge of the pure theory of morality is *synthetic a priori*, and is therefore superior in character to anything that we may know that depends on our knowledge of ordinary causal regularities. Pure moral theory was also supposed to be superior to applied ethics in precisely the way that mathematical knowledge was thought to be superior to empirical.

In Sections 3.7 to 3.10, I shall consider some recent attempts to construct realistic metaphysics of morality. Michaels Smith's recent papers on moral realism are probably the best known, and most influential, of such attempts. Frank Jackson's theory is more abstract, but it derives from a view of the nature of reality that is, like mine, a physicalist one. But Jackson is metaphysically still a Humean, and so wedded to this eighteenth century view of the nature of reality. Therefore, his physical realism is very different from the one that I have developed in Ellis (2005, and 2009). To develop an adequate theory of the metaphysics of morality, I believe that one needs to be a realist not only about mental events, but also about causal powers—for reasons that should become clear. The moral theorists that are realists about causal powers are the moral value realists. Two such theorists are Torbjörn Tännsjö and Sam Harris. Tännsjö's book and papers on moral realism (1990a, 1990b, 1998) present us with a sound empirical foundation for many of the judgements we make about what is right or wrong, and about what actions or character traits are good or bad. But, as Tännsjö is well aware, these judgements do not justify moral principles. Tännsjö's view is that these principles have to be developed, much as

The Metaphysics of Causal Realism   65

scientific principles are developed, to explain the empirical data. Harris's book (2010) presents a development and forthright defence of the thesis that morality should become the science of human wellbeing and should be studied and promoted in the way that the science of human health has been. I agree. We should, he says, be able to identify empirically the practices that are most harmful to our wellbeing and those that do most to promote it. I agree with this, too. Moreover, Harris thinks, as I do, that human values are real and are shaped by the societies in which they evolved. And, human values, of course, are just a species of causal powers—viz. those involved in the determination of human preferences.

However, Harris appears to be confused about what he is doing. He is not trying to found morality on our *natural* human values, as he seems at times to be saying, because these values, whatever they may be, are primitive, and so are unlikely to be adapted to promoting human wellbeing in modern societies. Harris is talking about what our values *ought to be* in today's world: We need to adopt policies and practices that are likely to increase human wellbeing and eliminate those likely to decrease it. Therefore, he says, we can find out what our values ought to be. They must be just those values that would dispose us to make decisions that would promote what is good from this perspective and discourage what is bad. To argue that science has nothing to say about what this involves, he says, is just plain wrong. I agree. If there is a science of health (medicine), then, by parity of reasoning, there must be a science of human wellbeing (morality). And it is time we got on with it.

3.2   SEVENTEENTH CENTURY MECHANISM

René Descartes, who is generally credited with being the principal author of mechanistic philosophy, had a big influence on European thought. He influenced French philosophy directly through his writings, greatly influenced Sir Isaac Newton, and appears to have persuaded the Western world that minds and bodies are distinct and ontologically independent kinds of existences—mental and material. The mental world was supposed to be that of thought, reasoning, sensory experience, and feeling. It is the world to which our minds belong. The material world, in contrast, was that of material things—including our bodies, but not our minds. Descartes thought that our eyes and ears were our principal windows to this material world, and that the structure of our sensory experience gave us knowledge of its structure.

According to Descartes, the material world consists of matter in motion, and, since God is always constant in His ways, He must conserve in this world as much of matter and motion as he originally created. Descartes supposed, reasonably enough, that the quantity of motion must be proportional to the quantity of matter being moved, as well as to the speed of its

66   Social Humanism

motion. Thus, Descartes came to formulate, long before Newton, crude versions of some of the principles of mechanics that were later incorporated in a more refined way in Newton's dynamical theory, including the law of inertia, the principle of the conservation of mass, and the law of conservation of momentum. But note that these principles are all conservation principles. They do not imply that anything, of itself, ever does anything to anything else. They are not active principles of the kind required for causation. Indeed, this is precisely what most mechanists believed was true of the material world. It is, in itself, wholly passive.

For a mechanist, inanimate matter does not initiate any causal processes. Bodies, once set in motion, will continue to move uniformly in a straight line indefinitely unless they come into contact with other bodies that interfere with them, which, consequently, will assist, hinder, disperse, or deflect them in their motion. But although inanimate matter may be involved in such processes, it never does anything more than just pass on all or some of the impetus/momentum that has already been given to it. So, essentially, inanimate matter was thought to be passive. It was subject to the laws of nature and so moved as the laws of nature required. But only God could vary the laws of nature, and only human beings could initiate actions independently of God.

Newton's *Mathematical Principles of Natural Philosophy* (1687/1964) did much to establish mechanism as the dominant philosophy of the age. For, it presented a coherent picture of the known universe as a world whose parts were strictly governed by universal laws. It was a picture of a world that could, apparently, just go on doing what it was doing forever, much like a gigantic piece of clockwork with an everlasting spring. It is true that Newton sometimes spoke of a force of gravity, and therefore seemed to be suggesting that the planets were being pulled around by the Sun. But Newton himself emphatically denied that the Sun, or any other material body, had the power to do this. In a letter to Richard Bentley in 1693, Newton wrote:

> It is inconceivable that inanimate brute matter should, without the mediation of something else, which is not material, operate upon and affect other matter without mutual contact, as it must be if gravitation, in the sense of Epicurus, be essential and inherent in it. And this is one reason why I desired you would not ascribe innate gravity to me. That gravity should be innate, inherent, and essential to matter, so that one body may act upon another at a distance through a *vacuum*, without the mediation of anything else, by and through which their action and force may be conveyed from one to another, is to me so great an absurdity that I believe no man who has in philosophical matters a competent faculty of thinking can ever fall into it. Gravity must be caused by an agent acting constantly according to certain laws, but whether this agent be material or immaterial I have left to the consideration of my readers. (Thayer, 1953: 54)

The Metaphysics of Causal Realism 67

There seems little doubt that Newton believed God to be the source of the power required to maintain the planets in their orbits. David Hume, who was an atheist, responded to the challenge posed by gravity in a rather different way. He did so by effectively denying the existence of gravity. The planets did not move around in their orbits, he thought, because they are pulled around by forces emanating from the Sun. That goes well beyond anything that is, or ever could be, given to us in experience. The planets move around in their orbits, he argued, because this is what they must do, given the laws of nature. There is regularity in the motions, he insisted. And there is also causation. But this kind of causation really does not involve anything more than regularity.

Hume's 'regularity' theory of causation is well known to philosophers everywhere. It has been the dominant theory of causation in Western philosophy for over two hundred years. Hume argued that all knowledge is either of relations of ideas or matters of fact. It is, he said, relatively unproblematic how knowledge of relations of ideas is possible. For, we can analyse or compare ideas directly, or, if need be, we can derive them from more elementary relations of ideas that are known directly. But, our knowledge of matters of fact is more problematic, he said. For, there is no known deductive path from those matters of fact we are able to apprehend directly to those that cannot be so apprehended. What then, Hume asked, is the basis of our reasoning concerning matters of fact?

To answer this question, Hume claimed that all such reasoning must ultimately be based on knowledge of cause/effect relationships. But all such knowledge, he argued, requires knowledge of truths of the very kind that we are seeking to explain. A particular event c of the kind A is the cause of a particular event e of the kind B, if and only if c precedes e, c is contiguous with e in space and time, and events of the kind A are regularly conjoined (in the same sort of way) with events of the kind B. Consider Hume's own billiard ball example, in which the white ball strikes the red one (the event c), causing the red ball to move (the event e). The process is one of causation, says Hume, because c precedes e, there is contiguity in space and time between c and e, and events of the kind of which c is an instance are regularly conjoined with events of the kind of which e is an instance. But, says Hume, that is all there is to it. There is no necessary connection between the first event and the second. There is nothing to make the second ball do what it does. It just does it. As far as we know, or can ever know, A-type events may one day cease to be conjoined with B-type ones.

This theory of causation, or something very like it, was generally acceptable in philosophy of science for much of the twentieth century. It was agreeable to the positivists, because it stuck closely to what was empirically observable and did not go much beyond it. And it was acceptable to analytic philosophers, because it seemed to provide them with adequate truth conditions for statements of cause/effect relationships. But it left the problem of induction that Hume began by addressing unsolved. Indeed, it made it

68 *Social Humanism*

appear to be insoluble. Thus, the problem of induction became a major one for philosophers generally. They could neither ignore it nor solve it. The positivists, in particular, could not ignore it, because, without a solution to the problem of induction, the laws and theories of science, which made factual claims that went far beyond anything that was directly verifiable, would have to be declared unverifiable. But verifiability was a condition for empirical significance for the positivists. They prided themselves on their scientific approach to philosophy and thought that verifiability was the hallmark of scientific respectability. So, they could hardly accept that all of the great theoretical achievements of science were unverifiable. However, neither they nor anyone else could solve the problem of induction. No matter how hard they tried, there always seemed to be fatal flaws in their arguments.

Sir Karl Popper, whose influence in the philosophy of science was also profound, made Hume's theory of causation a cornerstone of his critical realism. Popper agreed with Hume that the laws and theories of science could not be shown empirically to be true, and, like Hume, he rejected the idea that they could ever be known to be true. But, according to Popper, this does not mean that the laws and theories of science should be dismissed as empirically meaningless, and therefore valueless. On the contrary, said Popper, the laws and theories of science are valuable as postulates, but not because they are known to be true. They are valuable, he said, because, although they are not known to be true, they have not yet been shown to be false. And this is the case, despite the fact that every effort has been made to falsify them. They are postulates that are all highly corroborated, he said—and this is what really matters.

But Popper's theory is highly counterintuitive. Why would you put your trust in the scientific view of the world to the extent to which we all do, if you did not think it was reliable and will remain so? It is not enough to know that it has not yet been shown to be false. Yet, according to Popper, there is no good reason to think that any scientific theory is reliable or will remain so. So, most philosophers of science today are not persuaded by Popper's case. There is a strong conviction that the vast majority of the laws and theories of the established sciences are, if not strictly true, then at least approximately true. That is, most philosophers of science are intuitively scientific realists. Most of them are convinced that the scientific image of the world, in most respects, is at least close to the way the world really is.

So, the tide has at last begun to turn against Humeanism. Philosophers of science are no longer as sceptical about induction as they once were and have begun to question seriously the mechanistic philosophy that led to their scepticism. For example, recent developments in the metaphysics of science have seen a strong revival of the idea that things have causal powers and are bound to act as they do just because they have these powers. This change developed in stages. Jack Smart and U. T. Place began by attacking the orthodox Cartesian mind/body distinction, arguing for what became known as the 'mind/brain identity theory'. It was also labelled 'central

The Metaphysics of Causal Realism   69

state materialism' or, in some places, 'the Australian heresy'. The argument centred on the question: What are sensations? Smart (a philosopher) and Place (a psychologist) argued that sensations are brain processes and fielded a wide range of objections to this answer. The extraordinary success of Smart's (1959) article was undoubtedly an important development in the philosophy of mind. It led, naturally enough, to a physicalist ontology, involving the belief that the world is fundamentally physical and that the mental is supervenient on it. Such an ontology was articulated by Wilfrid Sellars (1963).

The success of Smart's article also led to a broader attack on the whole positivist movement. In 1963, Smart published his *Philosophy and Scientific Realism*. This book broke new ground at the time. Most philosophers of science in the first half of the century doubted the reality of most of the theoretical entities of science, including not only the fundamental particles (such as electrons, protons, and neutrons), but also the supposed structures of the chemical elements and compounds. Their failure to solve the problem of induction, broadly understood as including inferences from observed effects to hidden causes, left them with no obvious alternative to scepticism about these entities. Most philosophers of science regarded the theories concerning these entities as models of reality that were more or less useful for predicting what will happen in the world, but thought that these theories had no claim to be descriptive of anything that really exists. Smart challenged all this, arguing that there is no good reason to doubt the reality of the atomic, molecular, and sub-atomic worlds. For, there is no doubt that the world is such that it is just *as if* the things described in the relevant physical theories are real existents. So, we are faced with a choice: Either this fact is just a cosmic coincidence or else the things that are postulated as existing really do exist. The best explanation, by far, is that the postulated entities really do exist.

But Smart's argument did not go far enough. For Smart's realism did not include realism about the natural kinds of things that exist or the natural physical properties that distinguish them. To make good sense of chemistry, for example, one has to suppose that there are more than ninety mutually distinct chemical elements, and hundreds of thousands of chemical compounds involving these elements, which are each distinct from every other. They are each distinct from every other both physically and chemically, since no two different chemical elements or compounds have the same sets of physical or chemical properties. The differences between the compounds can all be explained by the differences in their compositions and/or their molecular structures. But as we descend the scale to the chemical elements, we are forced to look for the sources of their differences at a deeper level, the sub-atomic one. The ninety-odd mutually distinct naturally occurring chemical elements may be distinguished by a corresponding number of different kinds of atoms, with different nuclei and different electron structures surrounding them. However, this process of explaining the distinctions

70 *Social Humanism*

between the kinds by distinguishing the structures of things of these kinds has its limitations. For, sooner or later, we must run out of structure. Therefore, we must eventually come down to things that cannot be distinguished by their structures. Let us just call them the 'fundamental particles' and leave it an open question what these fundamental particles are.

The question then arises: How are these fundamental particles to be distinguished from one another? The only plausible answer is that they are distinguished by their properties. But their properties, whatever they might be, cannot be structures. For, if they were, they would not be truly fundamental. Therefore, the properties of the fundamental particles must be unstructured properties that are to be distinguished from one another, not by what they are, as structures are distinguishable, but by what they dispose their bearers to do. That is, they must be dispositional properties, as causal powers are supposed to be. Therefore, to make sense of all this structure in the world, we must suppose that, at the most basic level, things are distinguished, not by what they are, but by their dispositional properties. The dispositional properties of things are their causal powers, capacities, and propensities. Therefore, at the fundamental level, we must suppose that things are distinguished from one another by these sorts of properties. Scientific realism thus implies a natural kind of realism, which in turn implies realism about the causal powers, capacities, and propensities of things at the most fundamental levels.

The causal powers, capacities, and propensities of the fundamental particles in nature cannot be functions of their relations to other things. For, if they were, the identities of the particles would be different in different locations. Therefore, the dispositional properties that determine the identities of things at the most fundamental levels must all be intrinsic to these things. These identity-determining intrinsic properties are called 'the real essences' of the things that bear them. They are the properties in virtue of which the things in question are things of the kinds they are. The real essence of an electron, for example, must include its mass m, its charge e, and its spin ½. For nothing could be an electron if it lacked any of these properties, and anything that has all of these properties (and whatever other defining properties electrons may have) must be an electron. The real essences of the other fundamental particles of nature, such as protons and neutrons, can likewise be given. In every case, the real essences of the most fundamental particles in nature are sets of dispositional properties, i.e. causal powers, capacities, and propensities.

Modern metaphysics has thus moved a long way from the anti-essentialism of the Enlightenment period and the sceptical philosophy of Hume. It embraces the natural kinds of structure of the world, and all of its essentialist implications, and it reasons about nature in such a way as to preserve its theoretical understanding of it. As many of today's metaphysicians see it, it would be irrational to reject any part of this structure without good reason. Certainly, one can easily imagine events that, if they were to occur,

The Metaphysics of Causal Realism   71

would upset much of what we now think we know. But it would be irrational to reject the theoretical picture of the world that we have built up over the years simply on the grounds that we can imagine what would falsify it. So we have no alternative but to work with the picture that we have of the world and project future, or otherwise unknown, events on the assumption that it is accurate. No adequate theory of causation today could reasonably identify it as a species of regularity, as Hume's theory did. In today's metaphysical picture of the world, a cause/effect sequence is always a display of one or more causal powers. And a causal power is always a dispositional property of its bearer.

As will be explained shortly, the concept of a causal power is closely related to that of an agent. For, causal powers and agents both have capacities to act. It is important that we should explore this connection, because our aim here is to develop adequate metaphysical foundations for morality, and the concept of human agency would appear to be central to this project. It will be argued in the following three sections that modern metaphysics is much less hostile to the concept of human beings as free agents than the Humean position, even though Hume's theory was the one that preceded and backgrounded the development of Kantianism. In what follows, it will be shown that a plausible theory of human agency can be developed that is fully compatible with modern causal power realism.

3.3   CAUSAL POWERS AND AGENCY[1]

By 'an agent', I mean an object or substance that has causal powers. It is, by definition, something that is capable of acting or reacting to cause something to happen. According to the eighteenth century French philosopher Nicholas Malebranche, God is really the cause of everything that happens in the world, even the things we (apparently) do ourselves. But the more common view was that there are really two kinds of agents in nature, divine and human. The mechanistic interactions of things were not thought to be examples of agency, but just the ramifications of actions taken originally by God or humans. If you poke something with a stick, they would say, then you are the one doing the poking. The stick is just the instrument you are using. Thus, in a mechanistic world of the kind that Newton believed in, there would be no agents at all, other than God and human beings. But in the kind of world that Hume believed in, there was no place for agency of any kind, divine or human. Things just happen. Sometimes things may happen with cosmic regularity. But they do not happen because things have causal powers. For Hume, all causal relations are necessarily between events, and objects are never the causes of anything.

According to the proposed definition of agency, the fundamental particles are all agents. For, these particles all have causal powers of their own that they will exercise when the circumstances warrant it. But the agency

72   Social Humanism

they have is fixed and very limited. For, the properties that determine what the fundamental particles can do are all fixed by nature. Moreover, the circumstances in which they can act, and the ways in which they can act, are also fixed by nature. So, really, there is no possibility of a fundamental particle doing anything other than what it must, or be likely, to do in the circumstances in which it is placed. You simply cannot teach a fundamental particle any new tricks. If a fundamental particle that we supposed to be an electron began to behave in ways other than the usual ones, then it could not be an electron. It would have to be a particle of some kind other than an electron. If the exceptional behaviour were otherwise compatible with the particle being a normal electron, then it would have to be considered to be a species of electron. If it were incompatible with it being a normal electron, then it would have to be something other than an electron.

But the identity conditions for physical systems become less stringent with increases in size and complexity, since different structures can evolve within complex physical systems, creating different dispositions to act. And these changes can occur without loss of identity. A piece of iron that becomes magnetised acquires causal powers it did not have before. But it does not cease to be a piece of iron. A piece of wire that is bent sharply backwards and forwards many times becomes brittle. But it does not cease to be a piece of wire. It is possible, therefore, for things of more complex kinds to acquire or lose causal powers, without ceasing to be things of the kinds they are. Learning and forgetting are cases in point. If an animal learns a new trick, it thereby acquires a new way of behaving. If it forgets something, it loses a capacity that it once had.

Most things of the kinds with which we are familiar would appear to have variable causal powers. They can be magnetised, electrified, stressed, and so on, and, consequently, their causal powers can be changed. Accordingly, these things must all have variable agencies, i.e. it is, at least to some extent, contingent on what they are able to do. There is, therefore, nothing very special about having variable agency. Everything that evolves, grows, or learns from experience has variable agency, because its causal powers must vary as it evolves, grows, or learns. Human agency is clearly variable in this way, as is almost every form of animal agency. Perhaps, an amoeba does not learn from experience. I do not know. But clearly, most animals do learn from experience. Hence their agencies are variable.

When an animal learns from experience it does not necessarily acquire any causal powers of kinds it did not have before. The animal's capacities to do things are likely to be improved in some ways and neglected in others. But there are more subtle changes that do occur regularly. When an animal learns by operant conditioning, what normally occurs is that it becomes more likely to respond in one way rather than another to a given stimulus. And this is a marginal change in the animal's causal power profile. Over time, a sequence of marginal changes of this kind can amount to a significant change in the animal's dispositional properties.

The Metaphysics of Causal Realism 73

If human agency is special, then it must be, at least partly, due to the kinds of processes that bring about changes in our causal power profiles. Like most animals, we readily learn behaviour that we find pleasurable or satisfying, and we learn not to do things that prove to be painful or dissatisfying. That is, we learn by operant conditioning. But human beings have many other ways of learning that are not available to most animals. Firstly, we have languages, in which we are able to record what we and other people have learnt in the past. Secondly, we have a capacity to reason that enables us to predict the likely outcomes of the various actions that we take. Thirdly, we have vivid imaginations that enable us to anticipate and understand how we are likely to feel about the effects of our actions. Fourthly, we have good memories, which enable us to recall better what has happened in the past in like circumstances and so learn from past experience. Fifthly, we are social animals and have a developed the capacity to understand how others must be feeling. Consequently, we are well able to adapt our behaviour to serve the needs of others, as well as ourselves.

This descriptive account of the kinds of factors that are relevant to human agency, as distinct from the agencies of things of other kinds, already explains its apparent uniqueness in the animal world. Nevertheless, the account is seriously deficient as it stands. For it says nothing about deciding and willing and gives an inadequate account of the phenomenology of these processes. The complex and cumulative processes that are involved in determining our causal power profiles may determine the kinds of actions that are available to us and the probabilities of their being taken on various occasions. But it is introspectively clear that we always have the option of choosing which of these available alternatives to adopt. The kinds of considerations that go into determining our causal power profiles are therefore rarely, if ever, determinative of what courses of action we will take. What then are these processes of deciding and willing?

I speculate that the process of deliberating, and consequently of deciding what to do, is one that is focussed on creating a specific disposition to act in some way.[2] Let Y be what the agent A has decided to do in known circumstances X. Then, since A now has this disposition, A will do Y, when A is made aware that X has occurred. Moreover, if A's disposition was acquired by deliberation, then, in doing Y, A must be deemed to have acted deliberately. Accordingly, it must be supposed that acting deliberately is nothing more than the occurrence of a planned reaction to circumstances of a certain kind. And, deciding to act immediately to do Y is just a degenerate case of this. If these speculations are sound, then the process of deciding what to do in given circumstances must be affected by what we may call a 'meta-causal' power, i.e. a power to produce a causal power.

There is nothing odd about there being meta-causal powers. For, as we have seen, the causal powers of complex things are normally variable, not just in the sense that the probabilities of their being realised may vary, but also in the sense that things may come to acquire wholly new causal

74   *Social Humanism*

powers. The piece of iron that becomes magnetised, for example, acquires a new causal power—one it did not have before. An active solenoid's power to magnetise a piece of iron is therefore not just a causal power; it is also a meta-causal power. My speculation that decision-making is the exercise of such a power is therefore physically plausible. The ingredients for deliberative decision-making are all there, or, if they are not all there, they can easily be supplied. We only have to reflect on the range of alternative courses of action that are presented to us in consciousness and opt for one of them. Or, if we do not know what the alternatives are, we can initiate any or all of the processes that determine our causal power profiles to obtain an answer. Nor is it implausible that we should have a meta-causal power apt for decision-making. Its utility for beings that are as capable as we are of striking agreements with others, or of planning for the future, is obvious. Therefore, it is not surprising that it should have been selected naturally.

If this speculation concerning the nature of decision-making is sound, then what must the process of willing be? We naturally think of willing as doing something like issuing a command, an analogy that is naturally attractive to ontological dualists. However, I do not think that the trigger for the discharge of the dispositional property that we have created needs to be anything as specific as issuing a command to oneself—not even a *sotto voce* one. The apparent trigger might be just an occasion, such as the waiter's arrival to take our orders or our having the thought: 'Now would be as good a time as any to do what I have decided to do'. But there is probably just the one trigger in every case, viz. the occasion's being seen to be appropriate for implementing a decision that has been or is currently being made. So willing turns out to be a very ordinary event—certainly not the exercise of a metaphysical power of the kind that Immanuel Kant, and every other ontological dualist, must suppose it to be.

3.4   AUTONOMY

An individual free choice, as Isiah Berlin (1969) has argued, must be an act of choosing of which one is the sole author. It cannot be an event that somehow occurs in one's brain without any authorisation. It must be an autonomous act—something that we are able to do that disposes us to act in a way that we ourselves judge to be preferable, and is done for just that reason. But is there, on the new theory of causation, any such thing as acting autonomously?

Our capacity to act autonomously would seem to depend on our having the abilities to: (a) select our own objectives, and (b) form, monitor, and manage our dispositions to act according to our own circumstances to achieve them. If we lacked the power to select our own objectives, then we should be less free than most of us would like to imagine, because it would be tempting to argue that a person whose choices of objectives were

The Metaphysics of Causal Realism 75

determined just by their animal natures, or by the dispositions they have acquired just by their social or cultural interactions, would be slaves to their natures or circumstances, and so not really autonomous. Indeed, if we were unable to reflect on our objectives, or change them as we see fit, or form, monitor, or manage our dispositions to achieve our aims, we should be like a driver without a brake or a steering wheel, and therefore hostage to our circumstances.

Let A be a human agent, S an outcome that A wishes to achieve, and M a course of action that is believed by A to be a reasonable way of trying to achieve this outcome. Then A will naturally form the disposition to do M if A believes that taking the course M is the best way of achieving the desired result, and there is no good reason why A should not take this course. But, if A does M and the outcome S is not achieved, then A will have to decide whether to (a) abandon the aim of achieving S, (b) take a new course of action that A believes will achieve S in some other way, or (c) look for some achievable alternative to S and do whatever is necessary to realise this alternative. The question, then, for any student of human autonomy, must be: How are we able to do all these things?

It has already been sufficiently argued that we have the capacity to deliberate, and thus to form our own dispositions to behave. The process of deliberating is one that enables people to know what actions are most likely to achieve the ends they seek and results in the formation of dispositions to act in these ways, if or when it seems appropriate to do so. Less sophisticated capacities of this kind certainly exist in the animal kingdom. All animals that seek food or shelter or to procreate or defend themselves must know instinctively how to do these things and be disposed to do them as the occasion demands. Human beings too must have these basic instincts. But autonomy requires more than just basic instincts. It requires a capacity to develop new dispositions to satisfy new demands, and so achieve objectives that are different from, or even antithetical to, our most basic instincts.

Every intelligent animal with a causal power profile also has what I call 'an action profile'. That is, it has a certain set of objectives that has been refined or modified in the light of experience and a certain range of dispositions, which have been adapted to realizing these ends and are to be triggered in circumstances that are appropriate for doing so. An animal's action profile is subtly different from its causal power profile. Its causal power profile is focussed on its dispositions to act or react in specific circumstances. Its action profile, in contrast, is concerned with its intentions and the courses of action it is disposed to take to realise these intentions. But the action profiles of normal adult humans are superficially very different from those of other kinds of animals. The differences are not so great that human beings could not plausibly have developed the capacity to acquire them by natural selection. But many would doubt whether other animals have the capacity to act intentionally. For, intentional actions require having beliefs about what the consequences of their intended actions are likely to be, and hence beliefs about probable causation.

76 *Social Humanism*

But surely, it will be said, this is too sophisticated for any non-human creature to grasp. To be sure, human action profiles are extraordinary. The second order causal powers that are required to manipulate our action profiles are not well developed in other animals. There are, no doubt, some such powers displayed by some of the more intelligent animals that we know about, e.g. the anthropoid apes. For, these animals not only have the ability to learn from experience, but also to make some quite sophisticated decisions about how to achieve the things they want, e.g. by the use of primitive tools, such as sticks or stones. Nevertheless, human deliberative powers are in a class of their own, informed as they are by the powerful human capacities of reason, imagination, memory, and empathy. We even have a capacity (synderesis) to stand back imaginatively from a particular situation and view it dispassionately as an individual of no specific identity, and thus come to think about it from an abstract moral point of view.

When I speak of the power of reason and its relation to intentional action, what I have in mind is roughly what Hume meant when he spoke of reasoning about matters of fact. It is reasoning that depends on our having knowledge of the causes of things. This, as Hume was well aware, is precisely the kind of reasoning that is essentially involved in deciding what to do to achieve what we want. It is also involved in diagnosing mistakes, when actions fail to achieve what we hoped they would, and in correcting for these mistakes. Thus, reasoning about matters of fact is involved essentially, not only in forming our intentions, but also in monitoring and correcting them.

Therefore, the meta-causal theory of human agency does not detract in any way from the idea that our power of decision-making is a uniquely human. Certainly, there is nothing much very like it anywhere else in nature, other than a human collective of some kind. Collectives, like individuals, can plan ahead, monitor their progress, and make corrections as necessary to achieve their objectives. The only important difference is that the deliberations of collectives do not all occur in the one head. Normally, they occur around a conference table or in an assembly. It is true that the causal power and action profiles of collectives are as inherently unstable as their membership is, and this must inevitably complicate any legislation that may be designed to regulate collective behaviour. But, this detail need not concern us here. The main point is that, from the perspective of a causal realist, collective agents are the same as the individual agents in all socially and morally important respects. They form their causal power and action profiles in the same kinds of ways, for the same kinds of objectives, and must take responsibility for them in the same kinds of circumstances, for the same sorts of reasons. Moreover, the account given is clearly compatible with a plausible theory of individual and collective autonomy, which makes perfectly good sense of the idea that a society's effective decision-makers are all capable of being the authors of their own actions, and therefore morally responsible for them.

3.5 KANT'S PURE RATIONAL IDEALISM

Philosophers of the Enlightenment had good reason to think that human beings were not just passive participants in causal processes, as Hume was suggesting. For, unless they had a more active role than this would assign to them, they could not be responsible for their actions, except as the victims of circumstances. Kant presumably recognised this. In his *Prolegomena to Any Future Metaphysic*, he said of Hume's theory of causation that it had 'awakened him from his dogmatic slumber' and forced him to re-examine his views about human rationality and decision-making. Kant's response was to suppose that human beings all have wills that are determined by reason and desire but act as causal powers are supposed to act. They allow human beings to: (a) come to more or less well-informed decisions about what changes to the world they want to bring about, and what actions they would have to take to realise their aims; and (b) initiate these actions. The will, in Kant's philosophy, is thus an extraordinary instrument. For a mechanist, it would have to have both a mental and a material character. It must have a mental character, because it is determined by practical reasoning. But it must also have a capacity to act on material things, because it is through their wills that people are able to change what happens in the world. No wonder the will featured so centrally in Kant's metaphysics of morals.

Kant's identification of the human will as the agent that is productive of social activity allowed human reasoning its ultimate control in these areas. For, the will is itself responsive to the beliefs, desires, and values of its owner. As Kant understood it, the will was the supposed link between human thought and action; it could be influenced by human thought, but it could also act to implement human decisions. Thus, he spoke of acts of will. But human thought was a mental process, not a physical one. Hence, the will, the supposed link between thought and action, was *eo ipso* also a link between the mental and the physical.

To accept Kant's metaphysics of morals, one has to believe that there is at least one kind of causal power, viz. that expressed by an act of will. And this causal power, which we may call the power of human agency, must be the will itself, as it is informed by reason, desires, and attitudes. This view of human nature has no scientific basis and is metaphysically implausible. Nevertheless, it is one that has been widely accepted in Western philosophy and by many Western moral and political theorists since the eighteenth century. And there is good reason for this. Although Kant's metaphysics of morals is based on a faulty mind/body dualism, and the widely accepted, but false, view that nature is essentially passive, it is not really so very far from the account that a physical realist would give. For, these two mistakes more or less cancel each other out. Kant's postulates: (a) that the will has causal powers that can be shaped by reason and desire, and (2) is capable of acting on decisions made by its owner, is not an absurd theory. The modern doctrine

78 *Social Humanism*

is simply that people have causal powers that can be shaped by reason and desire, and that people are capable of using these powers to achieve their objectives. Thus, the doctrines that are most at fault in Kant's metaphysical theory are those of dualism and passivism, not his theory of the will, which he only needs for the purpose of neutralising his other mistakes.

The metaphysics of scientific realism thus allows the rational construction of a plausible theory of human choice and action that is, superficially at least, very like the one that Kant embraced in his account of the foundations of morality. Manifestly, it does not lead to the glorification of the will, which lies at the heart of Kant's theory. The will just turns out to be the power to act on decisions already (or simultaneously) made, which is neither mysterious nor profound. But according to Kant (1785/1946: 10),

> Nothing can possibly be conceived in the world, or even out of it, which can be called good without qualification, except a good will.

This is an extraordinary statement, when you come to think of it, and not at all what you might expect from an Enlightenment thinker. One might have expected 'happiness' or 'human wellbeing' to be the *summum bonum* of a moral theory, but not 'a good will'. For Kant, however, the will is the essential link between the inner mental world of reason and experience and the outer world of things. The will is the possessor of the power of agency, and the will is the thing that is, or could be, informed by reason. So, naturally, for Kant, the will is all-important. It is ultimately what determines what an individual does when acting responsibly. In the metaphysics of scientific realism, the will is nothing special. Human beings are themselves the possessors of all of the relevant powers of human agency. They are already in, and therefore parts of, the material world.

Having identified the will as the instrument of the mind for effecting changes in the world, and having argued that the only thing that is good in itself is a good will, the next question to be considered must have seemed obvious to Kant: What makes a will a good one? Kant's response was to argue that a good will is necessarily one that is intrinsically good. It cannot be one that is geared to any end that is extrinsic to it, such as human happiness or wellbeing. For, such a will would be, at best, only one that is good as a means to that end. Therefore, it can only ever justify hypothetical imperatives, such as: If you want the end you seek, then here are some good ways of achieving it. If, for example, you were seeking to promote human wellbeing as much as possible, then you might well develop and act on a strategy designed to achieve this end. But, Kant argued, a set of principles of behaviour designed to achieve such an end could never be a set of moral principles. For, moral principles are not geared towards ends such as these. And this would be so, he argued, however desirable the ends might be. A good will, he argued, must be a will that acts, not on hypothetical imperatives, but on categorical ones.

In answer to his own question, Kant thought that a good will would have to be one that always acted on principle. (Presumably, he means, whenever the interests of others may be affected.) And, to act on principle, he said, is not just to have a reason (or, as Kant says, 'a maxim') for one's action or inaction; it is to have a reason for it that could also be a reason for anyone else doing (or not doing) it in similar circumstances. Clearly, such principles can be debated and argued about. Is it, or would it be, a good reason for everyone in such circumstances? If so, then it would presumably be a principle that is at least a candidate for the status of a moral law. But, as I understand what Kant is saying, something more would be needed to establish that the principle is a moral law. In his famous *categorical imperative*, Kant's concept of a moral law is circumscribed by what he says it is not. Here is Kant's (1785/1946: 46) original statement of this famous meta-ethical principle:

> Act only on that maxim whereby thou canst at the same time will that it should become a universal law of nature.

But to act morally, Kant says, it is not enough for one to act on principles that one would consider to be binding on all people. One must act only on principles that one would consider binding on all rational beings, whatever their contingent natures. Kant repeatedly asserts that moral laws must have this broader scope. But even this may not be enough, it seems. For, every different rational agent might be willing to legislate a different set of principles and insist that these principles must be binding on all rational beings. So, if Kant wishes to have an objective moral system, it is not clear that his categorical imperative will lead him to it. He could say positively:

> Every rational agent must act only on principles that every rational agent would legislate for all rational agents.

This would guarantee objectivity. But Kant does not say this. And it would not be helpful if he did. For, unless the ideal of a rational agent were very considerably tightened, there might be very few such principles.

It must be concluded that Kant's metaphysical foundations of morality have so far failed to provide an adequate basis for morals. Nevertheless, there are many important lessons to be learnt from Kant. Firstly, the distinction between a principle of action and a reason for action needs to be preserved, because only the former could plausibly be a moral principle. Secondly, the conception of morals as principles of action or restraint that define the boundaries of good or acceptable social behaviour is sound enough, because this clearly implies that moral principles have the status of social ideals. It cannot be just that this is how I, or anyone else, may feel about these principles. The principles must be ones that everyone in society could reasonably endorse as guides to life. That is, they must be strong candidates for inclusion in the society's social contract.

80 *Social Humanism*

Perhaps Kant's greatest mistake concerning morality was to assume, as nearly everyone before and since has assumed, that moral principles must outrank social ones. So that if one is presented with a choice between whether to do what one thinks, or what most people think, is morally required, and obey the law of the land, then one ought always to do what one thinks is morally required. This is a form of what I am here calling the 'dominance principle'. To derive a conception of morality that would satisfy the dominance principle, Kant sought to justify his moral principles by pure reason. Only the categorical demands of pure reason, he thought, could outweigh the hypothetical imperatives of social policy. To keep this end clearly in view, he thought of moral principles as laws of behaviour that would, somehow, be necessarily binding on all rational beings, not just on humans. It was not that there were any rational aliens around whose behaviour had to be considered. Kant's extension of the franchise of morality was, presumably, just to stress his view of the complete irrelevance of human desires for happiness, or for life fulfilment, to questions of morality.

3.6 ALTERNATIVES FORMS OF RATIONAL IDEALISM

The Kantian and neo-Kantian alternatives to pure rational idealism do not extend the field of morally responsible beings to all non-humans, as well as humans. On the contrary, they restrict it to the normal class of all ideally rational, but socially responsible, ones. Kant himself made such restrictions by implication in some of his writings, where he wrote of moral laws as laws of nature, although he was seldom explicit about the reference classes for his laws of nature. For example, he asserts that 'it is wrong to act on some maxim unless we could rationally will it to be true that everyone accepts this maxim, and acts upon it whenever they can' (Parfit, 2011: 286). The kinds of agents to which this rule is supposed to apply, and the scope of the 'everyone' who is required to accept this maxim, are both left unspecified, but there is little doubt that the implicit references here are to normal adult human beings. So, this successfully eliminates the possibility that there could be ideally rational beings, whose views we had to take into account, which, for all we know, might have the morals of alley cats.

Rawls' (1971) version of rational idealism is similarly restricted in scope. Or, if this is not so, then I am not sure that I understand what Rawls' version really is. Parfit (2011: 21) summarises Rawls' position:

> Everyone ought to follow the principles to whose universal acceptance it would be rational in self-interested terms for everyone to agree, if everyone had to reach this agreement without knowing any particular facts about themselves or their circumstances.

The Metaphysics of Causal Realism   81

To make sense of this claim, it is perhaps best to construct a sort of mirror image of Rawls' veil of ignorance. Let us call it 'the lens of rational insight'. An ideally rational being A has the lens of rational insight into a society S if and only if: A is completely indifferent to the people in S, but is (a) completely knowledgeable about the consequences of adopting any of the various possible principles of social behaviour that might be accepted as moral principles in that society, and (b) knows exactly what the individuals in S should or should not be willing to agree to in their own interests. Then, if I understand Rawls' theory properly, Rawls' claim is that the moral principles that A would prescribe for S as being on balance in the best interests of all are the moral principles that should prevail in S.[3]

Thomas Scanlon's (1998) version of contractualism is also a form of rational idealism. According to Parfit's (2011: 340) account, Scanlon's conception of moral wrongness is:

> It is wrong for us to act on some maxim unless everyone could rationally will it to be true that everyone believes that such acts are morally permitted.

But, interestingly, Scanlon's position is one that comes close to recognising the fundamental importance to moral theory of a society's ideal social contract. According to the theory of social idealism (to be developed in the next chapter), our moral principles are just those codes of practice that we would wish to see included as norms or regulations in the ideal social contract of our society. For this to occur, the vast majority of people in the society would have to think as we do about this code of practice. A vast majority, or near consensus, would be enough. But a vast majority is not everyone. One cannot reasonably expect literally everyone to agree with anything much that one has to say. So, instead of social idealism, which allows for the possibility of rational disagreements about the principles that a people should adopt as moral ones, Scanlon opts to bar irrational objections. If no one could rationally disagree with a code of practice, he says, then it cannot be wrong to act on it.

But I don't think that this or any other form of rational idealism is what is needed for moral theory. Rationally idealistic foundations for moral theory normally involve one or other of the following assumptions:

1. The bearers of moral properties are assumed to be adult persons of sound mind who think that acting morally is acting rationally (a) in one's own long-term self-interest while avoiding those actions that are not, or (b) in accordance with one's own well-considered ideals of goodness while avoiding those actions that are contrary to these ideals. (Let us call anyone who would endorse 1(a) an *egoistic rational idealist*, and any supporter of 1(b) an *idealistic rational idealist*.[4])
2. The moral principles we should endorse are those that an ideally rational human being would endorse, (a) who has all of the required

82   *Social Humanism*

knowledge about the probabilities of the various possible consequences of actions, and (b) whose ideals of goodness are derived from that ideal person's comprehensive understanding of the effects of these consequences on human and other sentient creatures. (Let us call anyone who would endorse 2 a *consequentialist rational idealist*.)

Naturally, I endorse the efforts of those who would seek to better understand the rationale for morality, especially those in the idealistic and consequentialist camps of rational idealism. As Parfit has pointed out, idealistic and consequentialist versions of rational idealism are not incompatible with one another. Our own well-considered ideals of goodness might well be formed by, or depend on, our understanding of the likely effects of our actions on human or other sentient creatures. Indeed, I should hope that they would be. Parfit's (2011) Triple Theory is such a bridging theory. It is: (a) a form of rational idealism, and hence neo-Kantian; (b) rule-utilitarian, and hence consequentialist; and (c) rationally idealistic, in the way that Scanlon's theory is. But it is still not adequate as a metaphysical foundation for morality. Because it is Kantian, it is essentially individualistic, objectivist, and dominant. Consequently, it fails, as all Kantian theories must, to tackle any of the issues of so-called 'applied ethics', which, in my view, should be among the main concerns of moral philosophy. What is needed, I will argue, is a new metaphysics of morals—one that will effectively replace the Kantian one.

Social idealism is a meta-theory that is foundational for both morals and politics that is well able to serve in this capacity. It is a theory that is realistic about the causal power analysis of agency developed in Sections 3.3 and 3.4 above, and it accepts that a true anthropological description of any human society must make non-redundant reference to a wide range of kinds of social agents, having various and varying degrees of power and social influence, and that this complex will be regulated by laws and social conventions defining good behaviour and the limits to tolerable behaviour. The social agents involved will normally include a large number of collectives, e.g. governments, corporations, armies, universities, and so on; a wide variety of specialist agents, e.g. doctors, CEOs, pilots, teachers, and so on; and the social laws and conventions of the society will normally be specific to each different category. They will also refer to the normal category of 'socially responsible individuals' and to other categories of people considered to be morally relevant. All of this information will be included in the de facto social contract of the society, which evolves as the society evolves and adapts to changing circumstances or technologies. The theory of social idealism is then based on the thesis that an individual's moral system is the set of all social laws of conventions concerning the behaviour of society's social agents, which that individual would wish to see included in the society's social contract.

Two sorts of social ideals are evidently required for such a theory: ideals of society and ideals of good character, corresponding roughly to the

The Metaphysics of Causal Realism 83

distinction between politics and morality. But, the two are not really independent of each other, because those of good character should include the character traits that we think are needed to construct and maintain a good society, and good and well-regulated social institutions are certainly needed to develop and maintain good character traits. The aim of Part III of this book is to develop the theory of social idealism on the basis of the assumption that these two ideals are not really independent.

Traditionally, moral philosophy has been seen as being concerned mainly with good character development and as basically independent of political philosophy. But that is my main criticism of rational idealism. It treats moral philosophy as though it were independent of all political concerns, and it focuses on individual character traits as though they were of supreme importance. Neither is true. Good people need not only be good in a politically neutral way; they also need to have a good social conscience and to be good members of society. And a good society needs not only good people; it also needs good institutions and well-regulated social agents to serve the needs of all of the different kinds of people that the society must cater to. However, the customary disciplinary division leaves the social moral principles of applied ethics in limbo. They are not properly included in political philosophy, because they are not thought to belong there, and they have only a second-class status in moral theory, because they are thought to be derivative. Again, neither is true. The principles of applied ethics are central to moral and political theory, while those of so-called 'pure' ethics and/or government are peripheral. What is needed for the sound development of moral and political philosophy, it will be argued, is a common meta-theory that is realistic about the power of agency and would integrate these two disciplines as two interlocking branches of an overall theory of society. The theory of social idealism would do just that.

3.7 SMITH'S MORAL REALISM

A more recent, and much more plausible, attempt to provide adequate metaphysical foundations of morality is Michael Smith's, in which he construes morality as the branch of human understanding that is concerned with the influence of knowledge and rational reflection on our systems of desires and values. He identifies his position as a species of 'internalist moral realism', i.e. as a species of the kind of moral theory that regards the propositions of morality as (a) having truth values, and (b) being concerned with what we would wish for as a rational agent in a state of 'broad reflective equilibrium'. Specifically, he thinks that moral theory is concerned with what our desires would be in a state in which our beliefs are maximally informed and our desires perfectly coherent and unified. The search for moral truth must therefore be partly concerned with our knowledge of the world, and of the effects of our actions, and partly introspective, concerned

84 *Social Humanism*

with our basic attitudes. In the end, Smith thinks that there are just two forms of internalist moral realism that have this character and survive criticism—a relativistic form (RF) and an objective or a non-relativistic form (OF). According to the RF:

> RF: 'An action A is morally right in circumstances of kind C for a given class K of rational creatures R' is true, if and only if, for all x, if x ∈ K, and Mx (i.e. x has a maximally informed, coherent and unified set of beliefs and desires M), then x would desire to do A in C, and, for all y, if y ∈ K, x would desire that y would also do A in C. (Smith, 2004: 204)

The OF is:

> OF: 'An action A is morally right in circumstances of the kind C' is true, if and only if, for all x, if x ∈ R and Mx, then x would desire to do A in C, and for all y, if y ∈ R, x would desire that y would do A in C. (Smith, 2004: 205)

Smith's preferred analysis is the second, although he admits that he has no good reason to suppose that perfectly rational individuals cannot disagree about what is ultimately most desirable if they satisfy the condition of having a maximally informed, coherent, and unified set of beliefs and desires (M). I agree. And, if we turn our attention to social agents other than human individuals, it is clear that they would not always agree about what is ultimately most desirable. Consider the class K or perfectly rational cats. There is no good reason to believe that every member of K would not desire to torture mice to death, as they always have done, however well informed their belief and desire sets may be, and that they would wholeheartedly recommend this practice to all members of their species. Of course, there are no perfectly rational cats. But there are very rational and highly motivated mining companies operating in Western Australia who recently pooled their vast resources to defeat the Labor Government's mining super-profits tax so that they could continue to enjoy their super-profits at the expense of the manufacturing and retail sectors of the Australian economy. Was this position, therefore, a morally right one for the mining giants to take? It is, if RF is the correct analysis of moral rightness.

These examples show two things clearly: (a) that Smith's analyses of moral rightness apply, if at all, only to morally responsible individual human beings—not to non-human rational animals or to collectives; and (b) that even the weak relativistic version RF presupposes that morally responsible human beings whose belief systems are maximally informed, unified, and coherent must necessarily adopt a humanistic perspective. This assumption is obviously untenable for non-humans and human collectives, but it would also appear to be untenable for various kinds of subgroups in the human community. There is no good reason to believe that whites, blacks, males,

The Metaphysics of Causal Realism   85

females, Jews, Muslims, and Christians must all potentially be humanists, i.e. have maximally informed, unified, and coherent belief and desire sets that do not discriminate between classes of individuals, so that they would come to think of themselves, not as whites, blacks, males, females, and so on, but simply as human beings. As a humanist, I wish that this were so. But as a realist, I do not believe it is, because the social conflicts that plague our societies seem unlikely to be resolvable just by seeking out better information or reasoning more coherently. The differences derive from fundamentally different social attitudes, and there will need to be political upheavals to resolve them, if, indeed, they are capable of resolution.

Nevertheless, Smith's analysis has a number of attractive features. Firstly, it explains most of the important connections between moral judgements and moral attitudes of approval or disapproval. For example, it explains why 'X is morally right, but I morally disapprove of X' is a pragmatic contradiction. It is a pragmatic contradiction, because it is (a) attitudinally incoherent, but (b) not a formal contradiction. It is not a formal contradiction, because the truth conditions for 'X is morally right' and 'Ellis morally disapproves of X' are not inconsistent. Secondly, it explains the pragmatic contradiction between (a) 'X is morally wrong' and (b) 'I morally approve of your doing X'. It would be attitudinally incoherent for me to assert both of these things, even though their truth conditions are not at odds with one other.

But the attitudes implied by Smith's truth-conditional analysis of the proposition that X is morally right are sometimes at odds with what they should be given a commonsense view of the matter. Firstly, if it truly is morally right to do X in circumstances C, it does not follow that if I had a maximally informed, unified, and coherent set of beliefs and desires, then I would desire to do X in circumstances C. For, I might reasonably think that it would be silly for me to do X in circumstances C if doing X in such circumstances were not the established social norm. Suppose, for example, that I were a morally committed nudist and believed that morally no one should wear clothes. It does not follow that I would want not to wear clothes in the absence of any social agreement to this effect. Nor would I expect others to behave in this way and so make fools of themselves. The morally right thing might not be the rationally preferable thing to do.

Secondly, there are many different kinds of social agents within any community, and it would be wrong to ignore them, or to think that if we could solve the problem of what it would be right for an individual, qua responsible human being to do, we have therefore solved the problem of what it would be right for such human beings, qua surgeons or members of parliament to do. Individuals in specific social roles have role-specific moral responsibilities, and hence moral rights and obligations that other members of the community do not have. But this diversity of moral rights and obligations can only be accounted for on Smith's relativistic analysis, because it is manifestly inconsistent with his objectivist one. The sets of doctors, teachers, parents, policemen, and company directors whose belief

86   *Social Humanism*

and desire sets satisfy M are all proper subsets of R.[5] But then we should have to allow that their sets of moral obligations and prohibitions are different from each other's and different again from those of people with other social roles or profiles. Personally, I accept this implication. But it is not one that Smith could easily accept, because it would mean that there *could not* be a comprehensive moral system based on OF.

Moreover, there is no doubt that corporations and other collectives also have moral responsibilities. But I do not see how they could possibly be determined by any process that involves only seeking better knowledge or greater coherence. Boards of directors, shareholders, employees, customers, trading partners, and so on all have vested interests in how they collectively should behave, but each lacks the objectivity required to choose overall in the public interest. So there is no point in the members of any of these groups of individuals reflecting on how they would most want these organisations to behave. The members of these different classes would almost certainly give very different answers to this question, even if, perhaps even especially if, their belief and desire systems were maximally informed, coherent, and unified. The decision about what they ought morally to do clearly has to be a social one, not a consensus of individual decisions. So, plausibly, the lack of a social dimension to Smith's theory of morality is fatal to it.

Smith's theory of morality is essentially humanistic, which is fine by me. But it is also essentially individualistic. As such, it is the kind of moral theory that Anglo-American (as opposed to continental European) philosophers are most inclined to favour. But what is needed, I shall later argue (in Chapter 4), is a theory of morality that takes the social aspects of morality much more seriously.

3.8   RIGHTNESS AND REALITY

Smith begins his book on moral realism by arguing for what he calls a 'naturalistic' theory and against what he calls 'minimalist moral realism'. The minimalist theory, he says, is what one would arrive at if one had only a minimalist theory of truth, i.e. if one regarded the predicate 'is true' as nothing more than a device for indirect assertion. As such, it is certainly a useful linguistic tool, but it adds nothing to what is said to be true. For example, the economy of my saying 'Everything you say is true' is obvious, where my aim is just to commit myself to what you have said. But it does not elaborate on what you say or say anything different from what you have already said. So, given this minimalist conception of truth, the proposition that our judgements of right and wrong are either true or false really does not tell us much. It contextually implies that the sentences used to express such judgements are all capable of being accepted or rejected, using the device of indirect assertion. But this is about all it does. It does not ascribe a semantic property, i.e. a relationship between words and the world, to

The Metaphysics of Causal Realism 87

them, as it appears to. Consequently, if one asserts that 'Torturing babies is wrong' is true and attaches no other sense to 'true' than the minimalist one, then this is exactly the same as saying that torturing babies is wrong. It does not imply that to ascribe 'right' or 'wrong' to an act is to claim that it has some naturalistic feature that warrants such an ascription. But a naturalistic version of moral realism does require the belief that using the term 'right' or 'wrong' to describe an act would be justified only if the act in question had the relevant naturalistic right-making or wrong-making feature. Therefore, moral realism cannot be derived simply from the fact that moral propositions can be said to be true or false. Any viable form of moral realism must be a form of naturalistic moral realism.

Smith's own version of naturalistic moral realism is a species of internal realism and suffers from all of the philosophical problems associated with this position. In the internalist theory of truth that I once defended, I argued that the only philosophically defensible concept of truth is one of epistemic rightness. Specifically, I argued that truth is a mode of evaluation. It is the concept of truth that we standardly use to express the belief that a particular sentence says accurately what we think it is epistemically right to believe. The attribution of this property to a given proposition is thus an indirect way of commending its acceptance to others. That is why, I argued, it is a pragmatic contradiction to say, 'It is true, but I don't believe it' or 'I believe it, even though it is false'. These assertions are pragmatic contradictions, I argued, not because they are strictly contradictory, but because they are attitudinally incoherent. Clearly, there is no contradiction in anyone (other than me) saying, 'It is true, but Ellis does not believe it' or 'Ellis believes it, even though it is false'. Similarly, one of Smith's arguments for internalism about moral realism relies on the existence of pragmatic contradictions, e.g. between 'X is right' and 'I morally disapprove of X'. For this to be possible, he argues, rightness would have to be an internalist property that is reflective of moral attitudes.

To make out the case for internalist moral realism, Smith feels that he has to argue against the externalist version of this position. In doing so, he makes use of the so-called 'open question' argument. According to the externalist position, 'X is morally right' must be made true by the existence of some natural property that makes it right. The property might, for example, be that of having optimific consequences. Let this right-making property be P. An external moral realist will then claim that 'X is morally right' is true if and only if X is P. But this analysis is open to a serious objection. For there is no apparent contradiction in saying, 'Although X is P, I do not think that X is right'. It is perhaps worth noting that I once argued against correspondence theories of truth in the same sort of way. Specifically, I argued that if φ is the alleged truth-making relationship between a sentence S and reality R, it would always be an open question whether a sentence S that bears φ to R is true. For 'S bears φ to R' is a factual claim, not an evaluative one. Therefore, it cannot be a contradiction to say that

88 *Social Humanism*

although S bears φ to R, S is not true. Thus, my argument for internal realism in the philosophy of science maps quite closely Smith's argument for internalism about judgements of moral rightness.

For many years, I went along with internal realism, writing a number of papers, and eventually a book (Ellis, 1990), defending it. But I am now convinced that the internalist, or epistemic, concept of truth is not the only one. For just as there are two concepts of probability, an objectivist concept related to long-run relative frequency, and a subjectivist one concerned with the coherent distribution of degrees of belief over the propositions of a language, so there must also be two concepts of truth: an objectivist one concerned with the relationship of true propositions to the world, and a subjectivist one concerned with the coherent distribution of truth and falsity claims over the propositions expressible in the language. Science sets out to discover the nature of reality. But scientists, qua scientists, can never do more than discover what it is epistemically right for them to believe. Indeed, their methodology prevents them from considering seriously the question, which no additional evidence could possibly answer: What must the world be like for the theories we now accept to be true? What are their truth-makers? The evaluative theory of truth is all that is required for science. But a correspondence theory of truth is needed if we wish to go beyond science to answer these important metaphysical questions.

Smith seems to accept this criticism of internalism in the theory of moral rightness, because he cites Jackson's supervenience constraint on judgements of rightness and wrongness with evident approval. Right or wrong acts, he says, must have some naturalistic feature that warrants the ascription of 'right' or 'wrong' to them. But he does not follow up on this point, and the idea that what is right or wrong will eventually emerge through discussion among rational people, provided that all are maximally informed and aim to construct comprehensive belief and desire systems that are coherent and unified, is not very satisfying. What is needed, I think, is a rightness-maker theory that has something of the sophistication and persuasiveness of truthmaker theory in scientific metaphysics. Therefore, Smith's account of moral realism would fail to provide an adequate metaphysics of morals, even if all of the other objections to it could be answered satisfactorily.

3.9 JACKSON'S PHYSICAL REALISM

Frank Jackson (1998: 11) bases his argument for realism in ethics on the following global supervenience thesis:

> Any two possible worlds that are physical duplicates (instantiated physical property, law, and relation for instantiated physical property, law and relation identical) are duplicates *simpliciter.*

The Metaphysics of Causal Realism   89

Given this global supervenience thesis, which I would accept, he argues that, if moral judgements of right and wrong are descriptive of reality, then the following thesis must hold:

> (S) For all worlds w and w^*, if w and w^* are exactly alike descriptively, then they are exactly alike ethically. (Jackson, 1998: 119)

I argue that (S) is vacuous. There is no way that the world is ethically. There is a way the world is, and it is the aim of metaphysicians to describe it as best they can. But to say that there is a way that the world is ethically is to say that the class of moral judgements is a class of judgements about the way that the world is. I dispute this. My moral judgements are not about how the world is; they are about how ideally I would want the world to be.

In principle, it is possible to describe the world w in such a way as to convey what the various individuals in the world are trying to say. Let W_e be the set of all possible worlds in which my moral position e is realised. Let $I_1, I_2, \ldots I_n$ be all of the responsible adults in the world. Then, to describe the moral positions of every such person in the world, we should need to describe an n-tuple of sets of possible worlds $W_{e1}, W_{e2}, \ldots W_{en}$, where there is one n-tuple for each individual. Of course, one could insist that there is a way that the world w is ethically, viz. that its inhabitants $I_1, I_2, \ldots I_n$ stand in the relation of 'wanting ideally to realise' worlds of the classes of possible worlds $W_{e1}, W_{e2}, \ldots W_{en}$, respectively. But this does not even look like telling a moral realist what a moral realist really wants to know. For, Jackson wants us to conclude from his argument that simple moral properties, such as rightness, are analytically equivalent to more or less simple properties of actions. He thinks, for example, that the property of rightness might be analytically equivalent to 'productive of the greatest happiness for the greatest number', depending on how the moral debate about rightness unfolds. If, in the state of reflective equilibrium that is reached at the end of this debate, this turns out to be the case, then the statement that X is morally right will be analytically equivalent to X is productive of the greatest happiness for the greatest number. This, he thinks, would give the proposition a status similar to that of 'Water is H_2O', which he also believes to be analytic.[6]

It is possible that if everyone were perfectly well informed, then their preferred sets of possible worlds would all be the same. If this were the case, then we should expect to find that they were all being generated by the same moral principle or set of moral principles. For, it would be extremely unlikely that such moral agreement would occur by chance. In these extraordinary circumstances, then, we would be justified in believing that there was an objectively true morality, viz. the system that included just this principle or set of principles. In fact, I believe that if everyone were perfectly well informed, then their preferred sets of possible worlds would indeed have some things in common, viz. they would all be worlds in which the basic principles of humanism were adhered to. But these would not be

90 *Social Humanism*

likely to be the only principles that would be accepted as moral principles by perfectly well-informed people. For, as will be argued in later chapters, moral disagreements could, and probably would, still exist, even in worlds inhabited only by humanists.

3.10 HUMAN VALUE REALISM

Tännsjö (1990b) is a moral property realist. His realism is based on his claim that moral properties are directly observable and so must have a basis in reality. He does not think that moral goodness and moral badness are properties that would exist in nature independently of human or other animal perceptions. But he does think that acts of cruelty and injustice can normally be observed directly to be morally bad, while those of kindness and beneficence can usually be seen immediately to be morally good. These directly observable moral facts, he thinks, are the bases of all our moral theorising. And a good moral theory, he says, must be able to account for them. Therefore, he says, our moral theory must neither condone acts that are morally bad, nor discourage ones that are morally good. But, he insists, the principles of morality cannot be derived from the fact of our having the capacity to apprehend these moral facts. If they exist, the principles of morality must explain the facts, not give rise to them. The capacity to apprehend such facts is presumably one that was originally acquired by natural selection, as Peter Carruthers and Scott James (2008) and James (2009) have argued recently. For, what would be needed most for biological advantage would be: (a) a social structure that enabled the members of the tribe to act together intelligently in their pursuit of food and shelter, (b) discouragement of unjust and anti-social behaviour to avoid alienation and infighting, and (c) encouragement of friendly and socially cooperative behaviour to unite the tribe. So, we should at least expect members of the tribe to develop some familiar social attitudes. Moreover, we should expect them to be able to recognise good and bad behaviour by any member of the tribe in his or her social role and adopt the appropriate attitude towards it. It is very plausible, therefore, that we should have developed, very early in our history, natural tendencies to approve morally of acts that we judge to be socially good and disapprove morally of acts that we judge to be socially bad. It is very hard to disagree with any of this.

Tännsjö's moral realism is thus a bit like scientific realism. The moral facts, he argues, are best explained by the hypothesis that we all have certain natural moral values. Therefore, he says, these values must be real. Consider the analogy of smell. With very few exceptions, we are all able to distinguish disgusting from pleasant odours. No human being to my knowledge likes the smell of mercaptans, the pungent odours of rotting flesh. But nearly everyone loves the smell of freshly ground coffee or spices. To explain these facts, the simplest hypothesis is that we have evolved a

The Metaphysics of Causal Realism 91

dislike of the disgusting ones and have developed a natural liking for the attractive ones. Tännsjö's hypothesis is that, just as there are revolting smells, there are some events that are morally revolting. John's setting the cat on fire was morally disgusting. Susan's act of boiling her grandmother in oil and gloating over her screams was also morally repugnant. No normal person could witness such events without having the same reaction. Thus, says Tännsjö, there are moral facts, and these moral facts are reflective of basic human values.

The kinds of actions that elicit moral responses seem to occur within four broad categories—those of tribal loyalty, honesty, compassion, and justice, and their opposites. If this is true, then we should expect our natural human values to be classifiable under these headings. It is not difficult to see why the required moral attitudes to all of these kinds of actions might have evolved. Loyalty, truthfulness, compassion, and fairness are all required if a good society is to be created or maintained. Acts of these kinds are therefore likely to be encouraged or rewarded, whereas acts of disloyalty, lying, indifference, and injustice are likely to be hated or punished. Therefore, the idea that moral attitudes might have evolved by natural selection is not unreasonable. Nor is it unreasonable to suppose that this basic system is capable of development by discussion and argument, as most moral philosophers evidently believe.

Sam Harris (2010) is also a believer in moral facts and natural human values; like Tännsjö, he believes that they are, and should be, studied scientifically. So do I. But it should be stressed that our moral values are not necessarily the same as our natural values. Nor should they be. Our natural human values must have evolved to suit life in tribal communities, where tribal loyalties were at a premium, and tribal warfare and competition for scarce resources were savage and brutal. It is likely, therefore, that we are, by nature, militant racist bigots with strong group loyalties, who are willing to follow ruthless leaders into battle and fight to the death to secure victory. The moral task is to work out how we can live and work together in harmony in today's world, not to discover and promote our natural values. I do not question Harris's goal of promoting human wellbeing universally or his claim that we must use all of the resources of science to discover the best ways and means of achieving this objective. But I doubt whether there is a universal system of moral values that is somehow over and above our natural human values and stands in a position to correct them. However, I do not doubt that there are some moral facts.

3.11 PROSPECTS FOR A METAPHYSICS OF MORALITY

There is, as yet, no acceptable metaphysics of morality. Certainly, there is nothing that would provide us with truthmakers for moral precepts. And, since I do not believe that there are any truthmakers for any but the most

92 *Social Humanism*

elementary moral precepts, I do not intend to try to develop such a metaphysics. There are some objective moral facts and values, as Tännsjö has successfully argued. But these facts and values can do no more than limit the range of acceptable moral theories. They can effectively do this, because if an action is morally bad or an attitude morally vicious, then this can sometimes be discovered by observation or revealed in Socratic dialogue, and the range of prima facie permissible actions or attitudes can thus be restricted. But there is no good reason to think that this is enough to define an adequate metaphysics of morality. It is a plausible foundation for a theory of act-utilitarianism, perhaps, but it is not a foundation for an adequate theory of moral rights or obligations. Act-utilitarianism is not even coherent as a moral theory (Ellis, 2009: 156–159), and it has nothing useful to say about the utility of actions that involve significant trade-offs between good consequences for some groups of people and bad consequences for others, as most social transactions do. To construct such a theory, it is necessary to develop a social theory of morality, as Strawson (1961) and Harman (2000) have argued. A social theory is evidently required to provide adequate accounts of moral rights and responsibilities, and certainly no one has ever managed to construct an individualistic theory of these things. However, rights, obligations, and responsibilities are not dispensable in moral theory. There cannot be a sound doctrine of human rights in a world in which there are no such things as moral rights. However, the social theory that is required must be one that is restricted by basic human judgements about the range of prima facie permissible human actions or attitudes. In the following chapter, I will attempt to construct such a theory.

Part III
Social Idealism

Introduction to Social Idealism

Social idealism is a general theory about the nature of morality, on which, I claim, any and every plausible moral theory must be based. In some ways, it is like the theory presented by Kant (1785/1946) in his *Fundamental Principles of the Metaphysics of Ethics*. Its proposed role in moral theory is similar. But, whereas Kant's meta-theory was a species of rational idealism, mine is one of social idealism. Kant asked himself what an ideally rational society would be like. In particular, he asked: What principles of social behaviour would be required by (and for) a society inhabited by perfectly rational beings? My question here is this: What principles of social behaviour would be required by (and for) the best possible society inhabited by ordinary human beings?[1] If you accept my stance, then the basic structure of your moral position will be determined by your answer to this question. In my view, Kant's meta-theory is metaphysically flawed and is, in any case, inadequate to the task of providing a sound basis for morality. Social idealism is not metaphysically flawed and does provide a solid foundation on which many different moral theories can be built. Specifically, it provides a basis for social humanism, which is the form of humanism required for the development of charters of human rights and, as it happens, is the underlying moral theory of the welfare state.

The argument I will present here draws heavily on my own work in metaphysics over many years and extends the ideas developed in these earlier works (Ellis, 2001, 2002, 2009) to deal with the foundations of morals and politics. But readers should not be put off by my use of the term 'metaphysics' in this context. A metaphysical theory is just a meta-theory, which is sufficiently general to provide an adequate framework for theories in the field. To do this, it must be able to define the parameters, and set the agenda, for every substantive theory in the area that might be developed. To judge a system of metaphysics, one must consider (a) whether it does these things as well or better than any other meta-theory, (b) whether the proposed meta-theory is consistent with one's basic ontology, and (c) how well it compares with any other meta-theories that are also consistent with this ontology. The relevant background material was covered in Part II of this book, where it was argued that the metaphysics of causal realism

96 Social Humanism

should be regarded as fundamental. It was further argued that although the concept of free will required for moral theory could equally well be developed à la Kant or in my own physical causal realist way, Kant's theory was essentially dualistic and so unsatisfactory for this reason. But existing physicalistic meta-theories (e.g. M. Smith, Jackson, and Tännsjö's) all appear to be inadequate to the task. Therefore, the way is open for me to develop my own meta-theory for morals.

There are three chapters in Part III. The first, Chapter 4, develops the basic theory of social idealism, which is the proposed metaphysical foundation for morals. Social idealism defines the basic concepts of morality and sets the agenda for the development of substantive moral theories. It is not itself a moral theory, it should be emphasized—only a foundation for one. If this foundation is accepted, then there are many consequences for social and moral theories that need to be discussed. There are two groups of such issues. First, there are issues concerning the theory of individualism, which is the meta-theory that laid the foundations for the individualistic moral and political theories that were developed after the Second World War. This is the metaphysics that underpins the whole neo-liberal movement and most of the substantive political and economic theories that now dominate Western thinking. It will be discussed in Chapter 5. Second, there are significant implications of social idealism for the theory and method of moral inquiry, which should be particularly relevant to those concerned with the development of substantive moral theories. These implications will be discussed in Chapter 6.

The social theory of morality is the theory that morals are social ideals and the normative force of any moral proposition for any individual (or for any society) derives from the commitment of that individual (or society) to the ideal it expresses. A meta-theory of morals as social ideals was, I believe, first suggested by the late Sir Peter Strawson in his 1961 article, 'Social Morality and Individual Ideal'. But his suggestion was not well developed in this original article and was not in keeping with the prevailing moral theory of his time. Consequently, his theory was not followed up in the journals, and he did not pursue it. The aim of Chapter 4 is to develop the social theory into a firm foundation for the principles of morality that are primarily concerned with the creation of a socially ideal society. Specifically, I will use the theory of social idealism to define the basic concepts of morality, including those of moral obligations, responsibilities, rights, and formal powers. These concepts are all developed as idealisations of the corresponding social concepts. Consequently, the moral concepts, as they are here defined, all have clear links with the social conventions and legal systems of the societies with which we are concerned, and one can easily develop the theory to explain how moral theory can be used for the purposes of social or legal criticism.

Social idealism conceives of the function of morality as being to develop a better society democratically out of the beliefs, desires, and aspirations

Introduction to Social Idealism 97

of ordinary people. Individualistic moralities have always focused on creating better people, in the hope that if you did this properly, a better society would result. Socialist moralities have always focused on creating better societies, evidently in the belief that if this were done well, people would no longer be corrupted by the societies in which they lived, and their natural virtues would then be able to flourish. But both kinds of meta-theories are flawed. Individuals have some natural virtues, but not enough to overcome the influences of a corrupt or unjust society, and the imposition of a just society on an unjust one cannot sustainably suppress individualistic aspirations. 'Socialist man', i.e. one who was willing to work to full capacity to create a better society for nothing more than payment that was adequate for his or her needs, was always a figment of the imagination. This kind of person has never really existed in significant numbers. A moral theory needs to be individually realistic. We cannot, for example, expect everyone to be a saint, as some versions of utilitarianism seem to require. It also needs to be socially realistic. We cannot reasonably expect those who have benefited greatly from their existing society, or those who are still suffering from the traumas and indignities of injustice or discrimination to which it has subjected them, to behave well unless they are provided with hope that they, or at least their children and grandchildren, can flourish as respected members of a flourishing society.

In Chapter 5, I consider the claims of individualism. For, this is the metaphysical point of view that influences most people's thinking about morals and politics in my own society and in the societies of most other Western countries. I begin by distinguishing 'metaphysical individualism' from 'political individualism', because they are two very different things. Political individualism is a form of liberalism. In its most extreme form, it is a political theory based on the idea that everyone should be able to live as they please, without interference from governments or from anyone else, provided only that their ways of living do not interfere with the rights of others to live as they please. Neo-liberalism is a form of political liberalism that is built on a more radical conception of individual freedom that even the lowest taxing and most uncaring of states have shrunk from. It is, strictly speaking, a state in which the role of government is limited to just the protection of life, limb, and property. It advocates what is commonly known as 'the minimal state' (Nozick 1974: 16–18). In minimal states, there are no government welfare provisions, no safety nets, no government investments in infrastructure, no national radio or television, and no minimum wage settings.

Metaphysical individualism, which will be my main concern in Chapter 5, is the claim that individuals are the basic elements of society, in that they are: (a) *ontologically primary*, because all social or cultural changes supervene on changes in the beliefs, attitudes, and desires of their individual members; (b) *epistemologically primary*, because all explanations of social phenomena must ultimately refer to the beliefs, actions, and preferences

98   Social Humanism

of individuals; and (c) *causally primary*, because individuals are the sole agents in society and so are the primary causes of all social activity; they, and they alone, have the capacity to act with free will. This thesis is sometimes called 'primary agency individualism'. According to this thesis, other agents, e.g. corporations, governments, and so on, must all depend on human agency to drive them—which, of course, is true. But my objection to primary agency individualism is not that people are not crucially involved in shaping societies. They are. It is just that people are not really primary agents. People never act in a social vacuum. They have attitudes, preferences, desires, and belief systems, which are relevant to the decisions they reach, which are socially inculcated, and which they could not function without. Therefore, the actions they take are not primary, or uncaused, causes, as the theory of primary agency individualism suggests.

Metaphysical individualism was developed mainly in the 1950s and 1960s to counter sociological theories sympathetic to Marxism and other left-wing political positions. These theories typically spoke of social forces of one kind or another. In the most radical cases, they spoke of historical laws and inevitability. Such talk was labelled 'historicist' and was widely condemned. Social idealism does not speak about or imply the existence of historical laws, and it is not historicist. Nevertheless, it does talk seriously about social contracts—real ones, which are inclusive of social and moral rights, obligations and responsibilities—and suggests that most such contracts significantly influence what people may decide to do, even where there are no legal sanctions to back them. So there must be real doubts in the minds of many philosophers whether the social theory of morality is compatible with some of these widely held individualistic theories of social causation. In my view, the social theory of morality is indeed incompatible with some of these theories but is none the worse for that. In Chapter 5, it will be argued that metaphysical individualism is false, and that the political philosophies of individualism and neo-liberalism, which depend on this foundation, are destructive of conventional morality.

Chapter 6 is concerned with the derivation of ordinary moral principles, which social idealists might crudely identify as principles that define the limits of acceptable behaviour for normal adult human beings. The standard view is that the correct methodology for determining these limits is one of Socratic dialogue. Certainly, that is the procedure followed by almost every teacher of normative ethics (as opposed to meta-ethics) in the universities of which I am aware. Presumably, the aim of these dialogues has always been to discover the truth about the limits of acceptable behaviour, and what behaviour is good or morally right. But then, the question must arise whether there is such a truth. There is some plausibility in the assumption that the principles of morality that are answers to the question of how individuals should behave have a foundation in human nature, presumably because they are somehow encoded in the human genome. And, if this were true of all moral principles, then the methodology would be

Introduction to Social Idealism   99

justified. But it must seriously be questioned whether this really is true. For, there appear to be a great many moral principles that have a social origin, i.e. are justified on the grounds that they, or something very like them, are needed if the society is to function well to promote human wellbeing, or to protect the rights and freedoms of individuals. Hence, the standard methodology seems to require that we should able to resolve these social moral issues by discussion amongst ourselves. However, this assumption is almost certainly false. We can get a considerable way by this method. But, as will be argued in Part IV of this book, we may not be able to get much further than the accepted doctrines of human rights and responsibilities. Indeed, even some of these must be seen to be questionable.

In Chapter 6, I also discuss a number of different kinds of objectivist theories of morality, and I argue that the time has come to consider the social relativist position more seriously. In particular, I explore the consequences of a radically alternative set of hypotheses concerning the problem of how to determine the limits of socially acceptable behaviour for normal adult human beings: (a) that there is no comprehensive set of such principles that would characterise the social contracts of people's ideal societies; (b) that the principles that would be written into the social contracts that would ultimately be acceptable in different societies would normally be different, because they represent different social solutions to common social problems; and (c) that there is, nevertheless, a core of moral principles derivable by the Socratic method that should ultimately be acceptable to most people in most societies, viz. the humanistic ones that are simply derivable from what human beings need if they are to flourish. I argue that these assumptions have some far-reaching consequences:

(1) that the general principle of universalisability, which is often taken to be definitive of moral principles, must be rejected;
(2) that the social moral principles, i.e. those moral principles that derive from social solutions to social problems, can be expected to evolve and change with changing circumstances or technologies;
(3) that moral critiques of other societies should focus primarily on their records concerning social moral principles—while those, and only those, that are incompatible with universal humanistic principles should be rejected outright;
(4) that there is no unrestricted right of conscience;
(5) that doing what is legally forbidden, but is what you believe to be morally required, is never fully justified, unless the grounds for your belief are straightforwardly humanistic, or the society in which you live allows you no alternative.

In defence of these theses, it is argued that if morals are social ideals, then there is no good case for moral objectivity. That is, there is no good reason to believe that there is just one true and complete system of moral beliefs.

100 *Social Humanism*

However, if morals are not social ideals, then there is no viable secular theory of morality. They are not just rational ideals, as Kant believed. Nor are they just principles of rational self-interest, as metaphysical individualists seem to believe. Nor are they just programmed principles of social behaviour of the kind that bees or termites appear to have, i.e. principles that are biologically preferred because of their survival value. Nevertheless, there is clearly a huge difference between healthy, vibrant societies in which people are obviously flourishing, where instances of cruelty, oppression, and gross abuses of human rights are relatively rare, and failed states, or states ruled by ruthless clerics or dictators, in which such abuses are relatively common. A moral philosophy that failed to explain this obvious fact would be either worthless or dangerous.

4 The Social Theory of Morality

4.1 MORALS AS SOCIAL IDEALS

The positive thesis of Part III of this book is that morals are social ideals. Metaphysically, social ideals are generic kinds of dispositional properties. A person who has a social ideal X is disposed to behave in ways that will make the realisation of X more likely. From the point of view of a member of a society, they are the principles of social behaviour, which that person would wish to have included in a social contract of his or her ideal kind of society. From the point of view of a society, they are the social ideals that would be embraced by the vast majority of its members. Globally, they are the projected social ideals of a global social contract—one that is inclusive enough to accommodate most of the world's diverse social perspectives—united by a common humanitarian outlook and divided only by socially diverse rules that are consistent with this common outlook.

Briefly, the theory is this: Moral obligations are idealised social obligations: (a) for individuals, they are the social obligations, i.e. legal or conventional ones, that you would ideally wish to include in your ideal society's social contract; (b) for societies, they are the social obligations that the vast majority of its members would wish to see included in the society's social contract; and (c) globally, they are the social obligations that the vast majority of people throughout the world would wish to see included in their own society's chapter of the global social contract. Moral rights and moral obligations are to be defined similarly, as will be explained later.

This theory clearly has links to P. F. Strawson's (1961) social idealism and to Gilbert Harman's (1977) social custom theory. However, Strawson's social idealism is importantly different from mine. For Strawson, the social ideals of individuals are their conflicting more or less desirable images of what a human life might be like. Typically, they are images of communities of people living, working, building, creating, playing, or raising children together. For such images to be realised, Strawson (1961: 30) says there has to be some kind of social organisation. And,

102 *Social Humanism*

it is a condition for the existence of any form of social organization, of any human community, that certain expectations of behaviour on the part of its members should be pretty regularly fulfilled: that some duties, one might say, should be performed, some rules observed.

Strawson (1961: 30) then goes on to say:

We might begin by locating the sphere of morality here. It is the sphere of the observance of rules, such that the existence of some such set of rules is a condition of the existence of a society. This is a minimal interpretation of morality. It represents it as what might literally be called a kind of public convenience; of first importance as a condition of everything that matters, but only as a condition of everything that matters, not as something that matters in itself.

To capture what Strawson is trying to say here, I make use of the anthropological conception of a social contract,[1] which is a description of how a society works, including what its institutions, customs, and norms of behaviour are. But, unlike Strawson, I do not regard the regulatory part of this description as a minimal theory of morality for that society, although, in a free society, what is described in the social contract will probably reflect the moral system fairly accurately. For Strawson, moral systems are, minimally, just sets of rules of social interaction (demands, obligations, etc.), the normal observance of which are necessary conditions for the existence of societies of the kinds they characterise. But these demands, obligations, and so on could all, in principle, be social customs that are rigorously enforced in traditional ways and that, consequently, few people are willing to abandon, even though they would really prefer to live by very different rules. To define a system of morality, what is needed is an ideal social contract of some kind, not a de facto one.

In the end, I think that Strawson recognises this. In the final section of his article, Strawson links morality with the minimal systems of morality for ideal societies. But the suggestion is never clearly worked out. Almost every sentence used in the discussion of this point is qualified to the point that one is not quite sure what is being said in any one of them, except that it is all much more complicated than he is able to say in the short space of the article he is writing. Nevertheless, the suggestion is there, and it is basically a sound one. Moral obligations are social obligations of people living in socially ideal societies. But Strawson does not, I think, recognise that this is not a moral theory. It is just a meta-theory. It says what sorts of things morals are, but it does not say what they are in particular. If he is right, and I think he is, then every moral theory must have this same epistemic foundation. That is, it must be a theory that has the same kind of structure as the regulatory structure of the society for which it is intended.

The Social Theory of Morality   103

Harman is a moral relativist, but he is not a social idealist. Therefore, I am obliged to say that Harman's moral theory is not really a moral theory at all. On my account, the principles that Harman calls 'moral' are straightforwardly social. They are established social customs that are generally accepted in the community. A moral system exists, he says, in any society where there is a tacit understanding or agreement of intent about how people should relate to each other, and the morals of the society are just the principles of this agreement. But, isn't there a difference between a common social practice and a social practice that many, or even most, people strongly believe should be changed? I do not know what the numbers are, but the following is certainly a possibility: It could well be the case that most people in Australia strongly believe that greenhouse gas emissions should be sharply reduced. They would, in fact, strongly support any government that introduced legislation to put a significant price on carbon, because the majority believe that this is morally the right thing to do. However, it may also be true that most people will do nothing to reduce their carbon footprint if there is no legislation, because there is no consensus about what actions in particular they should take, and they are not willing to act to reduce greenhouse emissions unless there is a plan, and everyone else shows that they are willing to act according to it. Therefore, until legislation is passed, most people will probably just carry on as they usually do.[2] My social idealist analysis is this: I say that most people believe that morally they should reduce their carbon footprint but are not willing to abandon their customary practices until they are forced to do so. They are only willing to badger the government for being morally at fault for failing to stand up to the coal industry (and to an opportunist opposition) and to legislate to reduce greenhouse gas emissions. Harman's analysis would appear to be different. If the scenario I have described is true, then Harman seems committed to saying that the people of Australia are morally committed to continue as usual to emit large quantities of greenhouse gases until they are forced by government legislation to do otherwise. There is widespread agreement of intent[3] to continue acting in this way until the government acts to make us do something else. Therefore, by Harman's criteria, this is, for most of us, our considered moral position.

Socially ideal theories are, as far as I know, the only ones that can adequately explain the primary role of morality in social criticism. If the morality of a society is just the set of established social practices, then it is hard to see how one could possibly mount a moral critique of these practices. But surely this is one of the primary functions of morality. In a stable society, in which there are no challenges to the laws or customs that exist, the morals of the society may contingently be the same as the established agreements of intent that govern interpersonal relations. But even in a stable society of this kind, such agreements can always be challenged morally. They can be argued to be morally lacking in some way and so in need of reform. The standpoint of the moral reformer is clearly not the position described in the

104 *Social Humanism*

society's de facto social contract. It is the standpoint of someone wishing to improve the social contract—to forge one in which the principles of social interaction that he or she would wish to see established—are included.

To explain all this properly, it will be necessary to develop a kind of social contract theory, which, as far as I know, is new to the philosophical literature. Firstly, a social contract of the kind that is needed is not, as might be supposed, an original agreement. It is not an agreement made in a state of nature. Secondly, it is not a hypothetical agreement made by individuals working from behind a veil of ignorance, as Rawls (1971) supposed for the purpose of constructing a theory of justice. Thirdly, the agreement is not about what individuals should do or not do. It is an agreement, or rather a settlement, concerning the rights, obligations, responsibilities, and powers of the various classes of social agents. This social focus is important, because it means that the social contract could not possibly be an original agreement between individuals acting only on their own behalf. For, the parties to such an agreement would all, *per impossible*, have to be speaking and bargaining legitimately on behalf of whole classes of social agents, e.g. all citizens, children, parents, prisoners, or medical practitioners. It also means that the moral principles derivable by the processes of social evolution must all be principles of social behaviour applicable directly only to the members of these classes of social agents. Thirdly, the classes of social agents must range over all of the effective decision-makers in the community, not just over the individuals. For, collective agents, such as those participating in, managing, or directing governments, universities, and business corporations, are, and are likely to remain, the major social decision-makers in our society, and therefore they must have moral obligations and responsibilities qua agents of these kinds.

The common moral precepts include: having respect for persons, being fair and honest in your dealings with others, treating others as you would wish to be treated yourself if your situations were reversed, telling the truth, respecting the rights of animals, collaborating with others to protect the environment, and seeking to make the world a better place than the one you were born into. They also include some strong prohibitions, such as those against killing, torturing, maiming, and assaulting people; stealing or defrauding them of their property; bullying, humiliating, insulting, or degrading behaviour towards others; and abusing the rights of children, old people, or the mentally or physically disabled. These, and most other moral principles, are concerned with how ordinary members of the community should behave socially. The exceptions are rare enough to cast doubt on their status. The prohibition against suicide, for example, is frequently held to be a moral principle, presumably because of the old religious conviction that the taking of a human life is God's prerogative. But it is hard to think of a good social reason why people whose lives have become intolerable, and are without hope of improvement, should not kill themselves or seek otherwise to have their misery ended. Similarly with masturbating: It is

The Social Theory of Morality   105

said to be immoral, but the action is self-regarding, and the reasons for thinking it to be immoral are unconvincing.[4]

But if morals are social ideals, as I hope to show, they are not all of equal importance. We should regard some, mostly the prohibitions, as indispensable to any passably decent society. Consequently, they are, and are likely to remain, fixtures in the social contracts of all societies that have these basic ideals; however, anyone might wish that they would evolve. Others, though widely accepted, are of lesser moment, and deliberate violations of these principles are sometimes excusable. Others again are even more peripheral, and they have yet to gain widespread acceptance. On these peripheral issues, good societies can tolerate considerable differences of opinion. Defenders of such principles naturally believe that society would be better if these principles were generally recognized and acted on. But, as things stand, they can only hope to persuade others to change their ways by lobbying, arguing, protesting, or leading by example, e.g. by acting courageously on the principles being canvassed.

The idea that moral principles are social ideals is not new. It is, after all, the standard Kantian position. What is new about the theory is that it is based on the idea of a society with an evolving social contract. At any point in its evolution, we can ask whether the social system described in this contract is as good as it might be, from the point of view of the society's members. Does it give as much support and encouragement to the kinds of actions or outcomes that we regard as good? Does it discourage sufficiently the kinds of actions or outcomes of which we disapprove? If not (to either question), then the question arises: How should the social contract (including the social mores, the legal system, the procedures for resolving disputes, etc.) be changed to make the society better from the points of view of those who live in it? The moral principles we believe in include all of the social principles that are already incorporated in the society's social contract of which we approve, and all of those social principles that we should also wish to see incorporated in it, i.e. by becoming generally adopted.

Questions may be asked about the adequacy of characterising societies by their social contracts. Unlike Will Hutton (1996), I think of the social contract of any modern society as a complete sociological description of it, which, if it could realistically be described for a society as complex as ours, would be an enormous document. It would have to include complete information about how we are governed, how governments are chosen, how, if at all, improvements can be made to the social structure, what established institutions it has, what its laws and means of law-enforcement are, what sorts of collective and specialised agents it has, how these kinds of agents are regulated, and how these regulations are drafted, legislated, and enforced. The document would also spell out the complete sets of obligations, rights, and responsibilities of each of the various classes of social agents for which different regulations exist, and how these regulations are defined, administered, and enforced. It would also list the kinds of cases in

106　*Social Humanism*

which exceptions to the general rules may be made, describe the procedures for settling disputes about such matters, and the existing case law concerning such disputes. And this is just the beginning. Every modern society has a very elaborate social structure that defines and refines all of the standard social and legal rules and ultimately any laws or conventions that might be accepted, or proposed, as social principles.

No ideal society exists, and none ever will. But we can easily imagine ways in which, say, the quality of people's lives could be made better by changing the structure of the society or the norms of social behaviour within this structure. Hence, we may, if we wish, envisage an ideal society as a projected endpoint of a process of social improvement based on some particular conception of the good. The social principles that we think should exist at this endpoint, along with those we should undoubtedly retain, if we can, in any future social contract, are the ones we call 'moral principles'. If actions are taken that are contrary to any of these principles, then those who hold them seriously to be moral principles must also believe that these actions would normally be harmful, i.e. actions of a kind that would be likely to lead to an overall reduction in the good, or an increase in what is bad, for society's members.

4.2　REAL SOCIAL CONTRACTS

A real social contract differs in nature and function from any of the sorts of social contracts normally discussed in the philosophical literature. It is not an ideology (Gauthier, 1977), although any dominant ideologies in the society would have to be described in it. Nor is it the result of an ideally rational agreement made behind a veil of ignorance (Rawls, 1971), or any other kind of rational ideal. No, it is just a more or less stable historical settlement arrived at by ordinary people and their legislators, along with their administrators and legal interpreters engaged in their day-to-day activities. It describes the society's institutions, governmental processes and structures, justice system, laws, conventions, and normal social practices. It also describes how the society functions and deals with such issues as due process, how rights and responsibilities are spread around, and what these rights and responsibilities are. According to one tradition, that of Hobbes and Locke, the social contract of a society should be thought of as its founding document—an agreement forged in a state of nature to establish a system of government that defines the rights and responsibilities of its members, its sovereign body, and its principal institutions. According to another tradition, that of Rousseau and Marx, the aim of all progressive politics should be to replace a society's institutions and effective system of rights and obligations with better ones. This is nearer to the tradition to which this book belongs, because if morality is a system of social ideals, the moral quest must be to promote

The Social Theory of Morality   107

these ideals, with a view to incorporating them as far as possible into the real social contracts of societies around the world.

But the system to be developed here is not a utopian one. It does not seek to define an ideal state, with a view to gearing public policy towards its achievement. Therefore, it is more in the spirit of Rousseau (1968/1792) than of Marx. It envisages beginning from where one is and engaging fruitfully and pragmatically in the process of making things better from everyone's point of view. The real social contract of our own society is what I take to be our starting point. This is an anthropological concept of the social contract, although it is not one that is normally applied to whole societies of the complexity of modern nation states, because the task of describing it would be beyond the resources of any conceivable anthropologist or Department of Anthropology. Nevertheless, a notion akin to it is familiar in the literature of social commentary. Hutton (1996) outlines what he calls the social contracts of Great Britain and several of the mainland European countries.

My own concept of a real social contract is much more inclusive than Hutton's. At one point, Hutton remarks that America does not have a social contract at all. But that is not how I see it. America clearly does have a current social contract, as I conceive of it. It is certainly a fairly minimal one in terms of its social provisions, although not as minimal as Nozick (1974) would like. And, it is certainly exceptional in character, because it is firmly based on acceptance of the fundamental importance of individual liberty. Because of their obsession with freedom, many Americans are reluctant to embrace nationally funded social programs, which they see as depriving people of their fundamental right to spend their incomes as they please (beyond the minimum required to maintain some basic government services). But despite this, there is an established social structure in the US—indeed, a very elaborate one—and it is accompanied by an equally elaborate set of principles concerning how people (or other social agents) in their various social roles should or should not behave. And, where there are disputes, there are well-defined procedures for settling them. They may not be to everyone's liking, because, if the chosen procedure is one of litigation, it is likely to be very costly and heavily biased in favour of those with the most resources. Nevertheless, the American system comes clearly within the social framework we are discussing. It has a de facto social structure and a comprehensive system of rules for determining what are widely thought to be desirable social outcomes.

As I propose to use the term, the real social contract of a society is the historically generated settlement concerning the nature and structure of that society that defines the kinds of organizations it contains and the kinds of positions or roles that people may have within it or any of its organizations. The real social contract of a society also describes the proper distribution of rights and obligations of organizations, and of individuals *vis-à-vis* their social positions or roles in society, or within any of its

108 *Social Humanism*

organizations. The real social contract of a society is thus a true, comprehensive, and, in principle, discoverable account of the society's structure and mode of operation. As such, it should state which classes of individuals, or which kinds of organizations, are held to be responsible for doing what in society. It should say what the members think they have a right to expect of its governments, business corporations, trade unions, universities, hospitals, and so on. It should explain how professionals and tradespeople, i.e. doctors, nurses, plumbers, public servants, and so on, should behave in their respective roles. It should also state what the responsibilities are of its various classes of individual members, i.e. citizens, children, asylum seekers, pensioners, prisoners, warders, and so on, and what they must do to carry out their duties.

From the point of view of an outside observer of the society, the statement is purely descriptive; it just describes its structure and the normal roles of the various kinds of agents within this structure. However, from the point of view of an agent (individual or collective) who is a member of the society, the statement is normative, because social agents in a society must know what they will normally be held responsible for doing, to whom they will be held responsible, and what they will be expected to do to fulfil their obligations. Therefore, in the absence of special or exonerating circumstances, the agents will know what they should do as responsible social agents in that society.[5]

According to David Hume, one can never derive an 'ought' from an 'is'. So, no description of how society *is* organized can possibly tell us how it *ought* to be. This is true. Nevertheless, a full description of how rights and responsibilities are distributed in a society does tell us what the prima facie *social* rights and obligations of its various kinds of agents are *vis-à-vis* each other. Therefore, if you know what kind of social agent you are, and you know what social rights and responsibilities you have in virtue of being an agent of this kind in the society in which you live, then you must know what you ought, socially, to do. And, you will have these social obligations however you might think society ought ideally to be organised. You have them just in virtue of the fact that you have the position or role you have, and your society has settled on this particular social agreement.

But clearly your social obligations do not determine your moral obligations. For, according to the definitions offered in Section 4.3, what you take your moral obligations to be would have to depend on what principles of social behaviour you thought would be required of people of your or your organisation's profile in an ideal society. Where the two are the same, there is no moral dilemma. But where they differ, there is, because in every such case, the moral principles that you accept would conflict with your known social obligations. So, for you, the question would arise: Should I, or my organisation, act on principles that I believe to be morally sound, or should I act on principles that I know to be socially required? There is no easy answer; what it would be reasonable for you to do would depend on

The Social Theory of Morality   109

how strongly you believed in the soundness of you moral judgement, how important you considered the moral issue to be, and what penalties you (or your organisation, or perhaps both) would face for neglecting your (or its) social obligations. In practice, many of us would compromise. We might, for example, do as little as we can of what we are socially obliged to do, all the while protesting that it is unjust. Or, if we felt strong enough to resist the social pressures, we might do what we think we ought morally to do and be prepared to take the consequences.

Hume (1777/1975: 44) is also famous for his claim that 'Custom . . . is the great guide to human life. It is that principle alone', he said, 'which renders our experience useful to us, and makes us expect, for the future, a similar train of events with those which have appeared in the past'. I doubt this, because I do not accept Hume's theory of induction. But I do not deny that custom does generate rational expectations. Moreover, I think it has an important role in generating some of our prima facie social obligations, i.e. the sorts of obligations that are built into our real social contract. For, wherever there is a socially approved expectation that we should behave in the manner X in circumstances of the kind Y, and other people need to know for practical reasons what we will do if we find ourselves in such circumstances, we naturally have a prima facie obligation to act in the manner X. The wellbeing of others, perhaps a great many others, may depend on it. The obligation arises because we are, in fact, all necessarily dependent on the actions and testimonies of others, and our only basis for judging who is reliable, or what we may reasonably expect to be done in the circumstances, is how individuals, or people in various social roles, have behaved in the past.

If a person lies to us in circumstances in which we can normally expect her to be telling the truth, and, as a result, we act in a way that is harmful to ourselves or to others, then she must bear a large share of the responsibility for the harm inflicted. It does not matter that there was never any verbal or written agreement that she would tell the truth. For, the fact is that we were, with good reason, relying on her to give us true information. When the President of the United States and the Prime Ministers of Great Britain and Australia took their countries to war in Iraq on the basis of intelligence that many think they had good reason to believe was faulty, but pretended that it was beyond reasonable doubt that Iraq was rapidly developing a nuclear weapons capability, if those who think that this is true are right, then the three leaders effectively lied to their people and took them to war on false pretences. To the extent that people in the relevant communities believe this, their actions have undermined this understanding and weakened the social fabrics of their respective societies.

There is no doubt that custom can generate some prima facie social obligations. But as I understand them, it cannot generate moral obligations. The question, then, is how social obligations can become converted into moral obligations, or vice versa. The thesis to be defended here is that what

110   *Social Humanism*

we take our moral obligations of social origin, i.e. our social moral obligations, to be are just the actual or possible social ones that we suppose would ideally have to be binding on all agents within the relevant classes.[6] The social obligations we actually have must have arisen out of the historical processes that generated the real social contract of our own society. The social moral obligations that we think we now have are those social obligations that we do or might have that would be binding on all agents within the relevant classes in our ideal society in which the same kinds of actions could be performed in the same kinds of circumstances. The obligation to do what we think we are socially morally obliged to do is therefore not just contingent on the social contract of the society in which we happen to live: It is a social obligation that we think would be binding on us in an ideal society in which our roles as individuals are essentially the same.

According to H. A. Prichard (1937/1949: 94), a moral obligation (and therefore a moral right) has no nature that is capable of being expressed in terms of the nature of anything else: 'it is *sui generis*'. Prichard seems to have made a good case for this claim. For, none of the analyses he considers does justice to the concept of a moral obligation that we have inherited from our forebears. But his argument really only shows one of two things: (a) none of the many analyses that have been proposed over the years (i.e. pre-1937) is good enough, or (b) the concept of a moral obligation needs revising. I take the latter view. Our moral obligations have traditionally been understood within the churches, mosques, and synagogues as commands of God and, consequently, as (a) overriding all other obligations, and (b) binding on all members of the faithful. And the project of philosophy has naturally been to try to secularise and universalise such a conception. But, as Prichard has successfully argued, philosophers have so far failed to develop a concept of moral obligation that has the required dominance and is, at the same time, binding on all rational beings—or, perhaps, on all beings that share our human nature. Nevertheless, we urgently need a good theory of moral obligation. For, such a theory is required to focus debate about morality on the right issues and provide an adequate framework for a theory of morality. It is also needed to explain why we think morality matters. Moral judgements are much too important in human motivation and decision-making to be abandoned to Prichardian intuitionism.

It will be argued here that an important class of moral obligations are widely accepted because they are seen as being good for the health of society. Clearly, these obligations are capable of being analysed in a sort of way that Prichard thought impossible. But, in addition to these, many social obligations are widely accepted, because they reflect our ideals of individual behaviour, which we should naturally wish to see preserved in our ideal society, whatever its current structure. These are our 'individual moral obligations'. However, the same analysis applies to all moral obligations, whatever their source. All of them are social ideals that we should wish to see reflected in the social contract of our ideal society.

4.3 RIGHTS AND OBLIGATIONS

According to social idealism, our morals are the principles of social behaviour that we would wish to see embedded in our society's ideal social contract. It must be remembered that social idealism does not itself define a moral system; it is just the required metaphysics. Consequently, it tells us almost nothing about what the principles of morality should be. It does, however, allow us to define most of the key moral concepts, just as Kant's metaphysics did. For, if morals are social ideals, then moral rights, obligations, responsibilities, and powers must be just idealised versions of their social equivalents. This, it seems to me, is a powerful new idea. It makes sense of all of the most basic concepts of moral philosophy, and does so easily and naturally. But the same cannot be said for individualism in moral theory. Consider natural rights. From the point of view of a social humanist, natural rights are, if anything, the rights that are owed to people by the state, just by virtue of their being human. But, according to individualistic humanism, the state has no obligations other than those that its citizens mostly insist it exercise on their behalf. Usually, the citizens of any affluent state would insist that the state provide for their security, and for the security of their property. But only in relatively impoverished states is there likely to be much demand for the positive rights that are almost universally recognised as human rights. Hart (1955), for example, argues that there is only one natural right, the right to individual freedom. He does so on the ground that any encroachment upon individual freedom requires moral justification. Jeremy Bentham (1795/2002) notoriously described 'natural rights' as 'nonsense', and imprescriptible natural rights as 'nonsense on stilts'.

As the theory of social idealism is developed here, it lacks a category of natural rights, and is therefore not obliged to try to make sense of them. But in their place, it recognises that there may be human rights, i.e. social rights that people have just because they are human. And, if social rights exist in any society, then there is no reason why they should not be idealised and accepted universally as moral rights.

Here are the required formal definitions of social rights and obligations, and their moral counterparts.

A   Social Concepts

4.3.1   Social Obligation

x has a *social obligation* to Y in circumstances of the kind K in a society S with a social contract C if and only if x is a member of a class of social agents listed in C as having a prima facie social obligation to Y in these circumstances, and there are no good and sufficient reasons listed in C why x should not be held to be socially delinquent for failure to Y in such circumstances.

112 *Social Humanism*

4.3.2 Social Right

x has a *social right* to Y in circumstances of the kind K if and only there is some agent *z*, e.g. the government or the agent's employer, who has a social obligation to realise Y for *x* (or at least see to it that *x* is not prevented from realising Y) in these circumstances.

B Moral Concepts

Let C_{IDEAL} be the social contract of the kind of society S_{IDEAL} that *x* would consider to be ideal. Then, according to social idealism, the following definitions must be acceptable to *x*.

4.3.3 Moral Obligation

x has a *moral obligation* to Y in circumstances of the kind K if and only if *x* would have a social obligation to Y in these circumstances in S_{IDEAL}.

4.3.4 Moral Right

x has a *moral right* to Y in circumstances of the kind K if and only if *x* would have a social right to Y in such circumstances in S_{IDEAL}.

These definitions are interesting for at least four reasons. Firstly, none of them is individualistic. Social idealism is inconsistent with the view that the rights and obligations of individuals depend on their beliefs, attitudes, or preferences. The moral rights and obligations of individuals depend only on their positions or roles in their societies, given the circumstances they happen to be in. Secondly, the primary bearers of moral rights and obligations are not particular social agents in these particular circumstances; they are *classes* of social agents in similar circumstances. There is, of course, one class of social agents that embraces all socially responsible citizens in the community. We might call this the normal class N. Most members of any real society are bound to belong to N, although some may have additional responsibilities in virtue of their occupations, and others fewer responsibilities in view of their failings or immaturity. Thirdly, the bearers of these properties may be collectives. Collectives are competent deliberators, just as normal individuals are, and there is no reason why they should not be considered to be agents that are capable of acting freely, i.e. exercising free will. Fourthly, the definitions of moral properties are all highly subjective. So, most philosophers would probably consider them to be unsatisfactory. For reasons that will become more evident later, the subjectivity of these definitions is a good thing. It allows for some limited cultural relativism in morality. But it is also consistent with there being a class of moral principles that are universal, because they are firmly grounded in human nature. In

The Social Theory of Morality   113

general, the individualistic moral principles, which are pre-cultural or multicultural are universal, but the social moral principles may not be.

These definitions of moral rights and obligations all focus attention on the one central issue: They require us to consider what social obligations or rights we would wish to see created or preserved in the social contracts of our ideal societies. And this, ultimately, is what makes social idealism, and the definitions to which this theory gives rise, so important. If you can answer this question satisfactorily, then you should be able to answer all of the big questions of morality. Moreover, you should also be able to answer the big questions of political philosophy, because your first task, whatever kind of philosopher you are, must be the same: You must first decide the directions in which you would wish your own society to evolve. If you are a political philosopher, then you are likely to be concerned with more than just the evolving rights and obligations of social agents. You are, for example, likely to also be concerned with the evolving social structures of governments, governmental organisations, and the health of social institutions. For, clearly, C_{IDEAL} is not a real social contract; it is a projected limit of social evolution. But what is important is that moral and political philosophies are, and need to be, co-evolving systems. Social idealism thus brings moral and political philosophy together. A sound political philosophy must have a good moral philosophy to back it up, and conversely.

Every political theory that has been developed as a guide to social policy must be based on some form of social contractual utilitarianism. They can differ from each other only in their social policy objectives, or how they are ranked. Every moral theory that is capable of defining the sets of moral rights and obligations of the various classes of social agents in a given society must also be based on some form of social contractual utilitarianism. Such fully-fledged moral theories can also differ from each other only in their social policy objectives, or how they are ranked. Social idealism therefore allows one to say whether the political philosophy of a given society is compatible with its moral philosophy. It will be compatible if and only if the two sets and rankings of objectives are compatible. This is an important point, because it will later be argued that social humanism, which is the underlying philosophy of the theory of human rights, is the natural moral companion of the philosophy of the welfare state. And these two philosophies certainly do fit nicely together. But there is no plausible moral theory that would fit with either communism or capitalism. The welfare state is therefore a uniquely moral state. One does not need to adjust one's priorities or values as one moves from the political realm to the moral one. Plausibly, the welfare state is the only such state.

Our social rights and obligations include any that are established in our laws or customs as they are determined by precedents in our society. There are many variations on the above definitions, most of which are too obvious to bother with. For example, we may define guaranteed social rights, prima facie social rights, or optional social rights, and correspondingly

114 *Social Humanism*

there are definitions of guaranteed moral rights, prima facie moral rights, and optional moral rights. Thus, we have the following definitions.

4.3.2.1 *Optional Social Right*

x has an optional social right to do Y in circumstances of the kind K if and only if x is a member of a class X of social agents all of whom may do Y in such circumstances, and every social agent z has a social obligation not to interfere with X if x should attempt to do so.

4.3.2.2 *Guaranteed Social Right*

x has a guaranteed social right to Y in circumstances of the kind K if and only there is some agent z (e.g. the agent's employer) who has a social obligation to realise Y for x in these circumstances.

Given these definitions, we may immediately derive their moral equivalents:

4.3.4.1 *Optional Moral right*

x has an optional moral right to do Y in circumstances of the kind K if and only if x is a member of a class X of social agents all of whom may do Y in such circumstances, and every social agent z has a moral obligation not to interfere with X if x should attempt to do so.

4.3.4.2 *Guaranteed Moral Right*

One should accept that x has a moral right to Y in circumstances of the kind K if and only if there would be some social agent z in one's ideal society who would have a moral obligation to realise Y for x in such circumstances.

These definitions may be criticised on a number of grounds:

1. They may be said to be too subjective. S_{IDEAL} is, after all, a subjective concept. However, there are two good reasons for preferring subjective definitions such as these. Firstly, there is no evidence that satisfactory truth conditions for statements of moral rights or obligations are possible. Truth conditions for the corresponding social rights and obligations can certainly be stated, because the existing social contract of the society is a reality. One could state truth conditions for an S_{IDEAL} that reflects the society's moral stance. However, I am not sure that the resulting objective definitions would have any useful content. For, given the range of unsavoury people in the community of any modern society, there may well not be many social rights or obligations that would occur in the social contracts of most people's ideal societies. Some people's ideal societies might, for example, include a licence for Arabs to kill Jews, or

The Social Theory of Morality   115

vice versa, or at least allow or demand of them some very different rights or obligations from those they would allow or demand of their own kind. Even if the range of ideal societies were reduced to those that were democratically agreed to, the approved principles could be pretty horrendous. When hatred takes hold in a community, it can produce some very nasty results. Witness Nazi Germany. It is better, it seems to me now, to have subjective definitions of rights and obligations that would allow us to isolate any extremist moral principles and treat them as outliers or monsters. My own ideal society is one that would require anyone who advocated ideals like those just mentioned to be prosecuted for racial vilification, or some like offence, and anyone convicted of acting on such principles to be locked up somewhere, where they could do no harm. Other issues concerning moral subjectivity are further discussed in Part III of this book.

2. It may be objected that the definitions of prima facie rights and obligations are too vague to carry the weight required of them.

In developed societies, the issue of when a prima facie obligation becomes a real one may be settled formally by case law or informally by rational argument. That is, the social contract of the society provides several mechanisms for determining whether a person or an organisation is in breach of its obligations or whether it has the rights it claims it has. Hence, the vagueness of the statement accurately reflects the status of most human and organisational rights and obligations in the real world. Very few such rights or obligations are absolute, and those that are, such as the prohibition of euthanasia, are arguably immoral. Indeed, I and many others would say that terminally ill people should ideally have a prima facie right to euthanasia and, hence, that its absolute prohibition is morally wrong.

3. The definitions do not specify to whom social and moral obligations are owed or who are the guarantors of social or moral rights.

Social and moral obligations are conceived here as being owed to a society as a whole, since they are required by that society's social contract. And, this too represents a considerable break with tradition. A social or moral obligation might be an obligation to aid an individual or keep a promise to a particular organisation. Let us say that the individual, who has a right to be aided in the circumstances, or the organisation, which has a right to expect the promise it has received to be fulfilled, are *the beneficiaries* of these moral obligations. But, in an important sense, what is owed, the giving of the aid or the keeping of the promise, is not owed to the beneficiaries; the giving of the aid and the keeping of the promise are owed to society as a whole, because the institutions of aid-giving and promise-keeping are socially important, and everyone in the society, whether they are ever the recipients of aid or the receivers of promises, has an interest in preserving them. Similarly, social and moral rights are conceived as being guaranteed

116 *Social Humanism*

by the social contract, and hence by all members of the society that are assumed to be parties to this contract. If an employee has a moral right to compensation from a business corporation (her employer) for some work-related injury, then society as a whole has an interest in this business corporation honouring its obligation to provide such compensation.

4.4 POWERS AND RESPONSIBILITIES

Powers and responsibilities are definable in terms of obligations, but they differ from rights and obligations in a number of ways. As I shall define them here, responsibilities are role-specific sets of obligations. If you have a duty of care, for example, then you have a responsibility. But there is no social or moral principle that you must obey to act responsibly. If you are a caregiver, then your duty of care just requires you to be alert to any dangers or needs that the person or animal in your care might face; decide what, if anything, needs to be done about them; and act on your decisions. The responsibility of a journalist, to take another example, is not a specific obligation that could be summed up easily as a social or moral principle. It is to investigate what appears to be newsworthy and report accurately on what happened without political bias. This is certainly a social responsibility and, I would argue, also a moral one. But it is not just the obligation to be honest. It also involves an obligation to be objective—to tell the whole truth, not just that part of the truth that one's readers, political friends, or advertisers might like to hear. The first of these obligations (to be honest) is arguably a moral obligation. But the requirement of objectivity is not. Or, if it is, then every politician is in breach of it every day. The responsibilities of general practitioners and specialists are different again. They have a duty of care for their patients. But, more than this, they have a responsibility to make professionally competent and considered judgements about their patients' medical conditions or surgical requirements and to act on them. Ministers of state, governors general, magistrates, barristers, school teachers, scientists, and other specialists all have their own responsibilities, which, in every case, consist of a set of obligations to investigate, consider, decide things, in fulfilment of their duties, and act on these decisions.

Corporate and collective agents, such as the managers or directors of banks, non-governmental organizations, insurance companies, manufacturing firms, governments, senates, TV stations, universities, and so on, all have responsibilities too that are sets of role-dependent obligations to the communities they serve. But, in my view, there needs to be a lot more work done on the social and moral responsibilities of such collective agents. We have tended to think of them as being run by individuals and to reason that if we are clear about the rights and responsibilities of individuals, then we do not need any separate discussion of the rights or responsibilities of collectives. But this is a mistake. The social and moral positions taken by collectives are not derivable from those of the men or women who run them. For example, the positions

The Social Theory of Morality 117

taken by political parties in Parliament do not depend just on those of their members; they also depend on the attitudes of voters, which depend on the positions taken by the opposition parties, which depend on what they think the media will run with, which depend on what they think will sell papers or bring in advertising, and so on. Similarly, the social decisions taken by corporate boards of management are not just a function of the moral positions of the individuals involved in making them. For example, they may ignore the implications for the workforce, the nature or quality of the goods produced, and so on, even though as individuals they may be socially as concerned as anyone else. Probably, their decisions will depend heavily on what they think their corporate shareholders, especially the institutional ones, would want, which in turn will depend on the returns that the boards of these other companies think they will be able to offer their investors, and so on. Yet, as we have already noted, the collectives are by far the most powerful social agents in today's world, and there is no reason to think that their decision-making is any less free than the decision-making of individuals. On the contrary, since they are both more powerful and much less constrained by the social contracts of their societies, they are much freer to act as they choose. To my way of thinking, there is an overwhelming case for socially regulating the decisions and actions of all the important collectives in our society, and elsewhere in the world, and, if possible, reducing the moral pressures on individuals. People in positions of great formal power, such as the Queen, the Governor General, or the captains of industry or the media, need to be regulated tightly in the interests of everyone else.

Consistently with this discussion, I define the relevant formal concepts of social and moral powers and responsibilities

4.4.1.1 *Formal Social Power*

A social agent x has the formal power to decide how best to deal with issues of the kind Y in circumstances of the kind K, and to act on these decisions, if and only if x (or x's appointed representative) is the unique member of a class of social agents all of whom have been assigned this power by the social contract of the society.

4.4.1.2 *Formal Moral Power*

A social agent x has the formal moral power to deal with issues of the kind Y in circumstances of the kind K if and only if x's formal position (as agent or appointee) in society would give x this power in S_{IDEAL}.

4.4.2.1 *Formal Social Responsibility*

A social agent x has the formal social responsibility for dealing with issues of the kind Y in circumstances of the kind K if and only if the society's

118 *Social Humanism*

social contract assigns to x (in virtue of x's position in society) the formal social power to so.

4.4.2.2 *Formal Moral Responsibility*

A social agent x has a formal moral responsibility for dealing with issues of the kind Y in circumstances of the kind K if and only if x's social role gives x the formal moral power to do so in S_{IDEAL}.[7]

It is important, however, to recognise that most social and/or moral responsibilities are not as tightly regulated or formal, as those of the Queen and the Governor General. Mostly, they are acquired by changing circumstances. One might, for example, acquire social and/or moral responsibilities by becoming parents, buying a pet, learning to drive, or becoming a member of parliament. Or, one might acquire social and/ or moral responsibilities accidentally, e.g. by finding oneself in a position where one is the only person who is able to rescue a child from drowning. Powers and responsibilities still go together as they do in the formal cases. And the distinction between social and moral responsibilities still depends on the difference between the society's de facto social contract C and what would, for most people, be C_{IDEAL}. Here are some more or less plausible definitions of some of these informal social and moral responsibilities.

4.4.3.1 *Occasional Social Responsibility*

A social agent x has an occasional social responsibility for dealing with an issue of the kind Y in existing circumstances of the kind K if and only if the de facto social contract of the society would give x the social power, in such circumstances, to decide freely within the range of socially permissible options what to do on that occasion about Y, and to act accordingly.

4.4.3.2 *Occasional Moral Responsibility*

A social agent x has an occasional moral responsibility for dealing with an issue of the kind Y in existing circumstances of the kind K if and only if the social contract of S_{IDEAL} would give x the social power, in such circumstances, to decide freely within the range of morally permissible options what to do on that occasion about Y, and to act accordingly.

There is, however, a sense of moral responsibility that is radically at odds with these definitions of the social moral concepts, viz. the traditional one used for defining guilt and consequently for laying blame. This traditional concept is the confused product of Cartesian dualism and the metaphysics of individualism, and it should be rejected. This traditional concept may be defined.

The Social Theory of Morality 119

4.4.3.3 *Traditional Moral Responsibility*

A human moral agent x is traditionally morally responsible for having done Y if and only if x was the *primary agent cause* of doing A, of which Y is a natural and foreseeable consequence, and x did A of x's own freewill, while of sound mind, and in full possession of his or her senses.

Cartesian dualism was discussed briefly in Chapter 3 and found wanting. The concept of primary agency causation will be discussed in the following chapter (on the metaphysics of individualism). The theory of primary agency individualism, in which the concept of traditional moral responsibility is embedded, is a relic of Kantian metaphysics, which, as we have seen, is untenable. The concepts required for the theories of guilt and just punishment are those of *personal* and *collective* responsibility. It will be argued later (in Chapters 5 and 6) that the concept of personal responsibility is an adequate replacement for the traditional concept of moral responsibility, and that the concept of collective responsibility is a much needed one. The traditional concept just lets collectives off the hook and makes the individuals, who should be made answerable to the wider community for the collective crimes they commit, much more difficult to prosecute than they should be.

4.5 SOCIAL AND MORAL PRINCIPLES

4.5.1   A Social Principle of a Society

S is any true statement of any of the social, or prima facie social, rights, obligations, or responsibilities of any of its social agents. These statements would necessarily include any true statements about such matters that are implied by the laws, customs, or case law of the society S, all of which must be included in the social contract of S. Some may prefer to describe them as the socio-legal principles of S.

4.5.2   A Moral Principle of a Society

S is any statement of any social principle of S that would be held by the vast majority of members of S to be morally, or prima facie morally, binding on members of the relevant classes of social agents of S, including the government.[8]

There is no clear definition of 'vast majority' in Section 4.5.2, and, consequently, there is no sharp distinction between social and moral principles. The moral principles of S, as they are here defined, are all socio-legal ones. The differences are that the moral principles are by definition (a) more widely accepted than the non-moral ones, and (b) generally held by the members of S to be more highly desirable features of the society's social contract than any merely socio-legal principles.

120   *Social Humanism*

4.6   SOCIAL AND MORAL ATTITUDES

By the social and moral attitudes, I mean to include those of approval and disapproval, which we normally express using evaluative terms such as 'good' or 'bad'. These social or moral evaluations need to be defined. Formally, there is little difficulty in doing this. For, the existing social attitudes of a society would have to be recorded in its social contract. So, there is no need for us to do anything here other than define the moral attitudes. Accordingly, I would offer the following definitions.

4.6.1   Moral Goodness

One should accept that X is morally good if and only if one would include the judgement that X is good from a social point of view in the social contract of one's ideal society.
Similar definitions can easily be constructed for all of the other moral evaluations (badness, evil, excellence, etc.).

Given these definitions, we may go on to define the moral virtues and vices. I do so for individual agents.

4.6.2   Moral Virtues

One should accept that X is a moral virtue if and only if, in the ideal limit, one would include the judgement in the society's social contract that, from a social point of view, X is a morally good quality for anyone to have.

It should be noted that, even if these definitions are restricted to individual human agents, this definition of the moral virtues may be class sensitive. Courage, for example, may be morally virtuous for people of one kind, e.g. soldiers, but not morally virtuous for those of another, e.g. social workers. The social concept of morality may thus involve some stretching or limiting of the classical concepts of the virtues. But I see no great problems here. Most of the classical concepts of virtue described by Aristotle were thought of as estimable qualities of the free adult male citizens of Greek city states, not of people generally.

In moral discourse, it is common to talk about the distinction between right and wrong. As in the above definitions, I shall distinguish between what is socially and what is morally right or wrong.

4.6.3   Socially Right and Wrong Acts

An act X by an agent x in circumstances Y was socially the right/wrong thing to do if and only if X was done in accordance with/ contrary to x's social obligations or responsibilities at that time in these circumstances.

4.6.4 Morally Right and Wrong Acts

An act X by an agent x in circumstances Y was morally the right/wrong thing to do from the point of view of an agent/society z if and only if X was done in accordance with/contrary to what z accepts as x's moral obligations or responsibilities in the circumstances Y.

4.7 INDIVIDUALISTIC ETHICS

Traditionally, morality has been thought to be concerned primarily with the rights and obligations of responsible people, i.e. individuals who are mature and rational enough to have developed a workably good understanding of the distinction between right and wrong. Consequently, the methodology of theoretical ethics has often been thought to involve the rational discussion of issues and the gradual development of one's moral position—to shore it up against counter-examples, and to make it overall a more coherent and more unified system of beliefs. This, I suppose, is the most widely accepted methodology, and an ethical position that has been arrived at in this way may be, and commonly is, described as one of 'broad reflective equilibrium'. Michael Smith's theory of moral realism, for example, clearly depends on his view that moral truths can eventually be discovered by this procedure. This methodology is certainly useful in moral reasoning. Indeed, I support it strongly as a strategy for developing and rationalising moral theories. But there is no good reason to think that it can cross all cultural barriers. Social moral principles arise from politically generated solutions to social problems and enter the moral debate in a very different way from, say, the individualistic principles that are grounded in human nature. The Socratic methodology of aiming for broad reflective equilibrium by rational dialogue will be discussed more fully in Chapter 6.

Others, especially the act-utilitarians, have worked on the assumption that the correct methodology of ethics is like that of game theory. Their strategy is first to identify the good that is to be maximised, e.g. pleasure, happiness, or preference satisfaction, and then identify some useful rules (said to be 'rules of thumb') for achieving this objective. But all act-utilitarians would stress that these rules do not have a status any more significant than that of being mere rules of thumb. They are useful if one does not have the time or capacity to calculate exactly the prospective utilities of our actions. This theory is both individualistic and pseudo-scientific. It is individualistic, because each person, in theory, is supposed to do his or her own calculations of the utilities of the prospective consequences of his or her acts and then act to maximise probable benefit. It is pseudo-scientific, because the range of possible consequences of actions is ill defined, and the probabilities of their realisation are often incalculable. Moreover, it is easy enough to prove that, even if we could identify the range of possible

122 Social Humanism

consequences of actions, and the probabilities and utilities of their realisation were known to everyone, there would be circumstances in which the prospective utilities of X doing A and Y doing B might each be high and positive, while the prospective utility of the joint action, consisting of X's doing A and Y's doing B is strongly negative.[9]

The theory that morals are social ideals has some links with each of these traditions. The social ideal theory is compatible with a broad reflective equilibrium theory. But I see no sufficient reason to believe that there is just one position of broad reflective equilibrium. It is possible, I suppose, that the social contracts of all societies would eventually converge to one another, given enough focus on social issues in cross-cultural relations. Hence, their social ideals could also converge. So, ultimate agreement about morals is theoretically possible on the theory that is being proposed. However, I doubt whether many broad reflective equilibrium theorists would have thought of it this way. For, their use of the term 'reflective' suggests that the processes they had in mind are supposed to be ones that can be followed by an individual thinking carefully about his or her own experiences and reflecting on the judgements of right and wrong to which they give rise. But, for reasons to be explained more fully later, this methodology is unlikely to succeed in reaching cross-cultural agreements about morals. The members of each culturally distinct society may just go on reinforcing their own social ideals. And no one, in any society, who follows this methodology is likely to have anything much to say about the moral responsibilities of governments, collective agents, or specialists.

At the same time, the theory of morality as a social ideal is a utilitarian one. It is not an act- or rule-utilitarian theory, as these theories are normally understood. It is a social contractual utilitarian theory. It is utilitarian because the development of one's social moral theory necessarily involves discovering the ideals of social structure and behaviour for a society, in which people would be best able to live well, grow, and develop to their full potential. But these objectives go well beyond any that are envisaged in ordinary utilitarian theories. For, the ideal social contract would have to spell out the responsibilities of governments and other collective and specialist agents, too, and say how each would be ideally obliged to behave towards others and to the individuals with whom they must deal. Social contractual utilitarianism is formally most like rule-utilitarianism. But, according to the social contractual theory, it would be a mistake to try to evaluate rules individually, without considering the system of rules and other conventions to which it is to be added. In our society, affording offers of equality of opportunity would be considered to be good. But in other societies, they could well be fatal (literally). For a social idealist, the process of determining social ideals that go much beyond the simple demands of humanism is a piecemeal, social evolutionary, one. The optimal kinds of social structures, institutions, and conventions have to be discovered largely by political trial and error, and some, at least, of the

The Social Theory of Morality   123

conventions of social intercourse that would be recommended for one's ideal society are likely to depend on what social structures or institutions are already in place.

4.8   PROFESSIONAL AND INSTITUTIONAL ETHICS

The social theory of morality brings what is usually called 'applied' or 'practical' ethics in from the cold. If the social theory of morality is accepted, professional and business ethics must now be seen as being continuous with the area traditionally regarded as basic. For, no one has any moral responsibilities just because he or she is human. Qua human beings, our responsibilities always depend on our social roles or positions. Infants, for example, have no moral responsibilities. And, there is no point at which they suddenly acquire them. Moreover, the moral responsibilities that children have, when they do start to acquire them, are not all the same. They may, for example, depend on their age, their linguistic capacities, their ethnic grouping, whether orphaned or not, and whether their parents are normal, insane, or in jail. The moral responsibilities of intelligent adults in the community are not all the same either. Those of doctors are not the same as those of auditors, and both sets of responsibilities are different from those of judges or the members of juries. Further, the responsibilities of citizens are not the same as those of foreign visitors or refugees. Also, our social and moral responsibilities may diminish with the inevitable decline in our physical and mental capacities. For example, a man who is suffering from Alzheimer's disease must become less and less responsible for what he does, and a woman who is crippled and bedridden cannot be socially or morally responsible for the care and protection of her children.

So, fundamentally, all moral theory is applied to particular groups of social agents. There is a kind of normal field of application N, which is that of rational, healthy people who are sufficiently well acculturated to have a good sense of what most sensible people in the community would consider to be right or wrong. And, most of those who would count as professionals, tradesmen, or members of other specialist groups would also be members of N. Therefore, any responsibilities that people might have in virtue of their membership of N would almost certainly be included in their responsibilities as professionals, tradesmen, or specialists of other kinds. So there is a sense in which N is a fundamental grouping. Indeed, it is of special interest also in the ethics of business, politics, government, hospital treatment, university education, and so on. For, those who are engaged in pursuing the goals of these collective agents, as managers, board members, MPs, nurses, university professors, and so on will normally be members of N, and therefore share the moral responsibilities of this group, before we even begin to consider what extra responsibilities they may have as a result of their work.

124 *Social Humanism*

Therefore, the distinction between pure and applied ethics is not entirely misplaced. Nevertheless, this way of thinking about the distinction clearly suggests that applied ethics (which is concerned with the responsibilities of the various kinds of collectives and specialities) stands to normal or 'pure' ethics (which is concerned with the responsibilities of the membership of N) as applied mathematics stands to pure mathematics or applied science stands to basic science. But this suggestion is plainly false. Applied mathematics is founded on pure mathematics and applied science on basic science. But applied ethics is not founded on pure ethics. Pure ethics is just that branch of ethics applicable to all of the members of N. Applied ethics includes business ethics, which is applicable to the teams of managers or directors of public companies, financial corporations, and so on, and it is not derivable from pure ethics. Nor is pure ethics foundational for business ethics. Businessmen in our own community have the responsibilities of members of N. But the responsibilities of the companies they manage, direct, or finance are not derivable from those of the membership of N. On the contrary, the special responsibilities of the managers, shareholders, and directors of these companies all derive from the social roles of the companies they serve. Between them, these executives are required to ensure that the companies meet all of their social obligations and, ideally, to ensure that they meet all of their social moral obligations.

The distinction between pure and applied ethics is a bit like one that could conceivably be made between pure and applied forestry. Pure forestry, it might be said, is the study of the temperate rainforests of Europe. Applied forestry, it might be said, includes the study of tropical rainforests, forests of the Antipodes, and so on. In my view, all of these studies are just aspects of the one general study, namely, that of forests. There is nothing that is pure about the study of temperate rainforests, and there is nothing applied about the study of these other forests. They are just different areas of the one basic study. The same is true for pure and applied ethics. There is no good reason for us to pick out the class N of social agents in our community or to label the study of their social attitudes 'basic' or 'pure'. The study of the social ideals of the group N within our own community is important and interesting, because it is the group to which most educated people belong. But it is not the only group whose attitudes are relevant to the issues to be discussed in moral philosophy.

What is most distinctive of the responsibilities of collective and specialised agents is that they are determined by what their social roles are generally conceived to be. If, for example, the primary social role of a business corporation is generally conceived to be just to make as much money for the company's shareholders as possible, then the interests of the community are likely to be very badly served. But this neglect of community interests would not be a moral failing of the directors. They would just be doing their duty, if that were all that was expected of them. Indeed, according to Milton Friedman, company directors would be morally in breach of duty

The Social Theory of Morality   125

if they were to accept that their companies had social responsibilities other than their duty to shareholders. Therefore, if we wish to make insurance companies, banks, and finance companies more answerable to the community, then we must write what we want them to do into the social contract of the society or into the nascent global social contract defined by international treaties. It is no good just appealing to the boards of directors of these companies to do the right thing. We have to first make it clear to them what we expect of them. And this involves defining the social roles of the kinds of companies they direct.

To define the social role of a kind of company, such as a trading bank, the obvious strategy would be to ask the banks themselves to draw up a charter to explain the responsibilities of trading banks to depositors, borrowers, government agencies, bank staff, auditors, and so on and seek to have this charter approved by the government of the day. When a Trading Bank Charter is ultimately approved, laws could be passed to ensure that it becomes binding on all registered trading banks in the country and that bank executives would be required by law to do their best to uphold it. If something like this could be done, then we should have a clear statement of the trading bank's responsibilities, with clear implications for the responsibilities of the boards of directors of these banks.

I have chosen to use trading banks as an example, not because I think they were the most irresponsible of the institutions that brought on the global financial crisis, but because I think they would be relatively easy to regulate socially. Their function is clearly not just to make money for their shareholders and never has been. They have many other very important social responsibilities. I could have chosen fund managers just as well. They have a clear responsibility to manage the funds invested in them for the secure benefit of their investors. But they also have great power as investors, and one would expect them to use these powers responsibly in the public interest. When, for example, they use their millions of proxy votes to override those of the overwhelming majority of shareholders present at annual general meetings, in order to confirm huge salaries and salary bonuses for the executives of the companies in which they are investing, it is clear that they are not sensitive to the wishes of the shareholders they are supposed to represent on the board. Nor is it clear that they are even acting in the interests of their own investors. Or, if they were, the decision would not appear to be based on any solid evidence that huge executive salaries are required for good company performance. In my view, the use of proxy votes held by those who have invested other people's money in shares should not be used at all unless the holder of the proxy has received explicit instructions from the relevant shareholders about how it should be used.

But in case anyone should think that I am just anti-business, I would not limit my demands for charters to financial institutions. I think that universities too should have charters that set out for all to see what the universities' role in the community should be. These charters should, like the others I

126 *Social Humanism*

have suggested, be prepared by the universities and approved by the relevant government Department of Education. In fact, I only wish that charters like these had been in place before the neo-liberal state and federal government of Australia set about corporatizing the universities and gearing their activities towards developing education as an export industry. For, I do not believe that the charters that would have been written thirty years ago would have allowed this vandalism to occur. Moreover, I am firmly convinced that many in the financial sector middle management would think much the same about their own institutions. Many of the bank managers at the branch level, for example, must look at what has happened to their industry with horror.

There are three principal reasons for advocating the writing of charters. Firstly, charters are the most direct and best way of defining the sets of responsibilities of collective or specialised agents. They are straightforward and to the point. Secondly, new charters could help to restore some of the losses that have occurred in the social contracts of our own, and most other, Western societies due to the neo-liberal revolution. Thirdly, the sets of social responsibilities, which we suppose the members of institutional and professional agencies to have, have normally been fine-tuned by case law in the civil courts. But the process of developing case law to define sets of responsibilities is very slow and can take many generations. Moreover, the social accord that can result ultimately from individual case determinations is easily destroyed, as the neo-liberal surge of the last few decades has demonstrated. The existence and formal social approval of charters for the various institutions and professions could plausibly slow down the process of trashing them.

4.9 RAMIFICATIONS OF THE SOCIAL THEORY

Many ramifications of the social theory of morality need to be discussed. For, the theory is clearly at odds with a number of orthodox positions in moral and political theory. Firstly, the theory is a social one and therefore at odds with the prevailing orthodoxy of individualism in ethics. The questions are whether (a) this matters, and (b) it has implications for political theory. These and related questions will be taken up in the following chapter. Secondly, there is the issue of moral dominance. My stand on this issue is bound to be controversial, because it is inconsistent with all of the well-known objectivist theories of ethics—Kantianism, intuitionism, naturalism, realism, and most forms of utilitarianism. Moreover, the methodology of social and legal criticism seems to demand moral dominance, i.e. the view that our well-considered moral duty necessarily outweighs our known social duty. Yet there is good reason to reject this view. Our beliefs about what is right should not always outweigh what is socially demanded of us. The Dominance Principle will be discussed fully in Chapter 6.

5 Individualism

5.1 POLITICAL AND METAPHYSICAL INDIVIDUALISM

The social theory of morality is not a theory about what is right or wrong. It is a second-order theory concerning the foundations of morality, which is compatible with a great many moral and political positions. Nevertheless, the fact that this second-order theory is a social theory must make it highly suspect in some circles. For, the kind of theory that is here being developed would appear to be incompatible with both political individualism and mainstream metaphysical individualism. Political individualism is a form of liberalism and is compatible with social idealism. It is the principle that everyone should be able to live as they please, without interference from governments, or from anyone else, provided that their ways of living do not interfere with the rights of others to live also as they please. If you believed strongly enough in this principle, you would, presumably, wish to see it written into the society's social contract. Neo-liberalism is a form of political liberalism that is built on a similar conception of individual freedom, but it is also applicable to business enterprises. It, too, is compatible with social idealism. If you would like ideally to live in a state in which all social services, infrastructure, and enterprises are privatised and business profitability is the main determinant of social policy, then you may freely advocate this policy and wish to have the principles of free market fundamentalism built into the society's social contract.

In contrast, metaphysical individualism is not a moral or political stance. It is the metaphysical claim that individuals are the basic elements of society, in that they are: (a) *ontologically primary*, because all social or cultural changes depend on changes in the beliefs, attitudes, desires, and so on of their individual members; (b) *epistemologically primary*, because all explanations of social phenomena must ultimately refer to the beliefs, actions, preferences, and the like of individuals; and (c) *the primary causal agents in society*, and so are the primary causes of all social activity, for they, and they alone, have the capacity to act

128 *Social Humanism*

with free will. This thesis is sometimes called 'primary agency individualism'. According to this thesis, all other agents, e.g. corporations, governments, and so on, must depend on human agency to drive them. History and society are powerless.

The metaphysics to be defended here has some similarity to Mario Bunge's (1979) theory, in that it is neither individualistic nor holistic. Bunge calls his position 'systemism', the principal metaphysical thesis of which is: 'A society is neither a mere aggregate of individuals nor a supra-individual entity: it is a system of interconnected individuals' (Bunge, 1979: 16) But Bunge puts some strong restrictions on what societies can do or achieve. He denies, for example, that a society can act on its members or interact with other societies, although he allows that a group of individuals can act severally on a single individual. However, this is to give far too much away to metaphysical individualism. Societies are much more like collective organisms. They evolve, interact with each other, compete for scarce resources, learn from experience, prosper, or decline. To say that their evolution does not affect the lives of the individuals who live in them, or will live in them in the next generation, is absurd. A society's laws, social customs, educational institutions, health-care provisions, retirement benefits, and so on all affect the lives and wellbeing of its members profoundly.

One may be puzzled why anyone would wish to deny this obvious fact. But one must remember that metaphysical individualism was developed in the 1950s and 1960s mainly to counter sociological theories sympathetic to Marxism and other left-wing political movements that advocated radical social change. These theories typically spoke of social forces of one kind or another. In the most extreme cases, they spoke of historical laws or historical inevitability. Such talk was labelled 'historicist' and widely condemned. The social theory of morality does not speak about, or imply the existence of, historical laws, and it is not historicist. Nevertheless, it does postulate and talk seriously about real social contracts, which are inclusive of social and moral rights, obligations, and responsibilities, and it suggests that most such contracts significantly influence what people may decide to do, even where there are no legal sanctions to back them. So there must be real doubts in the minds of many philosophers whether the social theory of morality is compatible with metaphysical individualism. In my view, the social theory of morality is indeed incompatible with this theory, but it is none the worse for that. It will be argued here that metaphysical individualism is untenable, and that the theory that the strident defenders of individualism and neo-liberalism developed in order to undermine their socialist opponents is destructive of conventional morality. Metaphysical individualism is destructive of conventional morality, because, if there were no such thing as social causation, the social contract of a society would necessarily be ineffective, and so would all moral principles that are not backed by the

Individualism   129

force of law. In this chapter it will be argued that all three of the theses of metaphysical individualism are false.

5.2   THE ONTOLOGICAL THESIS

As I understand it, the ontological thesis of individualism is that the social characteristics of societies, i.e. their values, customs, laws, institutions, social preferences, and so on, all supervene ontologically on the beliefs, desires, decisions, actions, and personal preferences of the individuals who constitute them. That is, the ontological thesis simply states that these facts about individuals are the determinants of the social facts, and that these same social facts could not exist without them.

However, there is no obvious pattern of causal influences in modern societies to support this general thesis. The principal individual and collective agents in society interact with each other, and both are evidently involved in bringing about social changes. Individuals interact and influence each other in their beliefs and attitudes, normal ways of behaving, judgements of right and wrong, and in many other ways. Collective agents do likewise. They too interact with each other, and with the individuals they regulate, serve, or seek to influence by advertising—and sometimes they also learn from the experience. But to suppose that individuals are ultimately the determinants of all social phenomena is to ignore the complex plurality and multi-directionality of social causation. Individuals' beliefs, desires, and attitudes are influenced by the collectives in society, e.g. by the media they watch, the advertisements they see, the firms that employ them, and the schools and universities they attend or have attended. And these collective agents, or their products, are managed or directed by their governing boards or assemblies, whose members are influenced by the collective agents in the society, e.g. by the media they watch, the firms that have employed them, the schools and universities they have attended, and so on. Therefore, collective attitudes, beliefs, and desires both influence, and are influenced by, individual attitudes, beliefs, and desires. They are reciprocally dependent on each other, and hence neither is supervenient on the other.

The causes of social change that directly involve human activity are multi-directional. On the whole, the collective agents, including governments, corporations, financial institutions, and the media, would appear to be the most powerful of those that are directly responsible for social changes. But behind all of these collective agents, there are usually some very powerful individuals whose decisions and actions initiate these changes. However, the chains of influence do not always appear to end at any obvious points. For, behind these powerful individuals there are usually some powerful organisations—political parties, business councils, and other elite groups that determine the compositions of the most important boards of management—and these organisations demand, or at least expect, these changes to

130 *Social Humanism*

be agreeable to them. Moreover, these powerful organisations themselves normally owe their power to patronage or to the achievements of the distinguished individuals who founded them. And these patrons or distinguished individuals may in turn have owed their positions or achievements at least partly to their family's influence—and so on, back into history.

Contrary to the ontological thesis, the social contract of any modern society would seem to be a force to be reckoned with. It is common practice, for example, to object to a government measure, or to an unwelcome social practice, on the ground that 'it is just not the way we do things here'. To object in this way is to make a direct appeal to the society's social mores. But this appeal would have to be ineffective if the ontological thesis of individualism were true. For what would it matter what the social mores of the society were? Clearly, it would not matter to a committed political individualist, since what other people do, or have done, is of no concern to such a person. Yet, for many people, it is a powerful argument. It was undoubtedly a factor in defeating the Australian Government's Pacific Solution to the perceived problem of unwanted asylum seekers—people arriving unannounced in rickety boats. It was unkind and 'un-Australian', many people said, to treat them so cruelly. It was also an argument that almost forced the US government to abandon its health-care reform bill in 2009. Certainly, there were no rational arguments against the bill that could possibly have justified the vehement and uncompromising opposition to it that was displayed in Congress and the Senate. The only really effective argument appeared to be that the measure was essentially 'a socialist' one, i.e. that it was 'un-American'. The idea that there is 'an American way of life' is indeed a powerful one. And it is not without content. It greatly restricts the freedom of American legislators to enact socially progressive legislation, however desperately it may be needed.

In my view, the structure of any society that is reflected in its social contract co-evolves with the mind-sets of its individual members. By the mind-set of an individual, I mean the individual's total set of beliefs and disbeliefs, social attitudes, and desires and aversions. By a social attitude, I mean one of approval or disapproval. I include it here, along with desires and aversions, because I do not think that they are the same. One can approve of something without desiring it, and one can strongly disapprove of something without being repulsed by it. Also, like Kant, I wish to allow for the possibility that one can be motivated to act independently of one's desires and aversions. The mind-sets of the individuals in a society are normally informed by the society's social contract. Thus, the public endorsement of what is generally considered to be good behaviour, and the overt constraints on behaviour that most people would regard as bad, can become, and often are, easily internalised by individuals, where they appear as attitudes of approval or disapproval in the individuals' mind-sets. However, people's attitudes of approval or disapproval can be strongly influenced by events that they have witnessed or read about. Good and bad

Individualism 131

things do happen to people, and if we think that what has happened is due to the bad behaviour of any individual or other social agent, then we are likely to say so. If enough people say so, on enough occasions, then the approval or disapproval of individuals can be translated into legislation, or it can just become accepted over time that actions of the kinds in question should generally be approved or disapproved. Thus, individuals' mind-sets can directly or indirectly influence their societies' social contracts.

If two systems co-evolve, and have done so since time immemorial, then neither can be said to be more fundamental than the other. The social contract of a society and the range of mind-sets of its individual members are, according to the argument of the previous paragraph, co-evolving systems. Moreover, in most stable societies, this appears always to have been the case. Some societies have relatively short histories; they were established by the violent overthrow of earlier regimes and the replacement of their ruling elites by ones sympathetic to the conquerors. Presumably, then, the original social structures, out of which many modern societies must have been created, were initially dictated by the conquerors. But none of this is relevant to the question of which has ontological priority, the social contract or its members. A stable society of the kind that has a social contract could not possibly have existed immediately following the conquest. The social contract, when it evolves, could possibly be much the same as the one that was originally dictated. But it would not have been a social contract at first. It could only have become one by the slow and painful process of acquiescence or settlement.

There is a simpler version of the ontological thesis that may seem at first sight to be both obvious and true: viz. that societies are ontologically dependent on their members. For, the normal criterion for ontological dependence is this:

> Things of a given kind depend ontologically on those of another, if they could not exist without them, but things of this other kind could exist independently of those of the given kind.

To illustrate, molecules depend ontologically on atoms, because molecules could not exist if there were no atoms. But atoms could exist without molecules. So, by this criterion, societies depend ontologically on people, because they could not exist if people did not exist, but people could certainly exist even if societies did not. However, the ontological thesis cannot be just the truism that human societies are ontologically dependent on *people*. It would have to be the more substantial thesis that a society depends ontologically on its *members*. But this is evidently not true. Every society can survive changes of membership. Some societies, such as the Chinese and Japanese societies, can and have survived complete changes of membership. Evidently, all that is needed for a society to survive a change of membership is a sufficient degree of continuity in its social and cultural practices. So,

132 *Social Humanism*

plausibly, the identity of a society depends, not on its members, but on the continuing stability of its social structure and culture.

Nevertheless, there is a clear sense in which the character of a society depends on the attitudes, mores, practices, and so on of its members. For example, the moral system that currently prevails in the society depends on the current levels of commitment of its members to creating and/or maintaining the various rights, obligations, and responsibilities they attribute to the members of the various classes of social agents in the society. The current value system of a society depends on the levels of approval or disapproval that various actions, practices, and behavioural traits enjoy in the society. The social customs of a society depend on the social practices of its members. In this sense, the characteristics of societies around the world depend qualitatively and quantitatively on the qualities of their members, and on the strengths of their views, attitudes, or commitments. But such dependencies are not ontological. The character of a society obviously does depend on the attitudes of its members. But it is also true that the ways in which people are likely to behave depend, in broad brush, on the character of the society and, more specifically, with the kind of micro-society in which they were raised. Supervenience is necessarily an asymmetrical relation. Co-dependence is not.

5.3 THE EPISTEMOLOGICAL THESIS

The epistemological thesis of individualism (ETI) is the claim that the only possible 'bed-rock' explanations in the social sciences are those that refer to the actions, choices, preferences, and so on of individuals.[1] This thesis is naturally associated with a methodological thesis, otherwise known as 'methodological individualism', according to which the only viable methodology in the social sciences is individually focussed. According to methodological individualism, social scientists should always proceed by investigating the actions, choices, preferences, and so on of individuals and seek to base their theories on what they can discover in this way (Scott, 1973). There is nothing to be learned, they say, by studying societies as wholes.

The ETI has a long history, as Steven Lukes (1973) illustrates. Karl Marx would certainly not have accepted it, since he believed in historical inevitability. Emile Durkheim, who believed in a kind of collective conscience, argued at great length against it. And it was firmly rejected by F. H. Bradley and other idealist philosophers, who thought of societies as social organisms. Nevertheless, since the Second World War, the thesis of methodological individualism has been strongly defended by a number of prominent liberals, e.g. Friedrich Hayek and John Watkins (O'Neill, 1973), who were concerned by the rising tide of democratic socialism. In this later period, the debate about individualism focussed mainly on the question of what

Individualism   133

kinds of explanations are possible in the social sciences—as though this was somehow at the heart of the dispute between liberals and democratic socialists. Are individualistic explanations the only ones that are ultimately satisfactory in these areas? Or, is there scope for holistic or 'mixed' explanations too?

It will be argued here that the debate has been misconceived. The issue is not one that needs to divide liberal individualists from democratic socialists; it is a dispute that is internal to the philosophy of the social sciences. A liberal individualist has no reason to fear explanations that refer to social attitudes, and a social democrat has no reason to reject explanations that appeal to the mind-sets of individuals. Such explanations can be equally legitimate. It is just a question of which details of epistemic location are required. And even here, it is of no great consequence. If you are looking for an explanation of a sequence of events that you think is not just a random sequence, then you may want to know what would generate such a sequence—what mechanism or what formula. If you think that the sequence is one that approximates to some underlying pattern that it would actually have displayed, e.g. if there had been no errors of measurement, then you would need to guess what this underlying pattern might be and check whether the supposed errors or misfits are more or less randomly distributed around it. Or, if you have what seems to be an anomaly of some kind, then you may want to know whether it can be adequately explained on current theories. Explanations in science are normally attempts to answer such questions, i.e. questions that are concerned with filling the gaps in our understanding. That is why I characterise explanation as 'epistemic location'. For, that is what it always involves.

The question raised by methodological individualism concerns the direction of explanation. To answer this question, we need to consider how much individual social attitudes are determined by society's social mores and how much the social mores are determined by individual social attitudes. According to methodological individualism, the social mores must be wholly dependent on individual social attitudes. We know this, because the methodology requires that all explanations of the social attitudes of individuals must be traced back to their beliefs and desires. Among the social mores, I include the socially sanctioned prohibitions of rape, murder, theft, child molestation, pornography, and so on, and all of the socially approved actions, such as those of keeping promises, acting honestly, and being fair, kind, or generous.

But the methodological individualist cannot stop at this point. For, an individual's social attitudes would also need to be explained psychologically—in terms of that individual's likes and dislikes, or hopes and fears. According to methodological individualism, one never acts just because one thinks it is socially the right thing to do unless one hopes to gain some benefit by doing so, and one never refrains from doing anything one wants to do that is socially wrong, unless one is afraid of the consequences of

134 *Social Humanism*

being caught or sent to purgatory. For, social attitudes have no force for a methodological individualist unless they are backed by hopes or fears.

Therefore, for a methodological individualist, there can be no such thing as internalising a legal prohibition, or the social approval or disapproval of any activity. For, these are all explanations that have the wrong direction. They are explanations of psychological states (of approval or disapproval) that are dependent on social facts (about what is legally prohibited or socially approved or disapproved). But there are such explanations, and they are manifestly good explanations. Therefore, methodological individualism is untenable. Indeed, it is no more tenable than the opposite thesis (which, as far as I know, has never been supported) that all psychological explanations must stem from social facts. The plain truth of the matter is that both kinds of explanations are legitimate, and neither can claim to be more fundamental than the other. And, the kind that is to be preferred depends on the context. I do not deny that some individuals may do the right thing, because they expect to be rewarded for doing so (either in this world or 'the next'), or that some people may refrain from doing evil just because they fear the consequences. Many people are amoral in this way. But one can hardly base a methodology of the social sciences on the assumption that this is what is true of everyone.

For a Kantian, a moral act requires a moral motivation. It is not enough just to do the right thing. One must, according to Kant's theory, do the right thing for the right reason. That is, one must do the right thing, because it is right and for no other reason. But no methodological individualist could possibly endorse this Kantian view unless he or she thought (as Kant did) that rightness could be discovered independently of the social consequences of our acts. For, if the rightness of acting in a certain way depended on the goodness of the social consequences of doing so, then the individual's social approval of doing such acts would be explicable in terms of their social consequences, contrary to the tenets of methodological individualism. But Kant's *a priori* theory of morality is untenable, and no other *a priori* theory that would successfully justify our attitudes of social approval or disapproval has yet been developed.

Nevertheless, the fact that methodological individualism has been so strongly advocated by neo-liberal economists and adopted by a powerful political movement (neo-liberalism) has ensured that the thesis has received wide currency. Consequently, the kind of amoralism that it implies has become widely accepted in the economic and political communities. It has not, I hasten to add, been accepted as being amoral. On the contrary, it is just seen as being common sense. Thus, neo-liberal economics is not morally neutral, since it is based on the assumption that people in a market economy should always act out of self-interest if they do not wish to distort the market. If they do the right thing, because they are being appropriately paid to do it, then that is what is to be expected. But if they do the right thing, even though they are not being paid to do it, then that is anomalous.

Individualism 135

It is a case of market failure, because it undervalues the work that the morally motivated worker does and artificially depresses the wages of those doing that work for a living.[2]

Politics too has been corrupted by neo-liberalism. For example, neo-liberals do not support legislation just because it is right and would benefit the community in the long run. They will support legislation only if there is 'political mileage' in it. That is, the support will be rewarded by public support that could make a difference at election time. And they will oppose legislation for the opposite reason. It does not matter that the legislation may be necessary for the long-term good of the country. It matters only whether opposing it will have greater electoral benefits than supporting it or otherwise allowing it to pass. That is neo-liberalism translated into politics.

The true view concerning the directions of explanation in the social sciences is that individual social attitudes are dependent on societal ones and societal attitudes are dependent on individual ones. That is, they are interdependent. This is precisely what we should have expected given the evident fact that the social contract of a society and the mind-sets of its individual members are co-evolving systems.

5.4   HOLISM AND INDIVIDUALISM

Holism is the view that the behaviour of the parts of a system of some kind can best be explained by their roles in achieving certain end-results for systems of that kind. Such explanations are common in biology, where they are normally referred to as functional explanations. There are, however, good reasons why such explanations should be useful in this field. For, there is good reason to think that many of the identifiable parts of living organisms have specialised roles and have become adapted over the course of their evolution to performing them well. Therefore, many of the problems of epistemic location that have to be solved in this area are concerned with identifying biological functions.

In most biological organisms, the functional parts are contained in a single body. But there are many biological systems that involve many bodies. There are, for example, many species of animals whose members live together in groups, where they coordinate their activities. The members of some of these groups (ants, wasps, bees, etc.) are very tightly knit together into colonies and are naturally divided into sub-groups (queens, workers, soldiers, etc.) that have group-specific roles that contribute to the survival of these colonies. It is almost as though the sub-groups were the parts of a single organism. Other groups of animals of the same species are to be found living together in much more loosely connected groups or tribes, with much more elaborate social structures, where there is much more role differentiation, but where the determinations of roles are not so rigidly fixed by nature. Human beings belong to this latter group.

136 *Social Humanism*

How then do human societies differ essentially from ant colonies? The standard answer is that to understand how an ant colony works, you need to know what the various kinds of ants in the colony do, and how their performing these various functions contributes to the survival of the colony. And really that is about all you need to know. You do not need to know anything about the particular ants that make up the colony or anything about the history of the colony other than how it has worked in the past. But to understand how a human society works, you need to know what institutions, laws, or customs it has; whose interests they serve; and how they serve those interests. At first sight, the task of understanding a human society might appear to be similar to that of trying to understand the workings of an ant colony, only much more complex. But there is one striking difference. Human societies can reasonably be supposed to serve, and to have risen in response to, human interests other than just the basic ones of survival and procreation. Therefore, to understand any society, it is necessary to understand the complex social roles of its laws, customs, and institutions and how, and to what extent, they serve the various interests of its members.

To complicate matters still further, there are collective groups in societies that have interests of their own that need to be taken into account. A good sociologist must therefore be concerned with the beliefs, attitudes, and interests of the members and the collective groups of members of the society under investigation. Holistic explanations of the kinds that can be offered to explain the structure and organization of an ant colony cannot successfully explain the structure and organization of a human society. For, there is no common set of beliefs, attitudes, customs, and interests that any successful society must accommodate, and, even if there were, there might be a large number of different ways of satisfying them.

Defenders of the epistemological thesis of individualism have been quick to notice this difference and to stress its importance. They have argued that if we forget the requirement that a society is built to serve the various interests of its members—not just their basic biological needs—then we are likely to end up with a society that ignores some of the things that are really important to people or makes no adequate provision for them. And we are then, as Hayek (1976) warns us, on 'the road to serfdom'. But in defending methodological individualism, Hayek, Popper, and Watkins (O'Neill ed. 1973) have all misdiagnosed the problem. Holistic explanations are successful in explaining the structure of ant colonies because the ants in the various sub-groups are specifically innately programmed to carry out their social roles, which have evolved to promote the success and survival of the colony. They have social roles as worker ants, queen ants, or soldier ants, and the success of the colony depends on their all doing what might seem to us to be their duties. There is no good reason, therefore, why holistic explanations should not be just as useful in those areas of human endeavour, such as economics, once we recognise that the purchasers of goods and

Individualism 137

services have some common social interests that are distinct from those of the sellers of goods and services.

In the physical sciences, holistic explanations are usually contrasted with realistic micro-theories. The best-known examples of such explanations are probably those of thermodynamics. In the eighteenth century, thermodynamics was considered to be part of the caloric theory of heat. But it proved to be independent of this theory, and it survived the transition (in the 1840s) from the caloric to the dynamical theory of heat. The investigations of Boyle and Gay-Lussac had established the basic equation of state for gases under normal conditions of temperature and pressure.[3] In the early nineteenth century, specific heats at constant volume and at constant pressure were defined and determined for various gases. For every different gas, the difference between these two quantities was found to be quite substantial. In the 1820s, Sadi Carnot described a theoretical heat engine, now known as a Carnot cycle, that would exploit this difference and was able to prove the remarkable theorem that the efficiencies of all perfectly reversible heat engines working between the same temperature limits must always be the same, however they might be constructed. In the 1840s, this result led Robert Meyer to postulate a law of conservation of energy (the first law of thermodynamics) and later to H. A. Lorentz's discovery of the principle of entropy for adiabatic processes (an early version of the second law of thermodynamics). Thermodynamics continued to develop after the 1840s, when the dynamical theory of gases was developed, but by that time it had already proven its worth as a scientific theory and had done so independently of the micro-theory on which it was ultimately shown to depend.

In general, realistic micro-theories are preferred in science to holistic macro-theories, even though they may explain all and only the same phenomena. They are preferred, because they (a) are potentially more informative, and (b) have greater potential for theoretical development. Holistic theories generally depend fairly directly on the observed or postulated dispositional properties of the macro-systems under consideration. The micro-theories that explain these same phenomena normally do so by proposing a mechanism that would explain the dispositional properties of the macro-systems in question. Valencies, for example, were the supposed dispositional properties of chemical elements postulated to explain why these elements combined with each other in the proportions they did. It was a tolerably successful holistic theory of chemical combination, which survived until the twentieth century. The micro-theory that eventually replaced it is one that identified valencies with electron availabilities, making use of Bohr's theory of the atom. It was unquestionably a much better, more comprehensive, and much more fruitful theory.

Nevertheless, holistic macro-theories have important roles in science. They can discover order in apparent chaos and develop useful concepts for future elaboration. Such theories are to be found in most areas of scientific study. Economics is no exception. The theories of macro-economics are

138   *Social Humanism*

classical holistic theories. They describe and relate the collective economic responses of people living in free market economies and relate these to the various factors that would inhibit or stimulate aggregate demand or lead to increased production of goods and services. They allow the construction of economic models that enable economists to analyse huge quantities of data and predict with reasonable accuracy the overall economic effects of various social policies. It is true that economists would love to have a micro-economic theory that was firmly based on empirical studies of individual economic motivations and behavioural dispositions—studies that they could use to back up their macro-economic theories. But they do not have such a micro-economic theory, and it seems unlikely that they ever will, because the social roles, motivations, and mind-sets of individuals and collectives in modern societies may vary enormously from culture to culture, depending on what institutions they have and what they are socially required to do.

Macro-economics clearly presents a difficulty for the ETI. One could adopt the ETI's recommendations for the social sciences only if one were prepared to scrap macro-economic theory, if no satisfactory micro-theory could be found to replace it. But economists are not likely to do that—and for a very good reason. Therefore, there is no case for the total abolition of holistic explanations in the social sciences. Human beings are members of natural cluster kinds, just as all other biological species are. And there are a great many sound generalisations that can be made about them, just as there are about the members of most other biological species. Nor is there any good reason to reject holistic explanations anywhere else in science. There is nothing wrong with them, and they do a very good job as far as they go.

If the ETI is defensible anywhere, it would appear to be in the field of history. History is not a science and does not purport to be. It is not a science because it does not seek to explain generally the behavioural dispositions of the members of any specific natural kinds—where 'natural kinds' is broadly interpreted to include cluster kinds. History is concerned with human beings, but the historian's focus is not on any general characteristics or modes of behaviour of human beings. It is on how they behaved, and why they behaved as they did, in the particular historical circumstances in which they found themselves. General patterns of human biology and of personal and economic behaviour are studied in various sciences, but not in history. History's concern is with particular historical developments, especially those that appear to have had a considerable influence on the politics or culture of the societies in which they occurred. And such developments are nearly always *sui generis*. The complexity of any real-life situation is nearly always too great to allow any useful generalisations to be made. The worth of a historical explanation is consequently never evaluated in the same kind of way as a scientific explanation, since it does not rest on any general principles that can be independently tested. It must explain the

Individualism   139

facts as economically and plausibly as possible, just as any scientific explanation must. But there are no further tests that can be carried out to test the theory, e.g. by considering the histories of other societies. If one is in doubt, one can only gather more information about the particular society under investigation or cast about for a more plausible or better reading of the known facts about it. One does not test the worth of a historical theory by seeing whether it applies to another society or at another time to explain similar facts. The only tests that can be applied are whether the account deals as economically as possible with all of the known facts, and whether the motivations and capacities ascribed to the historical figures are sufficiently plausible, given the circumstances that then existed.

But the nature of historical explanation can offer little comfort to the defenders of the ETI. It certainly supports the case against historicism, but it does not support the wholesale rejection of holistic explanations in the social sciences or even the claim that such explanations are never 'rock-bottom' ones. One might plausibly argue, on the basis of a general preference for micro-theories, that holistic explanations are never, or should never be, regarded as 'rock-bottom' in any area of science. But, in that case, the lack of satisfactory individualistic or other atomistic explanations in a given area cannot be used to discredit it. Physics, for example, lacks satisfactory atomistic explanations of some physical phenomena. Therefore, if sociology, in particular, is to be discredited, a much better argument will be needed than the defenders of the epistemological priority of individuals in social theory have so far produced.

Sociology is the study of human societies and of human social behaviour in particular. The epistemological thesis of individualism is the claim that the only ultimately satisfactory explanations of human social behaviour are individualistic. Let us grant that this is the case for collective economic behaviour in a market economy. That is, let us assume that the collective economic behaviour of people in a market economy is predictable from the known dispositions of the members of that economy. For this to be the case, the known economic dispositions of the individual members of society must be strong enough, and consistent enough, to give the gross economic behaviour in question at least a high probability of occurring. All this is certainly plausible, even if some people only have these dispositions as a result of living in a market economy. But let us grant that living in a market economy has nothing to do with the formation of these attitudes, and that their origin is wholly biological or psychological. Then our economic behaviour would clearly not impugn the epistemological thesis of individualism.

What would then? The difficulty is that a counter-example to the 'rock-bottom' version of the ETI would have to be a clear case of a 'rock-bottom' explanation that was sociological. Newton's theory of gravity was a holistic explanation of gravitational phenomena. But a doctrinaire atomist need not be deterred by this. All that he or she would need to say is, 'So,

140 *Social Humanism*

Newton's theory does not give us a "rock-bottom" explanation of these phenomena'. The ETI in sociology can clearly be defended against any possible counter-example in the same sort of way. But the ETI is meant to be a bit more than a pious hope that sound individualistic explanations could eventually be found for all such cases. If good sociological explanations can be given in enough cases where no good individualistic explanations are available, this must be taken as strong evidence against the thesis. Putative counter-examples are not hard to find.

Example 1.

Social fact: Young women tend to buy clothes of kind X.

Individualistic explanation: Most young women like and can afford to buy clothes of kind X. They think they are attractive and make them look sexy.

Sociological explanation: Clothes of kind X for young women are now very much in fashion. The big brand-name fashion houses of the world have spent millions of dollars in promoting them. They have been very successful.

Comment: The individualistic explanation is reasonable, but the sociological explanation takes the next step. It explains why most young women think clothes of kind X are attractive and make them look sexy. The sociological explanation is mixed. It assumes the relevance of both personal desires and social forces to the observed outcome.

Example 2.

Social fact: By 2005, Australians were working the longest hours of anyone in the developed world.

Individualistic explanation: Every employer who demanded longer hours had his or her reasons, and every individual who agreed to work for longer hours had his or her reasons for agreeing to do so. These facts, together with the hours agreed on and the relevant employment statistics for Australia and the developed world, would together explain the social fact.

Sociological explanation: Industrial deregulation and changes in workplace relations laws have given employers greatly increased power over their workers, and it is in their interests to drive them harder. Workers, afraid for their jobs and caught up in a tide of consumerism and burgeoning debt, readily agreed to work for very long hours. These hypotheses, together with the relevant statistics, would explain the social fact.

Comment: The sociological explanation, if true, is obviously superior. For, it explains the trend in a way that no individualistic explanation of

Individualism 141

the social fact could possibly do. The sociological explanation's superiority derives from the fact that it recognises the existence of social forces, as well as personal ones, driving the increase in the number of hours worked.

Conclusion: There is no plausible case for the ETI in sociology. Most explanations in sociology are mixed. That is, their premises contain both social hypotheses and facts about individuals. If there is a case for the ETI at all, it exists only in history. But even here it is very weak. There are no holistic explanations in history, as far as I know, although there could in principle be some in economic history that are derived from macro-economics. So historicism is probably false. However, there are very few individualistic explanations in history, if by individualistic explanations one means explanations that satisfy the requirements of the ETI. Most worthwhile explanations in history are just like those of sociology—mixed. That is, some of their premises refer to the desires, values, beliefs, and actions of individuals, as the ETI requires. But most also contain premises describing the social forces that can reasonably be supposed to have been acting on individuals at the time, given their particular circumstances. For, in general, historians seek to explain the actions of individuals as being the combined effects of these two kinds of forces—of individual desires and ambitions that are hedged, modified, or encouraged by various social pressures, such as those arising from background political or religious convictions. So, even in history, the ETI is probably indefensible.

5.5   THE POWER OF AGENCY

Those who defended the ETI in history and sociology were all convinced of one thing: There are no forces of purely social origin. People exert forces, and a lot of people acting together can exert quite a lot of force. But, the forces that we call 'social forces' are not really forces originating in society. They must, somehow, be the products of forces originating in the decisions and actions of individuals. Consequently, these philosophers had no time for the belief that social forces could come into existence independently of the decisions or actions of individuals. To be intelligible at all, they thought, social forces would have to supervene on the forces that individual human beings are capable of exerting. Put this way, the individualistic thesis about social forces suddenly seems much more reasonable. For, the very idea that, by finding a way of living together socially, people are able to create an organism that can exercise control over their lives seems like nonsense. They felt, reasonably enough, that there could be no emergent causal powers. People, perhaps, had causal powers. But societies, which are human creations, could not have any causal powers that were not indirectly the expression of the causal powers of people. Any independent causal powers of societies would have to be regarded as emergent properties, which are intuitively highly implausible.

142 *Social Humanism*

Unfortunately, the defenders of the ETI chose to defend this insight as though it were just concerned with the kinds of explanations that are possible in the social sciences. They did so, I assume, because the theory of causal explanation that was then most widely accepted was Hempel's 'covering law' theory. Certainly, it was widely believed that to explain anything causally, it is at least necessary, if not sufficient, to subsume it under a general law. Therefore, if societies of any given kind were capable of exercising causal powers over people, and these powers were to exist independently of the powers of their members, there would have to be some general laws about how people would have to behave in any society of this kind. Therefore, if there were no such laws, there could not be any such causal powers. Hence, to rule out the possibility of there being any such laws, it would be sufficient if it could be established that there are no holistic explanations in the social sciences or, at least, none that was not wholly reducible to explanations involving only facts about the motivations, actions, and so on of individual agents. Thus, the important thesis of individualism, which is fundamentally a thesis about the causes of social evolution, became bogged down in a dispute about the nature of explanations in the social sciences.

The thesis that I believe to be of the essence of individualism is the claim that individuals are the *prime* movers in making and shaping their own societies. If this is true, then it is an important thesis in political theory. For, it makes individuals ultimately responsible for the development of the societies in which they live. But this is not just a thesis about the nature of explanations in the social sciences. It is about the causal powers of individuals.

If, as I argued in Chapter 3, one is a scientific realist, then one should be a realist about causal powers. That is, one should accept them as being what they purport to be, viz. capacities to make certain things happen when the appropriate conditions for triggering them are realised. The question then is whether we, as human beings, have any such powers that are under our own personal control. Ontologically, there is no problem about human beings having causal powers. Scientific realists must believe that all physical objects have such powers. The important question is whether we have any such powers that would make us free agents—agents of the kind we must be if we are ever to be held morally responsible for anything we do.

If you are a realist about causal powers, then you are committed to the view that all causation involves some kind of agency, and realism about causal powers involves realism about the activities of such powers. But human agency is supposed to be something very special. For, human agents must not only have causal powers, they must be able to monitor, adjust, and trigger them as they see fit. Prima facie, it seems impossible that we should have any such control over our own causal powers, because, if we did have such powers of control, these would be formally just like the supposedly independent causal powers of societies. They would be emergent. Therefore, any individualist who wished to embrace the powers of control required for

Individualism   143

moral responsibility would seem to be left with no good argument against a collectivist, who wished to embrace emergent social powers.

The causal powers of the most fundamental things in nature are all fixed. For, these things are all members of natural kinds that have all of their causal powers essentially. But, as we have seen, the powers of things that are constructed out of the basic ones are generally variable. The micro-structures of objects that are macro-scopically similar may not all be the same. Therefore, things of the same kind, even of the same natural kind, may have different or varying causal powers. Minor differences of structure do not generally imply any difference of kind. A piece of copper wire, for example, remains a piece of copper wire after it has been bent backwards and forwards to make it brittle. The temperature of a gas tends to rise if it is compressed, and it thereby acquires the capacity to heat up its surroundings. If wires made of two different conductors are joined together to make a loop, then heating just one of the junctions will cause a current to flow around the loop and therefore create a little electromagnet. Therefore, it is possible, even in inanimate nature, for things to have their causal powers changed, without ceasing to be things of the kinds they are. And, if this is possible in the inanimate world, it is certainly possible in the animate one. Most animals are capable of learning from experience. And the process of learning from experience is always one that results in changes in causal powers. When my dog went to 'Obedience Class', she learned to sit, lie down, stay, and fetch on command. In the process, she acquired certain capacities she did not have before. In fact, every instance of learning involves either the creation of, or an increase in, the capacities of the learner, and every case of forgetting or unlearning involves a loss of or decrease in such capacities. So, it must be accepted that the causal powers, capacities, and propensities of complex objects are generally variable.

Given that this is the case, we should naturally expect to find many 'meta-causal' powers in nature, i.e. powers that tend to produce changes in the causal powers of certain things when they are activated in appropriate circumstances. Stimulants, mood enhancing drugs, aphrodisiacs, analgesics, and so on are obvious examples of things that have meta-causal powers. But we do not need to delve into the pharmacy books to find examples of substances with meta-causal powers. For, many quite ordinary powers have meta-causal effects. A magnet, for example, carries a magnetic field, and any ferromagnetic substance within this field tends to become magnetised and so have its causal powers changed. Nevertheless, there is good reason to focus here on the meta-causal powers of things that can affect the capacities of living creatures. For, these are just the kinds of powers that must come into play when we have to make up our mind about something.

Firstly, I assume that we are all able to recognise situations in which we face a choice. We are in a restaurant, and the waiter asks us for our order. Or, we are buying a new television set and have to decide which of the many kinds of sets on display would suit us best. Introspectively, the process we

144 *Social Humanism*

then follow is one of considering the alternatives, of using our imaginations to visualise the effects of making the various choices, and of weighing the pros and cons of these choices—financially, socially, or in other ways. We might consider how much our preferred option would cost or whether we could really afford it. Or, we might consider how other people might be affected by the choice we make. If my preferred dish were raw beef but my dining companions were all vegetarians, I might think twice about my order. However, my consideration of the effect of ordering the raw beef might just strengthen my resolve to order it. The processes would be different for different choice situations. Imagination, for example, might have a greater or lesser role to play. But this is roughly what we think we are doing when we are choosing freely. And because we regularly go through such procedures when we make what we call 'free choices', we are very reluctant to believe that it is all a charade.

Yet there is a great deal of agreement in the philosophical community that there is no such thing as free will, and therefore no such thing as a free choice. It is argued that, if the world is deterministic, then there really is no choice to be made, and the procedure of considering the alternatives, weighing up the pros and cons and so on, is all determined too. If the world is not deterministic but lurches from one state of affairs to another, e.g. in the manner of a random walk, then no choice is possible. For, what happens eventually must lie somewhere within the range permitted by the stochastic laws of nature, but no possible action can determine where it will lie within this range. So, if determinism is true, we have no choice. And, if any degree of indeterminism is true, we have no possible way of choosing between the open possibilities. Nevertheless, these arguments must be wrong-headed. For, it beggars belief, as John Searle has argued, that natural selection would create an elaborate mock decision process that could serve no useful purpose. If the outcomes of our deliberations are already determined, why bother with them? If the show of making a rational decision is not real, why must we pretend to ourselves that it is?

Metaphysically, what has to be argued for is a compatibilist solution. If we are scientific realists, we must consider the processes of rational decision-making of which we are introspectively aware to be genuine biological processes that normally result in more or less rational decisions. Moreover, we must suppose that these processes serve useful biological purposes. Those who are better at rational decision-making, as we know it intuitively, must be at an advantage *vis-à-vis* their fellow humans. And human beings, who are evidently the only species of animals capable of such decision-making, must be at a considerable advantage *vis-à-vis* the members of other species, which, we may suppose, have no such elaborate decision-making procedures.

Firstly, we must suppose that the world allows changes in the dispositional properties of things to occur, because if the world were not of this kind, decisions involving new resolutions or changes of mind could not occur.

Individualism 145

What we call 'new resolutions' or 'changes of mind' could, in principle, be illusions, because we could in fact have had the relevant dispositions all along but not known about them. But this is biologically implausible. Why should nature conspire to make us think we are doing something that we are not? It is also ontologically implausible. For, few things are more common in the world of the higher mammals than learning from experience. But when we learn from experience, we change our dispositions. We learn new skills, become more adept at the things we practise, become quicker to respond to threatening situations, and so on—all processes of acquiring new dispositions or strengthening ones we already have. And this is not just a fact about human beings or other intelligent animals. Inanimate objects can and do acquire new powers or capacities, e.g. by becoming magnetised, or gain or lose capacities in various ways, e.g. by losing flexibility.

Secondly, we must suppose that our introspective knowledge of what is involved in rational decision-making is at least roughly true. When we imagine the consequences of decisions made in favour of the various options that remain open, we are drawing on our experiences of similar situations in the past in order to learn from them. And when we consider the effects that a decision made in favour of one of the alternatives will have on our budget or the looks on our friends' faces, we are again rehearsing past experiences in the hope of learning from them. But if this is really what we are doing, it follows that we are engaged in a process that we hope will lead to either (a) the creation of some new disposition to act, or (b) an increased resolve to act as one had previously been inclined to do. And, phenomenologically, these outcomes would appear to us as firm choices or resolutions. I postulate, therefore, that human beings have meta-causal powers that they are able to trigger on demand. If other animals have such powers, then they fairly clearly do not have them to the same degree. Most intelligent creatures certainly do have meta-causal powers, but not ones that they can trigger on demand. The meta-causal powers of animals are normally triggered by such things as the sight of predators, the presence of females on heat, the smell of raw meat, and so on, but not often voluntarily.

If it is true that human beings have this fairly unique power of being able to initiate meta-causal processes that seek to draw on past experiences to resolve problems of choice, then there is no doubt that this is biologically a very important property. For, it is a power that clearly distinguishes human beings from all other animals—if not absolutely, then at least qualitatively. I postulate that this is the power that we all know as that of having free will. It is distinctive of human beings, intellectual in nature, used in the process of rational decision-making, and capable of yielding effective decisions or resolutions. It is a power that has its biological origins in the capacities of all intelligent animals to learn from experience. But it differs from the animal powers because it can be triggered on demand and is able to draw on past experience (through imagination) and existing knowledge (contained in memory), but it is not primarily dependent or not dependent

146   *Social Humanism*

at all on current experience. Free will, thus understood, is biologically plausible and would appear to have all of the properties that would be required of any satisfactory theory.

The only question is whether it is ontologically plausible. If hard determinism were true, it would seem not to be. For, in such a world, if A has a disposition to X in the actual circumstances C at any given time t, A would necessarily have been predisposed to have this disposition at time t at every previous time. Therefore, it must always have been inevitable that if A were to be in the circumstances C at time t, A would X. Therefore, a temporally circumscribed disposition like this could not exist at one time and not have existed at every previous time in a fully deterministic world.

However, the biological advantages of being able to learn from experience in the unique kinds of ways that human beings can are independent of determinism and indeterminism. The biological advantages of being uniquely able to make un-coerced decisions based on our past experience, present knowledge, and the projected future are not mythical. They would exist in any world in which species originated by natural selection. Therefore, they would exist in any deterministic world in which human beings might exist and be able to enjoy this unique advantage. They would also exist in any indeterministic world in which these same conditions applied. For, any animals that had the unique meta-causal capacity of being able to create consciously controlled dispositions that suited the outcomes of their complex deliberations would enjoy a huge biological advantage over all other animals. And, this would obviously be the case, regardless of whether determinism was true.

We know now that the world is not fully deterministic. It is approximately deterministic on the macro-scale, but strongly indeterministic on the micro-scale. In such a world, the future is metaphysically underdetermined, i.e. it is a branching structure. The world preserves its macro-structure (more or less) whichever branch it enters. But its fine structure, and the things that depend on its fine structure, will be different in the different branches and diverge ever more widely from the existing fine structure as the universe tree is ascended. Consequently, there is no good reason to assume that the choices or resolutions that I make today were always the ones that I was destined to make.

I do not imagine that many scientific realists would endorse this theory of free will in its entirety. But it is at least as plausible as any other theory of personal freedom, and it has the advantage of being wholly naturalistic. One does not need to believe in what is called 'metaphysical freedom' or emergent powers of any other kind. The exercise of meta-causal powers is consistent with the world view of a scientific realist. Of course, to accept the theory, one would have to believe that we have insight into our own causal dispositions and that we have the meta-causal powers to change some of these dispositions as the need for change is seen to arise. The required insight is something that would need to be explained. But

Individualism 147

there is not much doubt that we have it. For, we are all able to describe our own beliefs, desires, and values in considerable detail. Nor is there any reason to suppose that organisms could not have become more self-aware and insightful through the normal processes of natural selection. For, there is also, presumably, considerable survival value in self-awareness. Nor is it unreasonable to suppose that the human capacity to change our own dispositions to act also evolved by natural selection. For, such a capacity would enable us to benefit more from what we do and so, presumably, would have excellent survival value. Nor, finally, is it unreasonable to suppose that the human capacity to trigger our own behavioural dispositions evolved in the same sort of way.

5.6 FORMS OF RESPONSIBILITY

5.6.1 Personal or Individual Responsibility

It is likely to be objected that this theory of free will does not do enough to justify our status as potentially autonomous agents who are capable of being morally responsible for our own choices and actions. Nevertheless, if we have the meta-causal power to choose between alternative courses of action and can exercise this power on demand, as I am supposing, then there is a clear sense in which any choice we might eventually make in this way must be our own. Let us say, therefore, that any choice that is made in this way is one for which we are personally responsible.

5.6.2 Collective Responsibility

Collective agents, such as Royal Commissions, Senate committees, boards of directors, and so on, are able to reach decisions about what should be done about a matter by processes that are formally similar to those that allow individuals to reach such decisions. They deliberate by reflecting on what has happened in the past, draw on their current knowledge and understanding of the situation under investigation, and implement the appropriate mechanism for taking the action on which they have decided. Let us agree to say that such agents are collectively responsible for the decisions they make. Clearly, collective responsibility, as here defined, depends ontologically on individual or personal responsibility, since the collective process of decision-making could not exist if the individual one did not. But the converse does not hold.

5.6.3 Legal Responsibility

A social agent A is legally responsible in a given society for having done or effected X if and only if A is personally or collectively responsible for

148   *Social Humanism*

having done or effected X and A acted freely in doing so in accordance with the principles of justice included in the social contract of that society.

Note that there is a significant difference between the legal concept of being or having been responsible for doing something defined here in Section 5.6.3 and that of being an agent of a kind that is held by the social contract of the society to be socially responsible for decisions and actions of various kinds as it was defined in Chapter 4 at Section 4.4.1. The legal concept is one of social answerability and is linked to the justice system of the society. The social concept in Chapter 4 has nothing to do with the justice system. It only has to do with the social expectations that we should demand of members of various classes of social agents. Some of the differences are striking. An individual or a collective may be legally responsible for having done something that he, she, or it has no social or moral right to do. For, the relevant legal concept is not class sensitive. Indeed classes of social agents may have social or moral rights to decide what to do in cases like this and obligations to implement their decisions. But then, again, there may not. If the kinds of actions for which X would be judged to have been legally responsible were criminal, according to this social contract, then no one in that society would be socially responsible, in the sense defined in Chapter 4, for performing such acts.

The connection between the two concepts of responsibility would appear to be this:

> An individual or collective that is a social agent of a given society, has a social right to do whatever is not proscribed by the social contract of that society, and is legally responsible for that action.

5.6.4   MORAL RESPONSIBILITY—THE LEGAL CONCEPT

Given the theory that has been developed so far, one would expect the moral concept to be definable:

> One should accept that a social agent A is morally legally responsible in a given society for having done or effected X if and only if A is personally or collectively responsible for having done or effected X and A acted freely in doing so according to the principles of justice included in the social contract of one's ideal society.[4]

But this is not the concept of moral responsibility that is used in courts of law. For, trials are not conducted according to the laws of anyone's ideal society. They are conducted according to the laws of the existing society. Therefore, the appropriate conception of legal responsibility is the social one, not the idealised moral one. Nevertheless, there is nothing wrong with this moral legal conception. It is just the conception of legal responsibility for which we should aim.

Individualism 149

5.7 RESPONSIBILITY AND FREEDOM

Individual and collective decision-making are formally similar. The same arguments may be considered, the same histories recalled, the same projections made, and so on. And each process leads to a decision to act, and the establishment of a mechanism for acting on that decision, either at once or at some future time. But there is one way in which individual decision-making may differ from collective that is worth noting, viz. that the triggers for individual decisions to be implemented or cancelled are always internal and immediately accessible to the person concerned. For example, a trigger for doing A might be my making the judgement that now would be right the time to do A. Or, a trigger for not doing A might be my thinking that the time has passed for doing A. Therefore, anyone who has just acted on a considered decision always has the clear impression that they could, right up to the last moment, always have acted otherwise. Collective decisions are not so easily changed and lack this apparent quality of last-minute reversibility. Consequently, many of those who have studied the free will problem are willing to argue that there is a kind of freedom of choice that only individuals are capable of exercising, viz. the kind of which the individual could truly say, right up to the last second, 'I could have done otherwise'.

Philosophers call such reversible free choices 'morally free', and the kind of responsibility that they call 'moral' is commonly identified as the kind of responsibility that one would have in making such choices. Of course, this concept of moral responsibility is very different from the one discussed in Chapter 4. For, this kind of moral responsibility is a refinement of the legal concept, not of the social one. There is not much doubt, however, that we have the capacity to make immediately reversible free choices. For, the introspective evidence that we have this capacity is likely to be true. The advantage to hunter-gatherers of having such a degree of freedom of choice is fairly obvious. Things can change very rapidly when one is hunting for food or fighting for survival, and any strategies that one may have adopted earlier must always be provisional and able to be dropped in an instant. But I do not believe that the concept of moral responsibility that would correspond to this conception of freedom of choice should replace the legal concept. For, there is no good reason to suppose that our ability to make immediately reversible choices would greatly affect our considered judgements of legal responsibility. But perhaps there are some differences. In that case, the relevance of our having the capacity to make immediately reversible free choices would add to the complexity of the social task of developing a satisfactory concept of legal responsibility. But one thing is certain. The evidence that we have a capacity to make immediately reversible free choices is not evidence that we have absolute freedom of choice. The exercise of this capacity cannot be our breaking into the causal order to change what would otherwise have happened. It must be a last-minute decision not

150 *Social Humanism*

to use the internal trigger. The concept of absolute freedom of choice has no place in modern metaphysics. We human beings cannot break into the causal order at will, and it would be absurd to suppose we can.

5.8   METAPHYSICAL INDIVIDUALISM AND SOCIAL IDEALISM

Metaphysical individualism is incompatible with social idealism. Firstly, metaphysical individualism denies the reality of social causation. Therefore, metaphysical individualists cannot believe in the efficacy of any elements of social contracts that are not legally enforced. But social idealism presupposes that social contracts can effectively put informal constraints on social behaviour and that unwritten social contracts can also encourage decent behaviour and so generate good will. Secondly, social idealism is probably the only satisfactory meta-theory of morality that is compatible with modern metaphysics. There could perhaps be some other kind of social theory that would provide a satisfactory foundation for morality. But there is no good reason to believe that any metaphysically plausible individualistic meta-theory is possible. Certainly, the philosophy of individualism discussed in this chapter is deeply flawed. So, it cannot possibly serve as a foundation for such a theory. Indeed, the whole idea of an individualistic meta-theory would appear to be an oxymoron. For, morality is fundamentally concerned with how people should treat each other. Hence, unless we are privy to divine knowledge about such matters or such knowledge is discoverable by introspection or *a priori* reasoning, a theory of morality could only be founded on a knowledge of how people could in fact interact socially and of what kinds of interaction we find acceptable or not acceptable.

The theory of absolute freedom that the metaphysics of individualism seems to require is also untenable and so cannot be the basis for a theory of moral responsibility. The idea that human beings are causal agents is not disputed. But, according to modern metaphysics, every substantive thing is a causal agent of one kind or another, because if it weren't we should have no way of knowing about it. This is not to deny that human beings have a special kind of agency—one that is unique in the animal kingdom. But there is nothing unintelligible about human agency. Its uniqueness derives (as explained in Chapter 3), not from any god-like powers, but from our extraordinary capacity for considered decision-making, and our highly developed ability to modify our own behavioural dispositions as and when we see fit.

As a meta-theory, social idealism is not itself a moral theory. It determines only the structure, or skeleton, of such a theory. We know that the required moral theory must be a form of social contractual utilitarianism (as argued in Chapter 1) and hence that the 'good' to be promoted must be one that could be possessed by a social contract. But there are many such

Individualism 151

goods that could be used to define a socially ideal society, and some of them are truly dreadful. Marxism had at least the flavour of a moral theory. For, Marx hoped to rid the world of poverty and injustice. But there is no good reason to believe that a grossly inequitable and unjust society can be made just and equitable by force, as Marx, Lenin, and their followers believed. Social contracts need to evolve. They cannot simply be imposed on a reluctant society. Historically, successful revolutions have tended to result in ruthless dictatorships or ruling elites who spend their time, their energies, and their nations' resources in shoring up their power and suppressing dissidents, whether real or imagined. In the view that is being urged here, a good moral theory should be founded on good values and evolve democratically to express those values in the society's laws, institutions, and social conventions.

Popper, Hayek, Watkins, and other radical opponents of social idealism have misdiagnosed the trouble with socially idealistic theories. The trouble is not that they are social or even that they are idealistic. Their own neo-liberal policies are both of these things, as are all moral and political theories. The mistake has been to equate social idealism with the collectivist philosophy of socialism. But it is not that. Nor is it supposed that the only goods are social goods. There are social goods, but there are also individual human rights and freedoms that must be respected in every good society. The moral thesis that is developed in this book presupposes that good social policy should evolve peacefully, and social policy goals should be continuously refined and redeveloped in the light of moral criticism to make this possible. For social policy to evolve peacefully, what is required is that we should live in a society in which peaceful changes in policy directions are possible. Therefore, we must live in either a democratic country or at least in one in which the government has the support of its people to make morally acceptable policy decisions and to implement them in moral ways. But, if one rejects all social theory, as philosophical individualists clearly wish to do, one must either reject all social morality or at least deny that it has a legitimate role in social policy development. Either way, morality is seriously undermined. And so is democracy.

6 Theory and Method

6.1 THE SOCRATIC METHOD

If morals are social ideals, as I have argued, how should we determine what our moral ideals should be? We can determine by introspection what our moral ideals are. We just have to ask ourselves what principles of social behaviour we should ideally like to see become or remain entrenched in our society's social contract. But a moral theory needs to say more than this, because our current social ideals are just our starting points. They are what we have to work with and try to improve or add to. Undoubtedly, we have certain social preferences or values that must come into play. And, as Tännsjö has convincingly argued, some of them are natural. In shaping our social ideals, we need to be clear about what they are and their relative importance. For, our aim must be to discover and press for the implementation of strategies for promoting our social ideals to achieve the best overall results.

We should all undertake this task as part of our continuing education. That is, we should think carefully about what is important to us in our lives, what implications these insights may have about how people should behave with regard to one another, and how they should treat animals. Many moral philosophers think that this is fundamentally what morality is all about—that there is nothing else. Their teaching focuses on examining the circumstances in which we may find ourselves and inviting students to consider how they would or should behave in such circumstances, and why. Thus, the methodology proposed is one of reflection on possible courses of action, in various possible circumstances, and determining what reasonable grounds, if any, there might be for choosing one course rather than another. This is the method of achieving 'broad reflective equilibrium' in determining our moral positions. Such a methodology requires a certain depth of knowledge of other people, and their needs and aspirations, a degree of understanding of how they would feel in such circumstances, and that we should have empathy with them. It also requires that we have various social values that we wish to act on, and that we know what courses of action would be required to do so. It is the Socratic method.

This Socratic method of seeking broad reflective equilibrium is widely accepted as the correct methodology for moral inquiry. It is a straightforward way that we can all understand, of seeking agreement about what should or should not be done, and it is often both satisfying and illuminating. The point of the inquiry is presumably to discover how we think we should ideally live together as members of society. In my view, this is an inquiry we should all make, and continue to make, throughout our lives.

Nevertheless, it must be asked whether there is in fact a right way of behaving, and, if so, what reason there is to think that this is the way to find out what it is. I do not think there is a uniquely right way. A moral stance that is developed Socratically would, no doubt, be sophisticated and well balanced. There would be a number of issues, such as abortion or euthanasia, on which widespread agreement could not be reached within our own culture. But it is not just for this reason that I reject moral objectivity. I do so because I see no reason to believe that there is a firm basis in human nature, or in any other aspect of the natural world, for how we should live. Arguably, some moral propositions are grounded in the human compassionate virtues and some in our sense of what is fair. It would be unfair, for example, to discriminate socially between people on the grounds of characteristics that they were born with and so cannot help having. For, these differences are not morally relevant ones. But these moral principles are, at best, just a subset of the social principles that are held with the kind of conviction that is characteristic of moral principles in any society.

Most people certainly believe there is a right and a wrong about moral issues. According to many, it is just that some of us are wearing the blinkers of religion or political loyalty, or are morally blind (depending on one's point of view), and so cannot see the truth, even when it is carefully explained. The differences over abortion, contraception, euthanasia, blasphemy, genital mutilation, water-boarding, the taking of hostages, abandoning one's faith, group punishment, homosexual practices, and so on are all thought to be explicable in one or other of these ways. But, even if one abstracts from the moral issues that divide people by religion or political faith, there are still very large differences in the moral stances of individuals that appear to be independent of religious or political faiths. Some are much more aggressive than others and are much more willing to take direct action to bring about what they believe to be right, or prevent what they believe to be wrong. Others would demand much higher levels of punishment than is normally approved for what they perceive to be wrongdoing. There are also big differences in people's attitudes to legal punishment. Philosophers have discussed theories of punishment for generations. But there is no broad agreement about what the aims of punishment should be, what kinds of punishment are justified, or how to determine what levels of punishment should be administered. Yet, every act of punishment needs to be morally justified. For, every such act is a deliberate infliction of harm on someone or some group of people.

154 *Social Humanism*

What reason is there to think that there is a right or a wrong about such issues? Nearly everyone speaks as though they thought that their moral positions were objectively right. But there does not seem to be much evidence that they are. The members of different cultures do not agree about morality, and there is very little reason to think that they could ever reach full agreement about moral issues by using the Socratic method. The exercise of engaging in Socratic dialogue on moral issues is important to us all. But it is more realistic to think of the aim of these inquiries as being just to articulate the moral implications of our own values, at least some of which have been culturally acquired. Protestantism and Catholicism, which are sub-cultures within our own culture, are unlikely ever to reach accord on the moral issues that divide them; and Jews and Muslims would be unlikely to reach agreements about any of the moral issues that distinguish them culturally, even if they could talk to each other without hostility. But the same is true also of other sub-cultures, which are not religiously based. Therefore, the realistic aims of Socratic dialogues on moral issues should perhaps just be seen as developing the moral positions of the participants in these dialogues. Realistically, trans-cultural agreements about divisive moral issues are unlikely to be achieved in this manner.

In his famous book, *The Structure of Scientific Revolutions*, Thomas Kuhn (1962) made the observation that most scientific research is paradigmatic. That is, it is carried out within frameworks defined by paradigms. Kuhn usually thought of a paradigm as a distinguished piece of research work in a field of study—a work that defined the field's conceptual framework, methodology, and basic presuppositions. Thus, according to Kuhn, a paradigm exists in a given field if the professionals working in this field are in broad general agreement about what has so far been established, what the main problems are, how one should go about trying to solve them, and what constitutes an acceptable solution. The researchers in such a field of study would normally have the same metaphysical stance, be committed to the same ways of doing things, and have the same convictions about what to aim for. Kuhn described those who were working within the same dominant paradigm as researchers engaged in 'normal science'. But sometimes, he said, paradigmatic research or normal science runs into what appear to be insurmountable difficulties. The accepted ways of doing things fail to solve the outstanding problems, and researchers begin to question what was previously taken for granted. Sometimes, alternative paradigms begin to develop. At this stage, said Kuhn, the profession may split into factions, working within different frameworks that are conceptually at odds with one another.

The members of different cultures or sub-cultures appear to be like this. For, they seem to have different social paradigms. The moral philosophers within these cultures are naturally mostly concerned to develop their moral theories according to their own basic assumptions. Consequently, they are able to teach moral philosophy within their own cultures. But,

Theory and Method 155

if they seek to engage with the members of other cultures, they may find that the examples they use at home draw different responses abroad and so lose their point. Kuhn remarked that, when the adherents of different scientific paradigms try to resolve their differences, they usually fail to come to grips with one another. As Kuhn says, they 'talk past' each other.[1] They do so, he says, because they have incommensurable conceptual frameworks. Consequently, what they say to each other may well be either not understood or misunderstood. Something like this seems to occur in cross-cultural moral discourse.

Those who, like me, advocate the Socratic method of seeking broad reflective equilibrium in moral philosophy must face up to this difficulty. It is fine for teaching culturally bound moral philosophy. But it may not be adequate for resolving trans-cultural or sub-cultural disputes. If the model of science is any guide, the solution to this problem will almost certainly require some radical rethinking of basic assumptions, of things that are normally taken for granted.

6.2 RADICAL ALTERNATIVES

Let us assume, contrary to complete moral objectivism, that there is no ideal set of principles of social behaviour that is complete enough to define how people should behave in the best of all socially possible worlds. This may not seem to many people to be a radical alternative. But in fact it is contrary to the view that most European, Latin American, Middle-Eastern, and Anglo-American philosophers would take. It is contrary to the European and Latin American traditions, which tend to be either Catholic and objectivist or Marxist and nihilist. It is contrary to the Middle-Eastern traditions, which tend to be absolutist. And, it is contrary to the Anglo-American tradition, which is conservative and individualistic, but still objectivist. Yet, the metaphysical assumption that a social idealist would have to make to justify such moral objectivism would appear to be manifestly absurd. Perhaps this is one reason why so few people are social idealists. But whether this is so or not, I think that the thesis of complete moral objectivism has to be rejected. There is no comprehensive set of principles of social behaviour that would characterise the social contracts of the best possible societies. The social contracts of the best possible societies are likely to differ in their social moral prescriptions almost as much as they do in the actual world.

The assumption that this is so is the premise of cultural relativism. It is not a popular thesis, but I think it is realistic and should be embraced. The view that there is more than one viable moral system accords well with the sociological facts, and, as we shall argue in the following sections, there is no good reason to suppose that it is false. On the contrary, cultural absolutism is simply not a tenable moral thesis. Nevertheless, the position

156 *Social Humanism*

of cultural relativism in morals is very different from that of moral nihilism. For, the claim that the sets of moral principles that are to be found in the social contracts of all socially ideal societies will often differ from one another must not be confused with the claim that there are no objective moral principles, as David Wong (1991) argues. For, there are some principles, viz. those of human rights, that nearly everyone thinks should be included in the social contracts of all civil societies. They include most, but not all, of the principles of The Universal Declaration of Human Rights, and most of the principles that are included in the other charters or declarations of human rights and freedoms that have been enacted since the Universal Declaration was made. The universal principles also include some primitive duties, which are no less compelling than the humanistic principles of people's rights. And there is good reason for this too: These principles are all grounded in the elementary principles of humanism, although in a somewhat different way, as argued in Chapter 1.

If, as I shall argue, there are some basic moral principles that we may reasonably expect to become included in the social contracts of all societies, then the unqualified thesis of cultural relativism cannot be accepted. It implies that there must be some moral principles that are accepted as universally valid and some that are not. How then is one to make this distinction? And what are its implications? The distinction that has to be made was developed in Chapter 1. It is a distinction between 'individualistic' and 'social' moral principles. The individualistic moral principles are the humanistic ones that derive fairly directly from our basic compassionate and humanistic values. These principles are the ones that ground our theories of human rights and obligations. Our social moral principles, however, are our deeply entrenched solutions to the problems of creating or maintaining well-serviced or well-functioning societies, in which people are able to live satisfying and fulfilling lives. As such, they are likely to have been arrived at politically. Characteristically, these solutions require trade-offs between goods and harms, where some individuals, or groups of individuals, will become worse off as a result, while others will become better off. But there is no universally acceptable way of making such trade-offs, and the issues involved are among the most common ones of political debate. So, of the two kinds of principles, the humanistic ones are arguably the more fundamental. For, these principles depend more or less directly on just our natural values of compassion, honesty, and fairness. Hence, they are principles that could, in principle, be argued for in a Hobbesian state of nature. But the social moral principles are not independent of how the state is constituted or how it works. They arise mainly from the attempts to make it work better.

The implications of this distinction are profound. Firstly, if one accepts that there are some moral principles that may not be universally valid, then one must also reject the principle of universalisability, i.e. the principle that nothing can count as a moral principle unless it is universal. The simple

Theory and Method   157

humanistic moral principles are universal, I believe, because the same considerations should be sufficient to establish their validity in any society. But our own social moral principles may not be. Secondly, since social moral principles are just widely accepted solutions to social problems, they are not fixed in time and may vary from culture to culture. We should, therefore, expect our social moral principles to evolve as new technology changes our circumstances. Thirdly, it implies that moral criticism of other societies should be based primarily on the principles of humanism, e.g. on whether they are acting contrary to the principles of human rights or not.[2] We should not simply be judging their practices by whether or not they are in accordance with our social moral principles. This also has obvious implications for any moral criticisms that we may have to make of past societies, when different social moral judgements were made.

Fourthly, acceptance of this distinction implies that there cannot be any unrestricted right of conscience. That is, it cannot always be right for a person to do what he or she sincerely believes to be the morally right thing to do. For, it would be wrong if the principle on which one was acting was (a) anti-humanistic, e.g. directly contrary to the principle of least harm; and (b) a proposed social moral principle that was not yet widely endorsed in the community. Fifthly, it implies that there cannot be an unrestricted dominance principle that would allow one to use the social moral principles of one's own society to critique the laws, mores, or social customs of other societies. By the dominance principle, I mean the assumption that underlies all moral critique, viz. that moral obligations must always over-ride all other kinds of obligations. But our moral critiques of the laws or practices of other societies cannot be based only on this simple principle. For, the laws and social practices of other societies will inevitably reflect different cultural histories and may therefore lead to different social moral principles being freely adopted. I do not say that no critique is possible. But, if it is to be made, it had better be focussed on violations of human rights rather than on violations of our own social moral norms.

6.3   MORAL OBJECTIVISM

A complete or unqualified moral objectivist is one who believes that there is just one true morality, i.e. a set of moral principles describing how people should ideally live together in the world.[3] Moral objectivists differ from each other mainly in how they think that knowledge of these principles is possible. But they may take heart from the similarities of roles of cultures and scientific paradigms in moral and scientific inquiry. For, science is clearly consistent with the belief that there is a way that the world really is, and that the ultimate aim of science is to discover it. Therefore, complete moral objectivists need not be too discouraged by the evident cultural relativity of present-day morality. The cultural relativity that exists in moral

158   *Social Humanism*

theory today may only show that different social paradigms are operative in different societies.

However, I do not wish to use the current existence of culturally relativity in morality as an argument against unqualified moral objectivity. Clearly it is not. My arguments against unqualified objectivism, and in favour of a qualified objectivism, will be more directly targeted. From the point of view of a social idealist, the primary question must be: Can one reasonably believe that there is a single and complete set of social principles included in the social contracts of all socially ideal societies? If there were, then there would indeed be a complete objective moral system. But this seems like a rather unlikely hypothesis. For, given a scientific world-view, this seems to imply that human beings must be essentially social creatures like bees, with genetically inbuilt programs specifying preferred norms of social behaviour. If you break up a beehive, it will rebuild it, much as it was before, with the same kind of structure and the same kinds of roles for the different kinds of bees. Human societies are naturally much more complicated than bee societies. But complete moral objectivism seems to imply that something like what is true of bees must be true of human beings. However, the world is not like this. If it were, then societies around the world would exhibit similar and stable patterns of social preferences and would quickly re-establish themselves in these patterns if they were ever disturbed, e.g. by a war or a great natural disaster. Cross-cultural moral disagreements would be rare and fairly easily settled. But this is manifestly not what is actually observed. From today's perspective, our own society is morally very different, not only from other societies, but also from what it was a hundred or two hundred years ago. Morality presents the image of an evolving structure of preferred social preferences for each social setting, not a uniform or stable one across different settings.

Complete moral objectivism and the Socratic method would make more sense as a package if one believed that morals were synthetic a priori truths, as Kant did, and M. Smith still does, discoverable by pure practical reasoning. For then, moral philosophers would be able to lead people to the moral truths in much the same way as a geometry teacher might be able to lead someone to discover a geometrical truth—as was argued in Plato's *Meno*. But the 'categorical imperative', from which Kant hoped to derive morality, has proven to be inadequate. One cannot derive more than a handful of moral principles by pure practical reasoning, and Kant himself was not able to do so. Nor can one, even in these few cases, demonstrate the truth of a moral principle with anything like the force that seems to compel a geometrical conclusion.

Complete moral objectivism and the Socratic method would also make more sense as a package if one were a moral intuitionist or a moral sense theorist. For, theorists of both kinds believe that morals have to be discovered by arguments to the best explanation. They believe that the facts to be explained are our primitive judgements of right and wrong, or of good and bad, and that the moral principles we are seeking are just the ones that would best explain these judgements. The Socratic method could then be justified as the most convenient and effective way of accessing the raw data with which we must work. This account has the merit of explaining the cultural relativity of morality satisfactorily. Its defenders would only have to say that the science of morals is still in its infancy, and that the members of different cultures are working with different paradigms. And, as with all paradigmatic research, a given paradigm carries with it its own observation language. Hence, moral disagreements between cultures must, just like cross-paradigm disagreements in science, often seem to be intractable. Thus, the model appears to work fairly well if the hypothesis that moral theory is still in its infancy is accepted. For, intractability is just what we find.

If the epistemology of morals were hypothetico-deductive, as most arguments to the best explanation are, it would follow that moral principles must, in general, have the status of hypotheses, and hence be acceptable as more or less probable. Linguistically, it is not usual to talk about moral principles as being probable or improbable. For, this way of talking seems to presuppose a reality with which a moral principle would correspond if it were true or fail to correspond if it were false. But, normally, principles of morality are regarded only as more or less compelling, or more or less exceptionless, as though the very idea that a principle of morality could have an objective truth-value were inappropriate. But this may be irrelevant. Plausibly, one could accept a pragmatic theory of truth for morals and argue that 'p' is true if and only if 'p' is ultimately rationally acceptable to an ideally well-informed Socratic inquirer.

For morality, this analysis may be good enough. But it would not solve the metaphysical problem for morals, since it would leave the point of the inquiry unresolved. In science, one can say that the point of the inquiry is to discover what is objectively true, i.e. what the world is like, independently of us as observers. But what could we say the point of moral inquiry is? If it were just to discover the limits of socially tolerable behaviour and define the character of good social behaviour, then the Socratic method might be well suited to the task. But if it also includes, which it must, what is required to create, service, and maintain a fair society in which human beings are able to flourish, then it might not be so well suited. Armchair philosophy could perhaps discover some principles of social behaviour, general acceptance of which would maximise human wellbeing, but it cannot plausibly discover what sort of social structure would be needed to achieve this result.

In the early Renaissance period, St. Thomas Aquinas and his predecessor Albert the Great had what was thought to be an answer to this metaphysical question. They would have said that the aim of moral inquiry is to articulate the Natural Law, which was given to us by God and is discoverable by reason. According to these philosophers, we have all been given a natural faculty or habit of mind called 'synderesis'.[4] This is a

160 *Social Humanism*

natural capacity or disposition to stand back and consider social issues impersonally—not just from our own point of view, but from a sort of common point of view. This abstract point of view was seen as being a natural counter to self-interest, which, it was thought, would otherwise dominate our thinking. The Thomists argued that synderesis provides us with knowledge of the Natural Law, which provides us with the universal premises required for moral reasoning. Aquinas believed that any actions taken freely in accordance with the universal premises supplied by synderesis would be acts of conscience, and therefore have special authority (D'Arcy, 1961). Secular moral objectivists do not, of course, believe in Natural Law theory or necessarily in the right of conscience. But many still believe that there is a set of objectively true moral principles that we could arrive at successfully, if only we were to cultivate the habit of thinking about them in this special way.

The 'view from human kind' inherent in the Thomistic theory of synderesis is essentially the same as Rawls's view from behind his 'veil of ignorance'. For, it is the view at which you would arrive by abstracting from your own position, characteristics, and so on and see yourself as just another member of the human race. It is what I would call 'the humanistic or cosmopolitan point of view'. It is much less abstract than Thomas Nagel's (1986) conception of a view from nowhere. But it is more abstract than what I would call 'the social point of view', which is just the view that you would obtain by thinking of yourself as simply another member of your own society. There are other abstractions too that lie in between the humanistic point of view and the view from nowhere. For, you could cut your human identity out of the equation altogether and see yourself as just another biological organism. This would yield 'the biological point of view'. To reach the view from nowhere, you would have to take the process of abstraction still further. For, to do so, you must abstract from yourself as knower and consider how the world would be in itself, independently of our perception of it. This process of abstraction is the one that results in what we call 'the physical point of view'. From this point of view, there is no normativity left to talk about. So, physically considered, there is no best of all possible worlds.

There is, however, an important question that we can and should ask: What principles of social behaviour would be best from a humanistic or cosmopolitan point of view? The question is important, because if any principle could be shown to be universally acceptable from this point of view, then it would have to be considered valid as a social ideal in all societies. But, to accept that a principle is valid as a social ideal is already to accept it as a moral principle. Therefore, to accept that a principle of social behaviour is universally acceptable from a humanistic or cosmopolitan point of view is already to accept it as a universally valid moral principle.

There is, at present, no global social contract in which such a principle could be embedded. Nevertheless, we can say, in advance of any attempt to

Theory and Method 161

construct such a contract, that if any such principles could be found, then they would have to be included as basic principles in this global contract. To lay the groundwork for consideration of this question, it is important to examine the slightly less abstract one. We should begin by asking how the members of our own society would answer this question. For, we know that any principles that would be accepted as ideal from a humanistic or cosmopolitan point of view would also have to be acceptable as ideal from a social point of view.

6.4   THE CONTAINMENT PRINCIPLE

As the Thomists were well aware, it is possible for normal adult human beings to look at things from different points of view. They can, for example, view them as individuals and think how they will affect them personally. Or they can stand back from this personal stance and consider how they would look from the point of view of some class of individuals to which they belong. Thus, one can look at things from the point of viewpoint of an academic if one is oneself an academic or has enough understanding and empathy with academics to be able to adopt this stance. Or, one can look at them from some more general perspective. Thus, points of view are more or less abstract perspectives from which individual members of groups can view the world.

The narrowest human perspective is one that is based on a singleton class of individuals, e.g. one's own or the perspective of any other individual. The broadest human perspective is the humanistic or cosmopolitan one, which is based on the class of all individuals. In between, there are, for example, the members of the British Commonwealth, the people of Latin America, the citizens of the United Kingdom, the residents of Australia, and so on. For, each of these groups may be said to have a point of view. Alternatively, we may divide the class of all individuals along different lines. For example, we may wish to talk of the perspectives of women, men, married people, or homosexuals in a given society. In every case, however, a perspective is defined by reference to an intentionally defined class of people who may reasonably be thought to have enough in common to have a common point of view on some of the issues.

If this is right, then it is arguable that the following principle must hold generally:

The Containment Principle:

6.4.1 If acceptance of a principle concerning social rights or obligations is morally or socially required from a given point of view V, then it should also be morally or socially required from every human perspective W that is contained within V.

162   *Social Humanism*

This principle has the following corollary:

> 6.4.2 If acceptance of a principle concerning social rights or obligations is morally or socially required from a humanistic or cosmopolitan point of view U, then it should also be morally or socially required from every social perspective S, since S is necessarily included in U.

The principle 6.4.2 is just a special case of 6.4.1 and is therefore valid if 6.4.1 is valid. Since the classes definitive of V and W are, by definition, intensionally defined, the members of V and W must each be equivalence classes, i.e. classes whose members are the same with respect to their defining properties. Moreover, W must be an equivalence class that is contained within V. For example, V might be the class of all socially responsible adult people in a given society and W the class of all socially responsible women in that society. Then what the principle says of this case is that whatever social or moral principles are held to be socially required of all people must be held to be socially required of all women. For example, whatever rights are possessed by all responsible adults are also rights possessed by all responsible women. And, whatever the prima facie duties or responsibilities of all adults may be, the prima facie duties or responsibilities of all women must include these. Women might have some special rights or responsibilities of their own, e.g. because of their biological differences with men. But the principle of containment allows for this.

Even a male chauvinist would appear to be committed to accepting the containment principle. A true male chauvinist could perhaps deny that there are any socially responsible women and thus argue that the class W is the null class. A female chauvinist, in contrast, could take the opposite view, viz. that the class of socially responsible adults is just the class W, and hence the V = W. So, the containment principle is neutral on the issues of male and female chauvinism, and hence on all positions in between these two extremes. But the containment principle has the merit of clarifying the issues. If, for any reason, a society does not accord full social or moral rights to women (or to men), it must be because the society denies that men and women (a) are social equals, or (b) have any, or many, rights or responsibilities in common. In any case, it seems to me that the governments that would claim that the men and women of their societies do, and should have, different rights and responsibilities should be required by the international community to make their case. Such a case could only be a social moral one, i.e. an argument that such discrimination is needed to create a good, just, and well-functioning society. In the absence of such a case, the presumption of social equality, and hence the injustice of social discrimination, must be made.

6.5   MORAL EPISTEMOLOGY

If the epistemology of a moral theorist is a hypothetico-deductive one designed to explain the moral judgements elicited by Socratic dialogue, the claim that every moral judgement is true or false need not be accepted. But it might, nevertheless, be accepted pro forma, as the corresponding claim in science would be. Therefore, a moral researcher who discovers a strong prima facie case of a deeply intractable moral disagreement need not give up hope and become a relativist. He or she can just continue to hope that new evidence, or a theoretical breakthrough, will occur that will solve the problem. Indeed, I am sure that this is the position of a great many moral philosophers. However, pro forma acceptance of objectivism in moral theory is not as plausible as in scientific theory. That our theoretical understanding will converge on the truth about the world is much more plausible than the hypothesis that our theoretical understanding of right and wrong moral judgements will converge on the truth about how ideally we should interact with each other in society. Why should there be just one way of doing this well? If we all thought it was God's will and we all believed in the same God, then we might think that we were pre-ordained to live together harmoniously according to His rules, as the Thomists seem to believe. But there is not much evidence that even the gods of the major religions are in agreement about how we should live together.

Furthermore, since our moral beliefs are usually thought to be about how ideally we should live, the criterion for moral truth is not in correspondence with reality. It is usually thought to be about what forms of social interactions are ultimately rationally acceptable to us. That is, moral truths are thought to be moral propositions that would be acceptable in the long run to any ideally rational human observer of moral situations, whose access to such situations was unrestricted. But there is no good reason to think that such observers would agree among themselves. Some might prefer a Rawlsian theory of justice. Others might, as I do, prefer Sen's (2009) analysis. Or, is it imagined that the ideal observers could somehow take in the total situation existing in a given society, compare it with what would have existed in that society if its social structure and social principles had been different, and then judge which of the two societies, the real or the imagined, would be better from a humanistic point of view? I think the question only has to be asked to reveal the nonsense of this moral objectivist position.

A further difficulty concerns moral motivation. As philosophers, we naturally seek the truth. But the truth alone is never enough to motivate action unless it is, or implies, a truth about which kinds of courses of actions are to be preferred over all others. There are two possibilities here. Either, we need a theory of which courses of action are intrinsically preferable. Or we need one concerning which courses of action have the least harmful costs

164　*Social Humanism*

or the overall best consequences. The first of these two possibilities points directly to Kantianism. For Kant's solution was to develop a theory that he thought would lead to choices that are essentially rational, and so strictly in accordance with human nature. The other alternative would presumably lead to some form of consequentialism, such as act- or rule-utilitarianism, because such a theory would have to be about deciding which courses of action have the least harmful costs or the best overall consequences. Therefore, any objective theory of morality would require a theory of the ultimate social good for humankind and a theory of the least harmful or best ways of achieving it. For Kant, the ultimate good for humankind is for everyone to be true to their rational natures and to act accordingly. For consequentialists, it is to pursue 'the greatest happiness for the greatest number', as most utilitarians would say. Or, perhaps it is just to act rationally in one's dealings with others to promote one's own long-term best interests, which is the position of rational egoism.

6.6　MORAL PERCEPTION THEORY

The Socratic method in moral philosophy pre-supposes that mature adults all have a natural ability to tell the difference between morally right and wrong acts. And it is evidently an ability that we have acquired with practice and encouragement, and can eventually improve upon. It must, therefore, be assumed to be something like the ability to read or recognise things. The precise nature of this ability is a matter of dispute among objectivist moral theorists. Some think that it is like the ability to see and recognise objects. Others think of it as an intuitive grasp, e.g. of the sort involved in learning the difference between grammatical and ungrammatical speech, or that involved in the recognition of harmony or disharmony. Either way, it yields judgements of right or wrong (or good or bad), and it enables Socratic dialogue on moral issues to take place. Those who see these primitive judgements as perceptual ones are called 'moral sense theorists', but for reasons that will become clear, I prefer to call them 'moral perception theorists'. Those who think that moral properties are *sui generis*, or non-natural, are usually called 'moral intuitionists'.

In the eighteenth century it was commonly supposed that our ability to distinguish between morally right and wrong acts was an acquired perceptual ability. On reaching the age of maturity, it was thought that everyone capable of sound judgement could make this distinction more or less directly by perception. This theory was the distinguished predecessor of intuitionism, i.e. the view was that moral concepts are *sui generis* (in a class of their own) and are known directly by our maturing ability to apprehend moral goodness and corruptness. Intuitionism, which we shall discuss shortly, was the most commonly held meta-ethical theory in the first half of the twentieth century, and it has shown some signs of revival again lately.

Theory and Method 165

The directness of our knowledge of moral principles was held by intuitionists to give them the required epistemic authority.

If our moral knowledge is based on a moral sense, as Thomas Reid and his predecessors supposed, then some basic moral perceptions must be possible. Consequently, it must be possible for individuals to judge particular cases and for moral philosophers to make plausible generalisations concerning such judgements and test them against experience. But the idea of our having a moral sense is metaphysically dubious. For, our moral sense, if we have one, cannot be like any of our other senses. It is not unreasonable to suppose that we alone in the animal kingdom are capable of moral understanding. But this fact does not validate Reid's 'moral sense' theory. For, moral perception, if it is possible, is clearly not like colour perception, shape perception, or any other kind of sense perception. There is no visible, audible, or other sensible quality that is perceived, which occasions the judgement. If you could remove all of the sensible qualities of the things involved in any event, then that event could not be observed. So, a moral property cannot be a quality that exists on a par with other directly observable qualities. Nor would it help if it were. For a sensually perceived quality would appear not to have the required normative force.

It can, however, reasonably be argued that moral rightness is a quality something like that of intelligent design, which, in a sense, is perceivable but is not a quality of sense. That is, moral rightness could be a sort of intellectual quality. If it were such a quality, then its perceptibility would have to depend on our having prior knowledge of the general profiles of right and wrong actions. The perceptibility of intelligent design, for example, presupposes that the perceiver has prior knowledge of the differences between a designed object, which is artfully built, and one that is naturally shaped and structured. So, if moral qualities are directly perceivable as intellectual qualities, it must be because we have some prior knowledge of the relevant moral distinctions to fall back on. But if this is so, then the intellectual perception of these qualities could not be used to create this distinction in the first place.

Nevertheless, the view that moral qualities are intellectual qualities is probably correct. For, all of the conditions required for their perception are satisfied. Moreover, our capacities to make moral judgements can be refined in just the ways that we should expect them to be, if it were true, as Davis (2006) argues. While there is considerable disagreement about how severe the punishments should be for those who disobey the laws or social customs of their society, there is a great deal of agreement that the punishment should be appropriate to the crime. It is also true that people in all societies are disposed to impose heavier penalties for crimes that they perceive to be (a) more obnoxious, or (b) more threatening to the social order and less for those that are perceived to be more benign or relatively unthreatening. So, all of the ingredients must be there in any society for an intellectual discussion about crime and punishment, and hence about

166 *Social Humanism*

what is just, and what is good or bad, or very good or very bad, in this area. Therefore, it is hardly surprising that our moral sensitivities should be capable of being improved by Socratic methods, e.g. by having someone point out similarities or differences between cases, about some of which we have already well-formed opinions.

Moreover, since crime and punishment must have existed since the very early days of human existence, such discussions must be almost as old as human language itself. And, since the point of punishing anyone in a primitive society must have been to preserve the social order or establish a new one, just as it is now, it is likely that the concepts required to maintain or create such a function were as much needed then as they are now. We should therefore expect laws and customs to have emerged very early in human history, and for early humans to have developed appropriate concepts of justice, injustice, and cruelty to evaluate its administration. We should also expect our stone-age ancestors to have developed capacities to recognise instances of just or unjust treatment and be able to recognise and empathise with those who are suffering greatly at the hands of others. Indeed, since human beings have always lived in tribes, we should expect them to have learned to think tribally from the very beginning, i.e. to think of what is good or bad for them, not as individuals, but as a tribe. For, clearly, if the members of a tribe can learn to live together and cooperate well with each other in their hunting, gathering, nurturing, building, teaching, and fighting activities, then they have a better chance of survival as a group than they would have if they acted as individuals in a Hobbesian state of nature and just looked after themselves and their immediate families.

It is not really surprising, therefore, that we should all (or nearly all) be able to recognise at once instances of bad, unsociable, cruel, or unjust behaviour. Nor is it surprising that we should be able to recognise instances of good, helpful, kind, or generous behaviour immediately at sight and not have to think about why it is good. So, it seems to me, that all of the ingredients are there for us to be able to perceive moral qualities directly, as intellectual qualities, just as we can perceive artefacts and distinguish them from naturally occurring objects. Moreover, all of the ingredients are obviously there for a Socratic dialogue to take place in search of a better, more comprehensive, and more coherent moral system.

However, there is no good reason to think that Socratic dialogue can solve all of our moral problems. For, many of them involve trade-offs between goods and harms, where those who benefit are different people from those who are harmed. Consider the issue of saving the Murray-Darling basin from destruction. If water is taken from the system at the current rate for irrigation purposes, there is good reason to believe that the system will collapse, poison the downstream lakes and wetlands, and destroy the Coorong at the mouth of the Murray. Of course, the long-term prediction that South-eastern Australia will become considerably drier due to global warming could be wrong. But the case for returning more water to the river system does not depend only on this. Water rights have been over-allocated in the past, and cuts to water allocations would be necessary anyway. The Murray-Darling basin is the food-bowl of Australia, and its collapse would be an ecological and economic disaster of considerable proportions. Reasonably, therefore, there should be a significant reduction of water usage from the system. But such a reduction would inevitably hurt the farmers and their families and workers, and hence the shopkeepers and other suppliers of goods and services to the people in the country towns of this area. However, if nothing is done, the result would very likely be bad, not only to the present population of Australia, but for future generations. So, we have a classic social moral problem on our hands. What is to be done? Clearly, the problem cannot be solved by Socratic dialogue. But nor can it just be left unsolved. So, what will ultimately be required is a political settlement, which strikes the best balance that is achievable.

6.7 MORAL INTUITIONISM

Several positions go by the name of 'intuitionism'. One of these is G. E. Moore's (1903) theory that moral goodness is a non-natural quality. It was supposed to be an objective quality that things or actions could have independently of human actions or appraisals, but which could, nevertheless, somehow be intuited. Moore insisted that goodness was not to be identified with any natural property, such as happiness or the capacity to make people happy. For, if it were, he argued, the proposition that happiness, or that making people happy, is a good thing would be an empty tautology. According to Moore, the rightness or wrongness of an action must depend on whether or not it has the quality of goodness and the degree to which it has it. So, the question arises: What is this fact, and how is our knowledge of it possible? Moore's answer was that we must have a faculty of knowledge that is adapted to the discovery of such facts. But, metaphysically, this theory is even less plausible than Reid's moral sense theory. Against Reid, I argued that if moral goodness is an objective quality that is not known directly by sense experience, it could only be one that is known indirectly by interpreting experience, i.e. it must be an intellectual quality. But any perception of an intellectual quality requires prior knowledge of the ways in which things that have this quality differ from those that lack it. Therefore, moral intuition, as understood by Moore, could not possibly be the source of our knowledge of right and wrong.

Another, much more popular form of intuitionism is the theory that we have an innate capacity to recognise the truth of true moral propositions once we fully understand them. They are, perhaps, like the axioms of geometry were once supposed to be, viz. self-evident and hence *a priori*. They are also, presumably, synthetic. For, if they were analytic they would be useless as guides to life. But the source of our knowledge of such

168 *Social Humanism*

principles needs to be explained. There are no plausible transcendental deductions of them; so they could not be known as Kant imagined the synthetic *a priori* truths of mathematics are knowable. Presumably, then, they must be capable of being known intuitively by reflection on actual or described cases. But how is this possible? Among the philosophers who believed that moral truths are knowable by intuition were H. A. Prichard, W. D. Ross, and C. D. Broad. All three accepted the idea that the moral concepts, as a group, are *sui generis*, and that moral truths all have a non-natural quality that we are able to perceive, which enables us to know them. They were also agreed that moral truths cannot be deduced from or defined in terms of non-moral ones.

Groups of concepts that are *sui generis* in this sense, i.e. inter-definable but not definable externally, are not unknown in other areas. They are said to belong to 'intensional circles'. The modalities of necessity, possibility, and contingency, for example, all seem to belong to a *sui generis* group that constitutes such a circle. The question then is whether the moral concepts of obligations, rights, responsibilities, and right and wrong acts also belong to an intensional circle. If so, then the moral intuitionists may have a good case. To solve their problem with the modalities, the logicians invented logically possible worlds. Given an ontology of infinitely many logically possible worlds, they were able to specify formally adequate truth conditions for modal statements and to develop logical systems that embraced them. And, if the moral concepts do indeed constitute an intensional circle, then perhaps it would be possible to develop a formal ontology of morally possible worlds that would enable moral theorists to think and reason about them just as if they were factually true or false propositions about the actual world.

But there is no need to pursue this speculation. The moral concepts of individuals in consensual societies, i.e. societies that have effective social contracts, are in fact definable with reference to what they believe to be the best possible ways of protecting or improving them. There is no need, therefore, to develop the logical apparatus that would be needed for dealing with a moral intensional circle, similar to that of the modalities.

6.8 CULTURAL RELATIVISM IN MORAL THEORY

If moral objectivism is untenable, as I have argued, then the most plausible moral stance is a qualified form of cultural relativism. An unqualified cultural relativism in morality would make all cross-cultural moral critique irrelevant and declarations of human rights and obligations irrelevant, too. But the view that is advocated here is respectful of all genuine human rights and obligations. I do not believe that any society has a right to abrogate any of these moral principles. With very few exceptions, the principles included in the various national and international declarations of rights are simply

Theory and Method   169

expressions of humanism. Mostly, they are humanistic, because they are founded more or less directly on the assumption that we should ideally all have an equal and unconditional concern for the wellbeing and dignity of everyone. Moreover, they should be culturally neutral, since they should not offend any country, civilization, or society that shares this unconditional attitude.

However, the humanistic principle that founds the doctrine of human rights is not a complete system of morality. It is incomplete, because it does not resolve social moral issues, i.e. issues that involve trade-offs between goods and harms. It cannot resolve such issues, because goods and harms cannot be measured on any one morally neutral scale, and therefore the kinds of actions that would do the greatest good or the least harm overall cannot always be decided in a morally neutral way. The only way that I know of resolving such issues satisfactorily is socially or politically. Normally, decisions have to be made by governments concerning how best to make these trade-offs. Where they are successful, they may just succeed in creating social ideals, which become accepted by nearly everyone as indispensable moral principles. But these trade-offs may not be the only ones that could have been made successfully. Therefore, the social moral principles of one society need not be the same as those of every other society.

Acceptance of such a limited relativism about morality is not without costs, because it implies a limited relativism about moral dominance. Classically, morals have nearly always been thought to be universal principles that stand above the laws and social conventions of any society. This was the supposed status of the Natural Law, the doctrines of human rights, and the accepted moral principles of every society. Consequently, morals were everywhere thought to set the standards against which the laws of the land, indeed of every land, must be judged. If Sharia law is immoral in any way, given our system of morality, then it is plainly and simply wrong; it is wrong without qualification. But likewise, if our laws or customs are wrong, according to the moral code of any Muslim country, then they too are plainly and simply wrong. But if one can only be justified in accepting a limited principle of moral dominance, then this may make some difference to how such disagreements might be resolved.

I am not, of course, asserting here that cross-cultural moral disagreements are all disagreements about social moral issues, i.e. moral stands that have deep social roots in the societies in which they are accepted. Some do, some don't. Nor am I suggesting that there are no moral principles in any society that deny basic human rights. Of course there are. But I am suggesting that these are the moral principles that should be the focus of world attention. For, these are the ones that must be abolished if we are ever to establish a global social contract. We shall return to consider this issue further in Chapter 7.

170 *Social Humanism*

6.9 THE DOMINANCE PRINCIPLE

There is no denying that morals are the standards of social behaviour that we appeal to when we are either criticising the laws and social conventions of a society or judging people's characters or actions. To be justified in using morals in these ways, we must believe that the morally required principles of social behaviour are at least as good as any conventionally or legally required standards. That is, our moral principles must be able to tell us whether a society's laws or conventions are good enough and, if not, what should be done about them. They must also be able to tell us whether an individual's behaviour is as good as it should be, or if not why not, and what would be acceptable. Therefore, a moral theory must be in the business of defining the ideals and limits of acceptable social behaviour, and our moral stance must be defined by the ideals and limits that we would accept. Our morals must, in this sense, be our social behavioural ideals. Indeed, it was for this very reason that I sought to develop the theory of social idealism in the first place.

The question then is: Why should morals have this critical role? Originally, it was supposed that morals were the commands of God, and that our obedience to these commands was therefore mandatory for all of the faithful. There was, of course, the question raised by Plato in the *Euthyphro* of whether the commands are morally sound because they are God's or whether the goodness of God is revealed by the nature of His commands, as these are revealed in scripture. Most theologians nowadays would probably say the latter. So, even for theologians, the interesting question is: Why should we, independently of our theological beliefs, consider our moral principles to be the standards against which our society's laws and social conventions should be judged? There are two sorts of possible answers to this question: (a) justificatory, and (b) non-justificatory:

(a) Our moral beliefs are acceptable as the standards of social critique, because they are the most rational, best informed, or most in tune with our better human nature;

(b) Our moral beliefs are, just by definition, the ones that express our most deeply held convictions about the kinds of social behaviour that should be encouraged or forbidden. So, they are, by definition, the standards we must insist on.

The first kind of answer seeks to justify the role that morals have in social criticism by arguing that our morals are really better known than the beliefs that once informed those originally responsible for establishing the laws and social customs of our society. But this is a very hard case to make out. If you were a Kantian rational idealist, for example, then you would have to believe that your predecessors were either working on the basis of the wrong meta-theory of morals or were less rational than you are. Or,

Theory and Method 171

if you were any other kind of rational idealist, then you would have to believe that your predecessors were either misinformed about the nature of morality, less rational than you are, or not sufficiently well informed about or sensitive to the effects of acting otherwise. The second kind of answer, in contrast, is non-justificatory. One only needs to introspect to find out whether one is sufficiently convinced of the principle being proposed to use it as a basis for social criticism.

But the two kinds of answers have different consequences. If you would answer the question in the justificatory kind of way, then you would be rationally justified in taking the law into your own hands and acting on your moral convictions. If you would answer it in the non-justificatory way, then you would not, thereby, be justified in taking the law into your own hands. You would only be justified in advocating appropriate changes to the laws or conventions of your society to the best of your ability.

The belief that morals are objectively true or false can thus give rise to what I am here calling 'the dominance principle', which is this:

> If one sincerely and reflectively believes that something is morally the right thing to do, then one always has a moral right to act on it, and insist that others should always be prepared to do the same in like circumstances.

This is the principle that is otherwise known as the right of conscience. It says that if one is sincere in one's moral beliefs, then one should always be willing to act on them, even if such actions would be illegal or contrary to social convention. The principle, which as Dworkin (1970: 291) points out is very widely accepted, derives from moral objectivism, because if one sincerely and reflectively believed that one's reasons for acting in a certain way were the most rational, best informed, or most in tune with our better nature than any that our legislators or ancestors may ever have had, then one would have compelling reasons for doing so, and no compelling reasons, other than fear of the legal or social consequences, for not doing so.

Yet, the dominance principle is a characteristic thesis of moral theory. Hector Monro (1967: 208–229) says, in effect, that moral dominance is a necessary feature of every moral position. For, it is precisely this, he says, that makes a moral attitude, conviction, or policy a moral one. If Monro is right about this, then for a moral objectivist, moral dominance must be the view that there is a true, and hence universal, moral theory, which, if known, would necessarily over-ride all contrary principles and invalidate any social or legal precepts that are inconsistent with it. In short, the dominance principle must be the view that:

> The true moral principles must be more strongly binding on the socially responsible members of any society than any merely social principles, and all sound legal or social principles must be consistent with them.

172 Social Humanism

We must, therefore, be very careful about making unqualified moral judgements if we are moral objectivists.

This view is one that is shared by moral philosophers of many persuasions, including intuitionists, realists, naturalists, Kantians, and utilitarians. Nevertheless, the dominance principle cannot be accepted as generally valid. It holds of moral beliefs that are indeed definitively established. It holds, perhaps, for the kinds of moral principles that do not depend on the social structure of one's society, i.e. for the kinds of principles that flow from the natural human virtues of compassion, honesty, or fairness, for which a sound case could be made, even in a Hobbesian state of nature. Plausibly, one has an unqualified moral right to act honestly, fairly, or compassionately if that is all that one is doing, and one is not acting for the benefit of some people at the expense of others. But, one does not have an unqualified moral right to act on one's moral beliefs just because one is sincerely and reflectively committed to them. The man who pushes a fat man off a bridge to stop a runaway trolley from killing workers further down the line is a criminal and should be treated as such. The Bali bombers, who killed hundreds of innocent people in a nightclub to rid the world of their evil influence, were murderers, too.

The dominance principle could perhaps be defended by arguing that social moral principles are not really moral laws. But this is highly counterintuitive. Consider bribery. Bribery is not obviously contrary to humanistic principles, since the participants in the bribe both normally benefit from it. It could be argued that bribery always gives the participants an advantage in their struggle to achieve good lives for themselves, and hence is always contrary to humanism. But so do many other fees for services. Hence, taking or offering a bribe is not obviously like treating someone with disrespect or with more respect than they deserve. It looks much the same as any other transaction. But it is not, of course. For, people can be bribed only if they have moral or social responsibilities. If they have no responsibilities, then they cannot be bribed. This is not to say that people without many responsibilities cannot be enticed or seduced. Bribery is necessarily a betrayal of trust. The practice is therefore one that inevitably has a corrupting effect on the institutions of society, and, in the interests of social justice, it is necessary to discourage this practice. But in another society, or at another time, the social response might have been to punish only those who accepted bribes or otherwise behaved irresponsibly in their public duties. Consequently, if the injunction against offering bribes has the status of a moral law in our society, which I believe it does, then it has this status because of a social decision that has been made in the past, not because bribery is inhumane. The same is true of the legal injunctions against many other criminal offences. They are nearly all crimes that the vast majority of people in our own society would wish to see kept permanently on the statute books, whatever other changes might occur. Therefore, they are, with few exceptions, all social transgressions that we should consider to be

Theory and Method 173

immoral. But the kind of immorality involved in some such transgressions need not be inhumane. Consider tax avoidance. It is not inhumane to avoid paying taxes. But it is immoral to do so, because the social services of our society could not be funded if too many people were to engage in it. The dominance principle cannot, therefore, be well defended by arguing that social moral principles are not genuine moral laws.

Yet, the dominance principle does seem well suited to explaining the place of morals in social and legal theory. When people say what they think their moral obligations, rights, or responsibilities are, as opposed to their legal ones, they normally go on to argue how the law should be reformed to accommodate their moral precepts. But no one ever argues that, if their moral obligations are not consistent with the legal ones, then their moral ones should be changed. Moral precepts thus seem to have a kind of dominance over laws or social conventions when they are in conflict. Laws and social conventions cannot impugn moral principles in the way that moral principles can impugn laws or social conventions.

How, then, is the practice of moral criticism to be justified? There are two basic ways of doing this. One is to suppose that there is an objectively true moral system, which includes some of our deeply entrenched social principles, which describes the best possible set of social attitudes for any human society. But, as we have seen, this seems highly improbable. The other is to argue that the morals we believe in are simply the principles that we should eventually wish to see built into the socio-legal system of our own society. That is, it is, effectively, just to accept social idealism as our meta-theory. Both hypotheses account well for the practice of moral criticism of our own socio-legal system. But social idealism provides the only plausible account.

Within any given society, it makes no difference to the practice of moral criticism whether the principle of moral dominance is rejected or not. Those social idealists who have strong moral convictions can continue to have them and argue for them before any audience that will listen. They can continue to demonstrate in their favour, take a stand against the law, and, if necessary, be punished for doing so. Their justification for doing such things will still be, as at present, that they are earnestly seeking to create a better world. In this respect, their motivations will differ from those of the moral objectivists. For, the moral objectivists are committed to arguing that the principles they wish to defend are ones that should be held to be valid in any society. They could not, therefore, be tolerant of a society that chose to deal with issues of corruption differently or had a different attitude to property ownership than ours. The moral objectivist must believe that there is a best of all socially possible societies that would be regulated by the one universally true morality. A social idealist need not believe this. That there is a socially possible development of our own society that would be better than this one is not hard to believe. But that there is a best of all socially possible societies seems *a priori* highly implausible.

Part IV
Global Humanism

Introduction to Global Humanism

Global humanism is the global form of social humanism. It is the kind of social world that every social humanist should aim for. It is a form of cosmopolitanism, but it need not be the same as the universalistic form that is usually promoted. A globally humanistic world would have to be one in which all states were humanistic, but it might also be one in which some states differed from others in their social moral principles.

Consistently with the approach to moral and political issues taken in this book, my overall approach to global issues must be to consider the possibility of constructing a global social contract. This strategy is clearly preferable to that of trying to achieve a world government, which I am sure most people in most societies would vehemently oppose. Even the construction of a global social contract is undoubtedly a very ambitious project. To achieve it, the basic task must be to develop a moral framework that is able to accommodate all of the different cultural perspectives that are morally tolerable. It would be necessary to do this, because, unless we have such an accommodation, we cannot hope to have lasting peace in the world. But, given the arguments of this book, a global social contract would not require that there should be complete universal agreement about moral issues. It would require only an agreement on moral principles that are either (a) directly grounded in our primitive human virtues, or (b) plausibly social moral principles derived from the need for a humanistic moral accord that the world is able to accept. In the final analysis, it may not matter much if some of these social moral principles cannot command universal assent. Initially, we need only get to the point where cultural differences in moral outlooks can sensibly be discussed and evaluated. What would be needed ultimately is something like the Universal Declaration of Human Rights. But this doctrine focuses on just one issue—the duties of the state to the individual. But, what is clearly needed is a charter that sets out a complete system of rights, obligations, and responsibilities for all of the different kinds of social agents, including governments, industrial corporations, media conglomerates, religious organisations, and so on—to each other and to the people they serve or otherwise affect. Cultural differences in the acceptability of some of these social moral principles are bound to remain,

178   *Social Humanism*

e.g. where there are arguable trade-offs between goods and harms that may not ultimately be resolvable. But these differences can always be attended to and discussed further, and, in the end, it may not matter much if they are not finally resolvable. The point is to get to the point where they can be seriously and reasonably discussed.

7 A Global Social Contract

7.1 THE PROBLEMS

Technically, the world has become much smaller, and the pace of change is must greater than it was, say, a century ago. Firstly, the revolutions in communications and transport have changed our horizons, so that events that used to be very remote are now seen to be relevant to what is happening here and now in our own part of the world. Therefore, we do not live apart from the rest of the world as we used to, and increasingly we have come to see ourselves as belonging to an integrated global network of trade and commerce. Secondly, our population growth and ever-increasing demands for energy and basic resources have dramatically changed our relationships to the natural environment. Whereas we were once able to assume that the world's resources were effectively infinite, we must now assume that they are not, and that at least some of them are in urgent need of conservation. Thirdly, the world has become economically and commercially connected in a way that it has never been before. Its economy has become dominated by global corporations, which are largely free to exploit the world's resources as they see fit. Until recently, it could reasonably be assumed that the principal social agents affecting the lives of people around the world were all national governments. But this is no longer the case. Some of the large corporations are now much more powerful economically, and hence socially, than many small countries.

As a result of these changes, there are at least three sets of problems that need global solutions. The first is most evident in the Middle East, where conflicts and national ambitions have led to crises that have clear moral dimensions. Among other things, it is a Jewish struggle to establish a homeland, an Arab struggle against the injustice of this imposition on them, an American fight to establish control of some of the world's greatest remaining oil resources, a desperate fight to rid the Middle East of the American invaders and their allies, and a struggle between Sunni and Shiite Muslims for control of the region and of one of the world's major religions. These conflicts have brought morality to the fore in ways that wars in the past seldom have, because they raise serious questions about everyone's moral standards. They raise questions about religiously-based systems of morality, and about how

180 *Social Humanism*

peace is possible in a world in which people's values seem to be so violently at odds with one another. Peace in the region cannot simply be imposed by military might. People whose moral perspectives on life would appear to be so different will have to find ways of living together with each other that are broadly compatible with their ancient cultures.

The second group of problems is due to new technology, which has created a highly integrated world of international trade, travel, communications, and technical interdependence. This integrated world is essentially a commercial one, ruled by multinational corporations with enormous social and economic power. Some of these corporations are thought to be too big to be allowed to fail. The damage to world prosperity that they would do by failing would cause a great deal of suffering, deprivation, degradation, and death. The global financial crisis (GFC) of 2008 highlights the need for greater social control in this area. But, currently, no single country has the power, the will, or the responsibility to regulate effectively the multinational corporations that caused this disaster or, for that matter, any other corporations that might cause similar disasters in the future. The nation states that one would expect to take charge and lead the way are weak and divided. Indeed, nation states are losing power almost everywhere. Their borders define the geographical limits of their state power, as they always did. But they have lost much of the substance of their power. They now have less, and increasingly less, control over their own resources, the cultural influences to which their people are subject, imports and exports, immigration and emigration, manufacturing and agriculture, and the social and moral outlooks of the members of their own societies. They will have to fight back if they are not to lose the battle against the global forces of corporatism.

The third set of problems consists of those due to human profligacy. Rapid population growth, better medical services, increased longevity, higher incomes, and increased levels of consumption of goods and services have all contributed to them. Our profligacy has already created a number of crises, such as those of atmospheric pollution, global warming, deforestation, loss of biodiversity, and a depletion of some of the world's resources (such as crude oil, fish of various kinds, and fresh water).

The global problems with which we are beset are very great and deeply interconnected. But there is no world government with the power or authority to deal with these matters, and no desire for one. No country would be likely to give up its sovereign independence to a world body, however dire the situation. On the contrary, the tendency appears to be for nations to split along ethnic or cultural lines, wherever such a split is geographically possible and the forces of nationalism sufficiently weak. What is urgently needed, I suggest, is not a global government, but a global social contract. For, that is surely the more realistic aim.

The behaviour of multinationals must be regulated globally as part of this contract, if we are not all to be dominated by them. At present, there is very little effective regulation of corporations even at the national level. For,

A *Global Social Contract*   181

the criminal law has never been specifically adapted for this purpose, and the civil law is much too weak. As Joel Bakan (2004: 79) explains:

> The corporation's unique structure is largely to blame for the fact that illegalities are endemic in the corporate world. By design, the corporate form generally protects the human beings who own and run corporations from legal liability, leaving the corporation, a 'person' with a psychopathic contempt for legal constraints, the main target of criminal prosecution. Shareholders cannot be held liable for the crimes committed by corporations because of limited liability, the sole purpose of which is to shield them from legal responsibility for corporations' actions. Directors are traditionally protected by the fact that they have no direct involvement with decisions that may lead to a corporation's committing a crime. Executives are protected by the law's unwillingness to find them liable for their companies' illegal actions unless they can be proven to have been 'directing minds' behind those actions. Such proof is difficult if not impossible to produce in most cases, because corporate decisions normally result from numerous and diffuse individuals' inputs, and because courts tend to attribute conduct to the corporate 'person' rather than to the actual people who run the corporations.

The civil law is too weak to control a corporation, because (a) a civil court can only fine, or award damages against a corporation—sometimes long after the event, when most of those affected are already dead, or too old to benefit; and (b) there is no government prosecutor for civil offences. The fines, amounts of compensation, and other costs that may be awarded against a corporation are rarely, if ever, borne by its managers or directors. Normally, they are fully indemnified by the corporations they direct. Its shareholders may sometimes suffer short-term losses on their investments. But normally the costs of these proceedings are borne by the corporation's customers (through increased prices) or the nation's taxpayers (due to loss of company tax revenue or the need for increases in unemployment benefits). The aim of the required adaptation of the criminal law must be to prevent corporate crimes, not just to compensate the victims of such crimes. The directors of corporations cannot be allowed to escape personal responsibility for criminal acts of tax evasion, fraud, negligence, recklessness, environmental damage, and so on. It is not enough just to compensate those who suffer as a consequence of them. The directors of criminal corporations must be sent to jail or at least be made personally liable for the payment of crippling fines.

7.2   THE NATURE OF SUCH A CONTRACT

A global social contract would have to be much more limited in scope than a national one. It would essentially consist of a number of international

182 *Social Humanism*

agreements about what to do about the world's increasingly urgent problems. But such agreements would have no force unless they were enacted by
national governments everywhere and backed up by appropriate national
sanctions. To achieve their purposes, these agreements would all have to
be accepted by the world's major powers and appropriate bodies set up to
monitor and verify that these agreements are being kept. There would also
have to be a range of common institutions, nascent forms of which, such
as the World Bank, the World Trade Organisation, and the International
Court of Justice, already exist. But what are urgently needed, beyond these
basics, are: (a) global agreements on how peoples of different cultures and
religions can live together in harmony, (b) a globally agreed set of con-
trols on international corporations and financial institutions and associated
ways of enforcing them, and (c) a series of global agreements on atmospheric pollution, management of scarce resources, protection of biodiversity, and so on. This book may have something useful to say about some of
these issues.

The first issue is currently being pursued by the Parliament of the World's
Religions. Their program, known as the 'Global Ethical Project', is aimed
at getting the world's religions to agree to a common moral position. But
the methodology being pursued by this body is fundamentally flawed. For,
it credits the world's major religions with authority in the field of morality—which it manifestly does not deserve—and it effectively allows them
to maintain their own archaic moral standards. But this is an unprincipled
approach to the problem. In its place, what is needed is a political program
aimed at achieving a secular reconciliation of the moral outlooks of the
world's different cultures. The 'Secular Moral Project' (SMP), as I shall call
it, does not aim at a common moral code, since that is probably not achievable, at least not in a way that would satisfy most people. Nor does it give
priority to the moral codes of the major religions. What is needed, I suggest, is a compromise that includes a core of widely accepted, and generally
acceptable, social and humanistic rights. This core, it will be argued, must
include all human rights, properly so called, and a set of political rights
and responsibilities that are together necessary for achieving the aims of
the SMP. These moral and political rights and responsibilities are ones that
must be insisted on globally for the purposes of the SMP. The rights other
than these moral and political ones that various states may wish to preserve
for their own societies must at least be capable of being respected and toler-
ated universally.

On the issue of corporate regulation, socially idealistic theories, such
as social humanism, are, to my knowledge, the only moral theories that
are directly concerned with the behaviour of collective agents, such as
corporations. It provides a metaphysical foundation for all moral systems
concerned with collective agents, including business corporations and limited liability companies, and it legitimises strong morally driven legislation to control these collectives in the interests of the general public. Social

A *Global Social Contract*   183

idealists are necessarily committed to the view that these organisations are directly responsible for their own free choices and actions, just as individuals are. Hence, they are committed to the view that business corporations and limited liability companies, not only have social responsibilities, but also moral ones. The people of the world must therefore be prepared to say what the global and local moral responsibilities of corporations and limited liability companies are and take whatever actions are required to ensure that they honour them. Moreover, they must be prepared to back their insistence on moral regulation with all necessary force. For, that is how we legislate to control individuals to prevent them from behaving irresponsibly. Therefore, there needs to be a full inquiry to determine what the social and moral responsibilities of business corporations and limited liability companies are, and national and international legislation must be drawn up to ensure that their managers and directors take whatever steps are necessary to see that these responsibilities are fully honoured, or else face fines or terms of imprisonment themselves. The practice that allows them to hide behind the corporate personality, and thus avoid all personal responsibility, must be ended.

7.3   A STRATEGY FOR MORAL RECONCILIATION

In the first six chapters of this book, I have been carefully preparing the ground for making a principled distinction between two kinds of moral principles: *essentially universal moral principles*, which are necessarily binding on individuals everywhere; and *social moral principles*, which are principally aimed at constructing or maintaining a good society. Social moral principles may also be universal. But, if so, they are universal accidentally, rather than necessarily. This distinction is the key to my way of prioritising moral principles and providing guidelines for those charged with the unenviable task of constructing a global social contract to cover the field of morality. Essentially, universal moral principles must, I shall argue, be given priority over social moral ones, because it is only with respect to the latter principles that we may agree to disagree with the members of other cultures.

The moral principles that are necessarily binding on individuals everywhere are those that I began by calling 'individualistic moral principles'. They are basic principles of morality derived from the assumption that our natural humanistic values of honesty, compassion, and fairness are the essence of humanity. This is the assumption that underlies all human rights doctrines, where everyone is assumed to have such values just in virtue of being human. Given this essentialist assumption, it follows that everyone must approve of exercising these values; to deny them would be to show oneself to be less than fully human. The individualistic principles are basic also in the sense that they require no more of us than that we should always

184 *Social Humanism*

try to act according to them wherever we can. The principles in question are simple, and normally there is no question of what actions would comply with them. They are simple because, as they are defined, they do not involve any trade-offs between goods and harms.

There are two species of individualistic moral principles: (a) the sentient ones of greatest good and of least harm, and (b) the non-discriminatory ones. Those of the first kind derive simply from our natural compassionate values and are directly applicable, not only to other human beings, but to all sentient creatures. Those of the second kind derive from our senses of concern and fairness in our social interactions. These principles, and the modes of behaviour they dictate, are universally binding, because their status does not derive from social considerations. They derive simply from basic assumptions about human nature and values that have nothing to do with the structure or culture of any society. The principles of greatest good and least harm apply to all sentient creatures and involve only our understanding of, compassion for, or empathy with others and our natural wish to express these feelings. The principles of social equality and mutual respect are ones of acceptance and inclusion, which must be offered to all other members of society, whatever their race, culture, sex, or sexual preferences. These principles, like the principles of greatest good and least harm, are straightforward expressions of our human social nature, and they too are founded in basic humanistic assumptions of the kind that underpin our declarations of human rights.

The social moral principles, in contrast, have a different origin and rationale. They derive from considering what must be done to create and maintain a good society, i.e. a society in which people can live well as human beings. To live well, one needs to have adequate food and shelter, good health and companionship, sufficient resources to meet one's needs and obligations, and a social structure in which one is practically free and able to develop a satisfying kind of life for oneself. Therefore, as a society, we should aim to ensure that these things are readily obtainable, or if any are not, then we must aim to provide them. Ideally, we should like to see people flourishing. But I do not know of any way of achieving this ideal other than by personal effort. For, a flourishing life needs a bit more than the basics. It needs excitement, adventure, or a sense of achievement; it needs depth and colour, as well as a sound basis. But depth and colour cannot be provided for other people. They require people to reach out for themselves and make the best of their talents and capacities. Perhaps the best a society can do is only to make provisions for people to develop their talents and capacities to the full, recognise them, and create a society that provides for their adequate expression.

As Bradley (1876/1959: 188) once argued, these two kinds of considerations are not independent of each other: They are, as he said, 'two distinguishable aspects of the one problem'. For, if traditional practices violate basic human rights and are allowed to persist due to the privileges they bestow on those in positions of power and authority, then the natural compassionate and social values of people in such societies may be denied full expression. But you can be sure that the beneficiaries of such unequal practices will have a rationale for them, based on the greater spiritual, economic, military, or social benefits that their continued dominance will guarantee. That is, they will have a social justification for suppressing some of our basic humanistic values. While social considerations are important for human flourishing, social considerations should not be allowed to dominate over human rights except in extreme circumstances.

Historically, there may well have been circumstances that would have justified our suppression of some of our fundamental human rights. If a tribe or city state is struggling for survival against the forces of nature or a ruthless enemy that will kill or enslave the population, then individuals may not be able to afford the niceties of civil behaviour towards one another. But these circumstances must now be fast disappearing, and every society must be strongly encouraged to move quickly to embrace the humanistic principles on which our doctrines of human rights depend. Therefore, in developing a global social contract, strong preference must be given to including humanistic moral principles in this contract as our most fundamental social ideals. But the optimal moral outlook for our society cannot be discovered just by our looking inwards to discover how ideally we should behave towards others given our basic humanistic values. We also have to consider what kind of society we want to live in, what institutions are required, who should be responsible for what in maintaining or developing these institutions, and what principles of social behaviour are required to ensure that they function properly. In other words, we need a set of social moral principles to supplement our basic humanistic ones.

These two kinds of principles have existed side by side in most communities, without much, if any, recognition of their different status or roles. For, it has been almost universally assumed that moral principles are all of the one kind, and the main problems of moral philosophy have consequently been seen as being to define them and to explain why they should be binding on all morally responsible members of society. But although some rational idealists since Kant have come much closer to solving these problems than he did, doubt must now arise whether moral principles are really all of the same kind. According to the theory that has been developed here, the assumption that moral principles are all of the same kind is false. It is true that they are all social ideals. But rules of social behaviour may be social ideals for very different reasons. They may be rules that we should insist on because our primary humanistic values demand them, or they may be favoured because they represent (to us) socially very acceptable solutions to important social problems.

The social moral principles of a society are clear for all to see. Typically, they are to be found in its systems of civil and criminal law in the various societies. The laws of theft, bribery, blackmail, privacy, breach of

186 *Social Humanism*

contract, fraud, tax evasion, bigamy, and bearing false witness, to take a few examples, are all clearly social moral principles. All of them are concerned to ensure the proper functioning of the institutions of the society in which they are enacted. Yet all of them are directly concerned with what are said, and understood by everyone, to be moral prohibitions. And these moral prohibitions do not arise from any direct conflicts with our natural human rights or obligations. They could, perhaps, be argued to be assaults on the person, or breaches of trust of various kinds. But the connections with our basic human rights or values, whatever they might be, are at best tenuous. Theft, for example, could not occur in a society without property rights, bribery could not occur in a society without office holders, tax evasion could not occur if there were no taxes, and bigamy could not occur in a society without an institution of monogamous marriage. So, plausibly, these are moral principles of a different kind from the essentially universal ones. Some of them might well be universal. But there is no necessity that they should be. For, if they are universal, it must be because the institutions they are designed to protect happen to be universal, and the means chosen to protect or promote them happen to be the same.

This distinction is important, I argue, because it provides a principled way of dealing with cultural relativity in morality—one that does not depend on bowing to religious authority. It is a rational and defensible strategy. But to complete the case for it, it is necessary elaborate on the distinction between basic human rights and social ones, and to consider some of the important political rights that Western people have and often include in their charters of human rights and freedoms. But many of these are at best only social rights. They are not, or not obviously, founded on essentially universal moral precepts.

7.4   BASIC HUMAN RIGHTS

Basic human rights are here understood to be essentially universal moral rights, i.e. rights that people should enjoy just in virtue of being human. The class of all human beings in any given society is a sub-class of the class of all agents in that society. The members of this class are not distinguished from collective agents in having the capacity to choose freely. Nevertheless, since the freedom of choice that collective agents are able to exercise is wholly dependent on human free choice, it is reasonable to include human freedom as a distinctive human capacity. But human beings are not distinguished from other animal species in being able to enjoy life or experience pain or suffering. So the principles of greatest good and least harm are not ones that are exclusively applicable to human beings. All sensitive creatures should be treated in accordance with these principles.

As well as freedom of choice, the most distinctive capacities of human beings are their intellectual and planning abilities, their capacities to

A *Global Social Contract* 187

communicate and work with others, the pleasure they take in pleasing or helping others, their abilities to acquire skills and apply them, their inventiveness, their aesthetic appreciation, their story-telling, and their vivid imaginations.[1] This list could easily be extended, but it should be long enough already to prove that there can be no simple formula for making people's lives better. Presumably, the best that a society could possibly do for its individual members would be to offer them as wide a range of opportunities as it can to develop their distinctively human capacities as they see fit, and to use them for any socially acceptable purposes that they may wish to pursue.

Ideally a government of any state exists to promote the good of its citizens. Therefore, an ideal government must aim to develop a wide range of educational and training opportunities and make them as widely available as it can. Since morals are social ideals, this must be a social responsibility of governments everywhere. A state may, because of poverty, be unable to fulfil this obligation satisfactorily, in which case it may have to limit the range of options it makes available or restrict entry to programs, presumably to those most able to profit from them. But there can be no doubt that it is a moral right of the citizens of any country that they be given such educational opportunities as it can reasonably afford. The other side of the coin is this: Citizens have a moral right to apply for, and be considered without prejudice for admission to, any educational, training, or work experience programs for which they may be eligible, and to put their natural and acquired talents to work to suit their own purposes, provided that these purposes are socially acceptable. We may assert, therefore, that no one should arbitrarily hinder, or make it impossible, for anyone to take advantage of educational, training, or work opportunities, or arbitrarily make it easier for some to do so at the expense of others. It would be a violation of human rights, therefore, to discriminate against anyone in their quest to develop or use their human potential on the basis of any considerations that are irrelevant to their abilities. Hence, racism, sexism, and all other forms of arbitrary discrimination in these areas are contrary to human rights.

Basic human rights derive from the principle of respect for persons and are insisted on to promote human wellbeing without regard to any specific groups. In general, the promotion of human wellbeing involves the removal of obstacles to its achievement in ways that do not favour any natively determined groups, i.e. groups into which one is born, except where they are designed to redress previous imbalances. That is, the policy must be either socially indiscriminate between natively determined groups or intended to achieve greater social equality between such groups. So, most human rights are concerned with the removal or reduction of impediments to social equality. Social equality is a concept that was explored in Chapter 2. It requires a realistic base that leaves no one trapped in poverty, and it is the kind of equality that should be sustained by 'social contractual egalitarianism'.

188 *Social Humanism*

Basic human freedoms are ones that people should have just by virtue of being human. There are two species of such freedoms—'freedoms to' and 'freedoms from'—which are written into most human rights charters, although not all of them are derivable just from universal principles. Many of the freedoms that people have in advanced countries should be regarded as social freedoms, rather than basic human ones. In the case of freedoms to, the state has a prima facie moral obligation to ensure that people are not arbitrarily prevented from exercising them. The freedom to vote in elections, stand for office, and travel within or out of the country and return to it if one is outside are standard examples of freedoms to that are written into charters of human rights. But these are all social rights; if anyone were to insist that they are moral rights, on the ground that they would wish to retain them permanently, then they would be social moral rights, but still not basically humanistic ones. In the case of freedoms from, the state has a prima facie moral obligation to ensure that people are not arbitrarily denied them and a moral responsibility to take corrective action if they are. Freedoms from fear, want, and persecution, for example, are good examples of basic human freedoms of these kinds. All of these freedoms are founded directly on the humanistic principle of respect for persons, and all represent basic human rights.

In his State of the Union address in January 1944, President Franklin D. Roosevelt announced approval of a Second Bill of Rights, which appears not to have had much publicity.[2] Here is the text:

> In our day these economic truths have become accepted as self-evident. We have accepted, so to speak, a second Bill of Rights under which a new basis of security and prosperity can be established for all regardless of station, race, or creed.
>
> Among these are:
>
> 1. The right to a useful and remunerative job in the industries or shops or farms or mines of the Nation;
> 2. The right to earn enough to provide adequate food and clothing and recreation;
> 3. The right of every farmer to raise and sell his products at a return which will give him and his family a decent living;
> 4. The right of every businessman, large and small, to trade in an atmosphere of freedom from unfair competition and domination by monopolies at home or abroad;
> 5. The right of every family to a decent home;
> 6. The right to adequate medical care and the opportunity to achieve and enjoy good health;
> 7. The right to adequate protection from the economic fears of old age, sickness, accident, and unemployment;
> 8. The right to a good education.[3]

A Global Social Contract   189

All of these rights spell security. And after this war is won we must be prepared to move forward, in the implementation of these rights, to new goals of human happiness and well-being.

America's own rightful place in the world depends in large part upon how fully these and similar rights have been carried into practice for our citizens. For unless there is security here at home there cannot be lasting peace in the world.

Of these rights, Numbers 5 to 8 are obviously universal, and Number 2 would be, too, if it were simplified to:

2* The right to adequate food, clothing and recreation'.

For, all of these principles (2* and 5–8) are grounded directly in our human needs and our compassionate prima facie duties.[4] The principles 1 and 3–4 are social moral principles. They were clearly compelling humanistic demands in a society of the kind that President Roosevelt was addressing in 1944, but they are not appropriate for a modern charter.

Children's rights are a sub-class of human rights. There are at least three freedoms from that apply to children and, indeed to all those who are unable to fend for themselves—the rights to freedom from molestation, neglect, and abandonment. Given our compassionate values and humanistic principles, the state clearly has a prima facie moral right to prevent such violations of children's rights from occurring and a prima facie moral responsibility to take appropriate action to protect or provide for children whose rights are violated. Children also have basic humanistic rights to nurture and protection, and the state has the moral obligation to ensure that these rights are adequately provided, if not by their parents or guardians then in whatever way is deemed to be appropriate in the circumstances. The same applies to other people who, for whatever reason, are unable to care for themselves.

Other principles that are sometimes written into charters of human rights are really not human rights at all as they are understood here. They are social rights. Property rights, for example, are not human rights, although many may wish to insist on them globally, because of their fundamental role in capitalist economies. In societies in which property rights are regarded as sacrosanct, viz. as rights that should not be seriously curtailed by wealth taxes, death duties, or any other means, the social principles that underlie these rights are, at best, social moral principles, not humanistic ones. And, as such, they are not necessarily universal, as humanistic moral principles are. Democratic rights present other examples. The right to vote, freedom of speech and freedom of expression, the right to know, the right to seek election, and so on are all democratic rights. But all of them are what we

190   *Social Humanism*

must here identify as social or political rights or, in our society, as social moral rights. For, while they are rights that we should all probably wish to insist on, they are not ones that are grounded just in human nature. Hence, they are not necessarily universal.

Finally, there are the rights associated with life and death. According to humanistic principles, everyone has a right, not only to live with dignity, but also to die with dignity, with full consideration being given to the fact that dying is normally a painful and distressing process for the patient, as well as for others who may be concerned. According to the principle of least harm, which is one of our most fundamental moral principles, dying with dignity often requires medical assistance. So, medical assistance in death is a prima facie human right, and it should always be provided unless there are overwhelming reasons why not. According to some moral theorists, the right to life applies to people whose lives are at an end in a very different way. For, this right is seen as implying that death should not be hastened, even at the express wish of the dying person. But this is simply to confuse rights with obligations. As human beings, we all have a right to life. Therefore, the state has a prima facie obligation to protect our lives as human beings. But we do not have a duty to go on living as long as possible. Therefore, if one is dying and there is no hope of recovery, and one earnestly wishes to die to end all the pain and suffering, then one should be allowed to do so. Moreover, if a dying person has decided that she wishes to die for such reasons, then, by the principle of least harm, she should morally be made the offer of medical assistance to die. She should not be made to starve herself to death. Death with dignity is a fundamental, and so non-negotiable, human right.

But what about the right to life itself? Does it apply to human foetuses? Biologically, a human foetus is essentially human, since it has a human genome. But a foetus is not yet a human social agent. Human rights, as I have defined them, are the moral rights of human social agents. So, the question of whether a foetus has human rights must depend on whether one thinks that the conception of a human social agent includes human foetuses. I think not. Foetuses are not plausibly parties to a social contract. A living human foetus is a potential bearer of human rights, perhaps. But it does not already have this status. Indeed, it could reasonably be argued that newly born infants are not human social agents, so that if foetuses do not have a right to life, then new-borns do not either. But that is not a position that I wish to defend. Even if newly born infants are not human social agents, I would consider it reasonable to extend the right to life to them *pro forma*. It is reasonable, because I think most people would not want to live in a society in which the practice of infanticide was readily condoned. Personally, I would condone it in some circumstances. I would rather a grossly deformed child be killed painlessly at birth, or soon after, than condemned to suffer an excruciating life. Nevertheless, I regard the right to life as fundamental to any good social contract, and would therefore consider that

A *Global Social Contract* 191

the right to life could well be extended to newly born infants as a matter of social policy.

By the same arguments, I would condemn the practice of performing late abortions—except in extreme circumstances, e.g. to save the life of the mother. The mother's life must always take precedence over the unborn child's, because she has an undoubted right to life as a human social agent. But an unborn child has no such right. Again, such a right might well be extended to it *pro forma*. It certainly has a right to be treated humanely, as any sentient creature has. Moreover, as a humanist, I think that every effort should be made to save the life of an unborn child, because it would be contrary to the spirit of humanism not to do so. However, my objection to the practice of late abortion is straightforwardly a moral one, not one that is based on the supposed rights of the foetus. Early abortions (say in the first month of pregnancy) are not objectionable on any rational grounds. They are not inhumane, they do not undermine the right to life as it is normally understood, and they do not negate the rights of unborn children. The difficult cases all occur in the middle months of pregnancy. In my view, there is no objective way of drawing a line between when abortions should be permissible and when they should not, and the only satisfactory way of resolving the issue is to do so democratically. The question of whether abortions are allowable, and if so when or in what circumstances, is not question of human rights, it is a social moral one.

The right to life is normally qualified to allow for armed self-defence, police protection, and military action in defence of one's country, since all of these things are almost universally considered to be compatible with the human right to life. It is almost universally accepted that a person has a right to self-defence or to be defended by others from violent assault. By the principle of least harm, the assailant should be harmed as little as possible in the process of defence. But, in some cases, killing an assailant may be the only viable option. Hence, the right to life is normally qualified to allow for armed self-defence. But this is just to scratch the surface of what is really a very complicated and difficult issue. At present there is no resolution in sight to the social moral problems that are posed by violence, and no such resolution is likely until people can learn to live with each other, respecting each other's different moral points of view.

Ideally, nearly everyone would like to live in a non-violent world. But, equally, *we as a people*, i.e. the vast majority of the national, ethnic, religious, or other natively determined groups with which we most strongly identify, would like to live in a world in which *we* are able to flourish. And that puts *us*, many would argue, at a gross disadvantage, because *we* are the victims of terrible injustices, of things that should never have happened, but did. Some people demand compensation, which they are unlikely ever to receive. Others demand liberation, which they are unlikely to achieve without a fight. Some, with a history of persecution, are deeply afraid and are currently engaged in acts of gross and aggressive self-defence. And

192 *Social Humanism*

then there are the terrorists, who are killing and maiming those they see as belonging to the enemies of their nation, religion, or culture, confident that God is on their side and that they are doing His will. None of these conflicts is likely to be resolved quickly, and the global aim of world peace is unlikely to be achieved until there exists a global social contract that reconciles the moral positions of people of all natively determined groups to each other. It is the aim of the secular moral project to achieve this end.

From what has been said in this section, it is clear that our perceptions of human rights are a function of our metaphysics of human nature. So, the metaphysics is important. If there are deep-seated differences of opinion about the metaphysics, there must also, to this extent, be deep-seated differences of opinion about human rights, e.g. concerning abortion. Therefore, it is important that people of all natively determined groups should focus on the metaphysical issues and attempt to resolve their differences. But this can only take us so far. For, where differences of conception of humanity are involved, there is no reasonable prospect of settling the relevant issues in the foreseeable future, and the status of the right to life, which is one of the affected rights, must remain unresolved. Consequently, secularists, and those who side with them, must be prepared to accept that religious groups may have fundamentally different views from theirs and conversely. Consequently, all should regard these rights as social moral rights, i.e. as widely accepted rights that have evolved to become embedded in the nation's social contract, not ones that are politically non-negotiable.

7.5   POLITICAL RIGHTS

Political rights are a species of social rights. Like all other social rights, they are embedded in the social contract of the society. They include all those rights that are concerned with the political processes of the society they characterise. Of particular interest here are the political rights enjoyed by people in democratic societies, the so-called democratic rights. These are not basic human rights, as I have defined them, but some of them are listed in charters of human rights and freedoms as if they were. Nevertheless, they are vitally important to the SMP. For, the SMP requires the community's acceptance of all basic human rights, and hence the elimination of all inhumane, discriminatory, or uncaring practices. And this requires the establishment of some form of democracy. For the elimination of these practices requires that all societies should at least become socially contractually egalitarian. And a necessary condition for this is that every natively determined group must have an adequate say in the determination of public policy—a say that is roughly in proportion to their numbers in the community.

So the first task of the SMP must be to develop democracies everywhere. That is, there must be a concerted campaign to establish governments in

A *Global Social Contract*   193

every society that are genuinely responsive to the wishes of their people, including especially those belonging to natively determined groups or minorities. There is, however, considerable room for differences in the forms of democracy that may be established. The English-speaking countries mostly have adversarial democracies, which are brash, crude, and sometimes very divisive. Some of the European countries, such as the Netherlands, have collaborative governments elected by proportional representation. And China is exploring alternative forms of democracy that are, supposedly, more in keeping with its ancient Confucian tradition, but, perhaps more plausibly, are for the purpose of perpetuating the existing power structure (Leonard, 2008). Nevertheless, different forms of democracy are likely to be better suited culturally to some societies than to others, and it would be a great mistake on the part of the dominant Western powers if they were to try to impose their own socially divisive kind of democracy on other countries, where the effects of rival political parties struggling for power, in the kinds of way they often do in Australia, Great Britain and the US, could well be catastrophic. For, what is important is not that they should be like the West, but that they should become socially contractually more egalitarian.

To begin this process, it is necessary that the democracies of the world should begin by putting their own houses in order. For, the democratic rights of these countries are not well observed, and the societies are not as socially contractually egalitarian as they should be. The democratic rights include the right to vote for the candidate of one's choice, the right to freedom of speech, and the right to stand for election. These rights are now mostly well established in Western democracies. But the right to freedom of speech has been seriously abused and needs to be revised. The classic defence of the right to freedom of speech was that of John Stuart Mill. In Mill's time, when freedom of speech was exercised by writing books and articles or talking in parliament or on a soapbox, it was reasonable to argue, as Mill did then, that truth would eventually triumph, and that our knowledge of it would be all the stronger for the fact that it had been contested. But at the present time, serious political argument has largely been replaced by spin, and news has been replaced by sensationalist reporting, or opinion masquerading as comment on 'the news', including sound grabs from politicians and a few carefully selected visual images. Powerful corporations, with vested interests in the outcomes of political debates, can, and often do, spend large amounts of money to spread confusion and hide the truth when it is better for them that the truth should not be known. The case is well illustrated by the tobacco industry, which spent a great deal of money funding research designed to spread the message that the case against tobacco was not yet proven. More recently, the coal and oil industries have invested very heavily in research to cast doubt on the growing consensus among climatologists about the causes of global warming. Their aim is to spread confusion about this issue by funding research that could

194   *Social Humanism*

be interpreted as showing that the case is still open to question. So far, they have been remarkably successful.

In the end, the truth about the causes of lung cancer became known, and the truth about the causes of global warming will also become known in due course. But freedom of speech cannot, and will not in future be able to, take any credit for making these findings known. It is more true to say that the discoveries were made known to the public despite the best efforts of the tobacco industry to prevent them from doing so. And the same sort of thing will be true about the causes of global warming. The coal and oil industries are doing everything they can to prevent the truth from becoming known, not because they are afraid of what the research may reveal, but because they know what it has already revealed, and their aim is to prevent the general public from knowing what they know. For, once the truth is accepted, they know that their industries will soon cease to be the main suppliers of energy in the industrialised world and will be reduced to supplying coal and oil to much more limited markets. So, freedom of speech is not working, as it was meant to work, in the interest of promoting knowledge of the truth. Increasingly, it is being used as a means of obscuring the truth, when the truth is threatening to powerful vested interests.

Mill's argument is therefore unconvincing. A modern democracy must place a very high value on ordinary people being truthfully and properly informed about their own society and about significant events occurring in the world. Given that many people in most modern democracies now rely heavily on newspapers and television for their information about important social issues, the question must arise whether the press and other media are doing what freedom of speech was originally supposed to do. Do they now truthfully inform people about important issues and achieve what freedom of speech was originally supposed to guarantee? Are the media providing their readers or viewers with a balanced view of what it is important for them to know about? Or do they just keep feeding the losing side of a technical debate with opportunities, just in order to keep the debate alive? The worry is this: Truth and balance in reporting are not the primary concerns of the commercial media. Their primary concerns are to sell newspapers and increase ratings. But if the truth is unpopular, dull, or uninteresting, it may not be in their interests to tell it. Like the metaphysicians of Tlön in Jorge Borges's famous essay,[5] the editors must be more interested in what is astounding than in what is true.

Professionally, journalists are not committed to reporting the truth about issues of substance. For, that probably involves making a judgement that they are not technically equipped to make. They are committed only to reporting what they call 'both sides of the debate' about such issues, which is a very different thing. It is very different for three reasons: (a) because a debate is not a search for truth, but a contest between competing sides; (b) because the aim of debate is not to arrive at truth, but to win an argument; and (c) because the issue may be a scientific one, about which there may be

A *Global Social Contract*   195

many unsettled questions, but no ongoing debate. Debate is for lawyers and politicians who are concerned with winning arguments, not for scientists who are seeking the truth. Consequently, most scientists are normally willing to concede points if they are sound. But politicians and lawyers almost never are. They are in the game to win the argument, not to arrive at the truth. And journalists, by and large, do not seem to understand this. They listen to scientists, hear all of their cautious qualifications, and conclude that the scientific case must be a weak one. The culture clash between the arts and sciences has never been starker than it has been over the causes of global warming.

The case against Mill's famous argument for freedom of speech is not, and is not intended to be, a case for abolishing it. On the contrary, freedom of speech is one of the social freedoms that is absolutely essential for the SMP to achieve its objectives. Without it, it would be virtually impossible for oppressed groups of people to make their objections known or get their governments to respond to their reasonable demands. The case against this classical argument is really just an argument directed at the blinkered attitudes of journalists, editors, and politicians in adversarial democracies. It is an argument to the effect that the focus of journalists on debate, and of politicians on the struggle for political power, is harmful to the process of adapting social policy to changing circumstances. They are attitudes that are more likely to obscure than reveal the nature of the challenges that these changes pose, especially if there are powerful vested interests intent on obscuring them. It is beyond the scope of this book to suggest a remedy for this defect. But Western democracies should be aware of the dangers that their adversarial systems would pose to rapidly developing economies, where major changes of infrastructure based on good science must be made just in order to satisfy the basic needs of their people. The West must be willing to encourage the development of new kinds of democratic institutions—ones that are not as destructive of rational planning as adversarial democracies undoubtedly are.

Other political freedoms that are essential to the SMP include liberty, freedom of movement and association, freedom of thought, religion, and belief, freedom of cultural and religious expression, freedom of peaceful assembly, freedom to vote for the electoral candidate of one's choice, freedom to participate in free elections, freedom to stand for elective office, and freedom from any coercion other than the minimum required to achieve a socially acceptable degree of compliance with the law. Of these, liberty, freedom of movement and association, and freedom of thought, religion, and belief are all arguably basic human rights, since they stem directly from the humanistic principle of respect for persons. The others are freedoms to which we have social rights, and plausibly also moral rights, which the SMP would seek to have included as social rights in the social contracts of all societies. There is little that is controversial in Western democracies about any of these freedoms, and most, if not all of them, are included in

196   *Social Humanism*

the charters of human rights that they have approved. But they are not yet universally recognised or approved, and much work has yet to be done to make them more universally acceptable. This is one of the primary tasks of the SMP.

7.6   CORPORATE REGULATION

The issue of corporate regulation is one to which social humanism may be able to make a significant contribution. For, it is a theory of morality that should motivate governments to either: (a) change the structure of corporations with a view towards making their boards of directors more socially responsible, or (b) adapt the criminal law to control the social behaviour of corporations. Concerning the first of these two options, we may wish to adopt some system of corporate democracy. For example, we could elect boards of directors of corporations to their respective positions, just as we elect members of parliament. Or, we could abolish or restrict limited liability in order to put real pressure on shareholders to consider the trustworthiness of the various candidates for office to uphold a socially approved charter of honesty and fair-dealing. This latter alternative would be my preferred option.

The possibility of amending the criminal law to deal adequately with corporate crime, which I was initially inclined to favour, faces many difficulties. Firstly, it requires that we should give up the idea that corporations are really individuals of a special kind. They are not individuals; they are organisations that are effectively controlled by executive board members. So there is no problem there. Secondly, it demands that the board members should be held collectively morally responsible for the gross behaviour of their corporations. This means that governments would have to amend legislation to recognise collective moral responsibility and be willing to charge the members of boards of directors with collective crimes, viz. the kinds of crimes that corporations themselves are currently being charged with. Again, I have no problem with this. Thirdly, it means that governments would have to legislate to recognise the legitimacy of collective legal sanctions in cases where the collectives are held to be morally responsible for corporate criminal behaviour. They might, for example, consider the possibility of corporate beheading as a legal sanction. That is, in the event of a court finding a board of directors guilty of a serious crime (of a kind that would need to be defined), the judge might order that all of the members of the board of directors who were actively members of the board at the time of the offence be summarily dismissed without compensation, and an interim board appointed to carry on the business of the corporation until a new board can be appointed at a special general meeting.

But the main difficulty with collective moral responsibility, and the reason I would oppose using the criminal law directly to bring down findings against the collective, is that it reverses the required direction of proof. For, it cannot be assumed that all members of a collective are equally responsible. Therefore, any collective punishment is likely to be unjust to some members of a collective and less than it should be for others. If, for example, a collective is found to be morally responsible for an action, which is really what is involved when a finding of guilty on a criminal charge is brought down on a corporate person, the members of the collective (in this case the board) must be assumed to be guilty, too, unless they can prove otherwise. It would be sufficient, I suppose, if one could show that one was not a member of the board at the relevant time, if the minutes of the relevant meetings showed that the member voted against the proposal, that he or she had spoken out against the proposal but was absent for the relevant votes, if the issue was not discussed and was passed by the board as an un-starred item, if the member was new to the board and unfamiliar with the issues, and so on. Therefore, there is a real problem with collective punishment, and it is no wonder that governments generally steer away from using the criminal law in this way. But, given that there is such a problem, it follows that it is fundamentally wrong to allow narrowly elected bodies, such as corporate boards, to make decisions that crucially affect the lives or wellbeing of the vast majority of people who have not been involved in their election, unless they are tightly bound by a corporate code of behaviour detailing the responsibilities of directors that every member or every executive board is legally sworn to uphold.

Currently, governments appear to be very reluctant to use the criminal law as an instrument for corporate control and even more reluctant to charge directors with criminal activity. They are reluctant to use the criminal law, because, as Joel Bakan (2004) points out, as the law stands, it is almost impossible to obtain a conviction of any individual for the commission of a corporate crime. If the crime is too blatant to be ignored, the government will charge the corporate 'person' with the offence, and, if the corporation is convicted, the court will fine the corporation. No other kind of sentence seems ever to be considered. Normally, governments use a Corporations or a Companies Act to regulate corporations. And, usually, the only penalties attached to failure to comply with regulations are again fines. But fines, whether for criminal offences or breaches of regulations, are normally ineffective for controlling behaviour. They are generally regarded as the costs of doing business—costs that can be passed on to customers or deducted from dividends or even from taxation returns if the fines are paid by outside insurers. Consequently, corporate crimes are rarely punished in the sorts of ways that other criminal offences are.

Business people are in business to make money for themselves or their shareholders, and the more they can cut corners, reduce costs, and persuade people to buy their products, whether they are any good or not, the better it is for them. Consequently, they are strongly motivated to act unethically, e.g. to lie about their products or conceal their faults. No one

198 *Social Humanism*

who was involved in the packaged mortgage scams that produced the GFC has yet, to my knowledge, been charged with any criminal offences. Nor has any financial corporation been charged with criminal behaviour. Presumably, the reason is that they can hardly pay money to these institutions to get them out of their financial difficulties while fining them for criminal offences. Yet, to the untutored eye of a layman, these are precisely the kinds of activities that should be prosecuted as criminal offences.

Perhaps the financial institutions involved in these scams broke no laws. They are legally persons, so it would seem that they could in principle be prosecuted under the criminal law. But, perhaps there are no criminal laws that the corporate persons have violated. In that case, I say, criminal laws to deal with such greedy, reckless, socially destructive, and grossly irresponsible behaviour urgently need to be created. To this, it could be replied that corporations cannot be punished as criminals. True. But their directors could be if they were sworn to appropriate codes of behaviour. I suggest, therefore, that every member of every board of directors of a corporation, or management team of a limited liability company, be required to sign an appropriate legally binding code of corporate or company behaviour as part of their oath of office.[6] For, given such an oath of office, the directors and managers of companies would at least know what their legal responsibilities were to their shareholders, workers, customers, the environment, and the government.

Such a move may not be enough to make businesses into good corporate citizens. But it is useless just to appeal to the moral consciences of managers or directors and expect them to do the right thing. When the treasurer of the Australian government urged the banks, which had had a bumper year in 2010, to keep their interest rate rises down to the increase in the lending rate set by the Reserve Bank, only one of the four major banks in Australia complied with this urgent request. One of them, the Commonwealth Bank, almost doubled the rate rise, thus increasing very considerably the mortgage repayments on home loans that ordinary people will have to pay. To be effective in regulating behaviour, moral laws usually have to be enforced if they make demands contrary to normal practice. Therefore, if your habit of mind is to think only of the bottom line in your business operations, then behaving as a socially responsible code of behaviour for your kind of business would require is likely to be something that you would try hard to avoid.

However, the scale of the problem of corporate greed is so great that something drastic has to be done about it. It is not unusual for corporations to offer bribes, spend the hard-earned retirement funds of employees, or cut their costs by neglecting safety measures, thus increasing the risks that people take with their lives. Nor is it unusual for them to cause considerable environmental damage and do nothing to repair it. But, most seriously, corporations have repeatedly failed to warn people of the dangers involved in consuming their products, or in mining the raw materials that they require to make them, and then compounded theirs crimes by actively participating in campaigns to suppress information about these dangers.[7] Yet often they are able to do all of these things with impunity, because they can so easily hide behind the corporate personality. The ordinary individual shareholders of corporations, who may, theoretically, have the power to control the executives, are usually widely dispersed and unable to attend annual general meetings. But even when such meetings are well attended and anger is high at the behaviour of the corporation, they are mostly powerless to control it, often because the controlling interests are in the hands of institutional or executive shareholders, whose votes in support of the executive can usually be relied on. Normally, the shareholders cannot even impose reasonable limits on the salaries or bonuses that the executives grant to themselves, because they are the ones who ultimately determine the rules they work by, and there is no clearly defined moral framework within which they are required by law to operate.

But it is not just corporate greed or corruption that we have to be concerned about. It is global corporate control and influence. If corporations cannot be controlled socially, then they are essentially out of control. Yet, as Bakan (2004) has argued convincingly, they are increasingly the primary forces in the world determining the directions of social development. We are, therefore, moving rapidly towards becoming a global 'corporatocracy', if I may coin an ugly word, in which we ordinary global citizens will have very little say about what happens, where it does, or how or under what conditions we may be employed.

Currently, the social control of corporations tends to be regarded as a civil matter. Nation states cannot effectively regulate multinational corporations, and they make very little attempt to do so. Mostly, it is left to individuals, or to individuals joining together in class actions, to sue for damages, where a corporation is thought to have been negligent or criminally reckless, and people have demonstrably suffered as a result. But, if there are no such suits, the government normally takes no action, and antisocial behaviour by corporations may consequently go unpunished. Or, if a corporation is forced to pay damages, it does not serve to enforce any principles of corporate behaviour that other corporations would be well advised to heed—unless it is just that they should all be careful not to inflict grievous injury on people, if these people are wealthy enough to pursue a class action, and likely to live long enough to become aware of the causes of their injury.

The problem is that the civil law is simply not designed to deal with criminal offences. It is really just an instrument for enforcing contracts or seeking compensation for damages or injuries. It is not an instrument for law enforcement designed or intended to prevent criminal activity. It acts after the harm has been done, but it is not designed to prevent the harm from being done in the first place. To control the actions of social agents, whether they are individuals or collectives, it is necessary to lay down the

200 *Social Humanism*

basic principles to which they must adhere and determine in advance what kinds or levels of punishment would be appropriate in the event of a felony being committed. If social humanists are correct in saying that collectives are morally responsible agents in exactly the way that normal adults are, then the criminal law must be applied to them or at least adapted to allow it to be applied to them. The directors of multinational corporations must not be permitted to hide behind the corporate personalities of their organisations and thus avoid prosecution for criminal offences for which they are collectively responsible.

7.7 IMPLEMENTATION

To deal adequately with the problem of regulating global corporations, there would need to be an international agreement on what basic principles of corporate behaviour multinational corporations should always be bound by, and what sanctions, or kinds of sanctions, would apply in the event of non-compliance. Appropriate legislation would then have to be drawn up for enactment of these principles by national governments. I imagine that there should also be an administrative body established to oversee corporate affairs, and two international courts should be established: a criminal court of corporate justice established for dealing with corporate crimes, and an international court of civil jurisdiction created to deal with international contracts, civil suits for damages, and so on, e.g. where an island state might sue an oil company for damages to its fishing industry, or the people of two or three different countries who have been badly affected by a nuclear accident might sue an international power company.

If such infrastructure were established, and the required legislation enacted in sufficiently many countries around the world, then adequate principles of corporate control and regulation could be established as part of a global social contract. I am aware that this may seem hopelessly idealistic. But if we wish to maintain workable democracies around the world, we must take whatever steps are necessary to civilise the corporate world. If we do not, then we shall almost certainly end up with an uncontrollable corporatocracy, and democracy will become, as Bakan warned us, 'Democracy Ltd'.

Conclusion

Social humanism is the political theory for arguably one of the most humanly successful kinds of state that has ever existed. Whether by design or by accident, the welfare states of Scandinavia and northern Europe are all very prosperous, very productive, and robustly egalitarian. Their citizens are very healthy, highly educated, and well informed by world standards, and by all accounts they are more compassionate, more honest, and more fair in their dealings with others than the citizens of other nations. The welfare states of the United Kingdom, Australia, New Zealand, and Canada were also, in their time, highly successful, although the class system was more deeply entrenched in the 'mother' country than in the dominions, and it persisted until Britain's welfare state began to be dismantled in the 1980s. Social humanism is also the moral theory that underpins all plausible charters of human rights. All anti-discriminatory principles in these charters are justifiable by the principle of social contractual egalitarianism, which is one of the characteristic theses of social humanism. There is, I would claim, no other moral or political theory that can claim such successes on both the moral and political fronts.

Social idealism, which is the metaphysical foundation for social humanism, is also unique in many ways. It is, as far as I know, the only metaphysics of morals, besides Kant's rational idealism, that yields adequate definitions of moral obligations, rights, and responsibilities. But these are the key moral concepts of social criticism; without them, we could have no plausible theory of human rights, no theory of the moral responsibilities of collective agents (such as states, corporations, universities, etc.), and no theory of the moral responsibilities of specialists (such as doctors, airline pilots, police officers, or public servants). We might, conceivably, have an individualistic ethics, such as act-utilitarianism, which could help us decide what particular actions are morally right or wrong. But there could be no adequate deontological theory, i.e. ethics of duty, without some well-defined concepts of moral rights, obligations, and responsibilities. Moreover, social idealism would appear to be the only such theory that is (a) compatible with a scientific view of the nature of reality, and (b) geared towards the construction of a moral theory that aims to improve the quality of

202 *Social Humanism*

life for all. Kant's rational idealism fails both of these tests: It is dualistic, and it is supposedly independent of the desires and aspirations of ordinary people. The first of these failings is not in itself very significant, because (as demonstrated in Chapter 3) the flaws in Kant's basic ontology (his dualism, and his theory of the rational will) cancel one another out. But the second is untenable. There cannot be an adequate theory of morality that is independent of what human beings need to flourish.

The theory of social idealism recognises the existence of two kinds of social ideals: ideals of character and ideals of society. Consequently, there are two kinds of moral principles: individualistic ones concerned with good character development, independently of the nature of the society in which one happens to live, and social moral principles concerned with the creation or maintenance of a good society. Neither is adequate by itself for a moral theory, because such a theory needs not only to define good people, but also the social structure required for a good society, and what principles of individual, collective, or specialist behaviour would be needed to sustain it.

The individualistic moral principles, i.e. those that can, prima facie, be justified independently of the nature of one's own society, are mostly primitive and pre-societal. They are primitive in the sense that our desire to express these principles in our actions derives from our natural values of compassion, honesty, and fairness. Our compassion, at least, extends to non-human animals and is the grounding for our moral concern for them. These values are pre-societal in the sense that the parties to such actions do not need to have any knowledge of the structure of the societies in which they live to understand and appreciate their importance. The principles they lead to include (a) the sub-act-utilitarian principles of greatest good and least harm, viz. our prima facie moral responsibilities to do as much good and as little harm to others as possible; (b) the most elementary principles of social interaction, e.g. our prima facie moral duties to be honest and true to our word; and (c) the most elementary principles of fairness, indicating a willingness to share and share alike with others. I speculate that these principles are all grounded directly in human nature and should, therefore, be universal. If they were not accepted in any given culture, there would have to be some culturally specific moral reasons for this. But, as I have explained in Chapter 1, I do not believe that there could be any such reasons that have lasting significance. There might be exceptional circumstances in which it would occasionally be justifiable to act contrary to some of these elementary principles, but there could not be any good culturally specific moral reasons for doing so.

Social moral principles are not primitive in the same way as the individualistic ones of compassion, honesty, and fairness. They are social in origin and intent. The moral injunction against bribery, for example, is a social moral principle aimed at preserving the integrity of society's institutions. The injunction against adultery is a social moral principle aimed at preserving the institution of marriage. The injunction against incest is a social moral principle of ancient origin, the aims of which are no longer transparent, but may reasonably be guessed at. The injunctions against theft, plagiarism, trespassing, and so on are all moral injunctions against breaches of property rights, which in turn are social moral rights. Freedom of speech and association are moral rights that are widely endorsed throughout the world, as is freedom of religion and the freedom not to be religious. But, these social moral principles are essentially different from the individualistic ones. Firstly, they are principles formulated in response to social problems that have proven to be successful in their aims and have gained widespread acceptance. Therefore, any attempt to construct a system of morality just on character ideals has a difficult task ahead of it. In my view, it is a hopeless task and should be abandoned. We should recognise the socio-political nature of these principles and adapt our moral theory to accommodate them. This, I claim, is what social idealism is able to do. It embraces the social moral principles under the umbrella of ideals of society and the individualistic moral principles under that of ideals of character, and it embraces both as social ideals of one kind or another in the meta-theory of social idealism.

If the two kinds of social ideals are not independent of each other, neither is either reducible to the other. The ideals of society held by any individual are the regulatory principles that that person would wish to see firmly entrenched in the social contract of his or her own society. The set of these ideals may well include a number of existing laws or social conventions. It may also include a number of other principles that are not yet widely accepted, e.g. ones concerning abortion, euthanasia, gay marriage, and so on. And, clearly, these sets of ideals will vary from individual to individual. Nevertheless, in any society, there is likely to be a core set of laws or social conventions that would be very strongly endorsed by nearly everyone. This set may be taken as defining the social moral principles of the society. For different societies, different sets of social moral principles are likely to be endorsed, because different societies have different histories and traditions, and are therefore likely to make different judgements about which laws or social conventions would need to be preserved or new ones to be added. Therefore, the social moral principles of different societies are likely to be different from one another and not easily reconciled. Consequently, it cannot be assumed that social moral principles are universal, as individualistic ones plausibly are. Nor can it plausibly be supposed that social moral principles can be derived from individualistic ones, or conversely, whatever facts about a society's institutions and regulative regime may be pre-supposed.

Yet, the long-standing tradition of moral philosophy has been to assume that morality is a fixed set of necessarily true and hence universal principles of social behaviour, that it has a foundation in human nature discoverable by introspection or by Socratic dialogue, and that social moral principles are either derivable *a priori* from this foundation or else are political

204   *Social Humanism*

principles rather than moral ones. But the social moral principles to which I have referred, and many others that I could mention, function critically as moral principles, are normally internalised as such in the societies in which they are effective, and are widely discussed and believed to be moral principles. Therefore, it seems much more reasonable to reject the view that moral principles are necessarily true or universal, as the elementary individualistic moral principles plausibly are, and to accept that the morality of a society evolves to accommodate new technology and improved understanding of the effects of our social policies on human and animal wellbeing.

Social humanism is a moral and political theory based on the foundation of social idealism. If one accepts a social idealism and embraces the ideals of humanism, then it is a natural next step to embrace a social and moral philosophy that seeks to enhance the quality of human life everywhere. Social humanism is a philosophy with such a general aim. It is a social and moral theory based on the principle of equality of respect for persons, which is understood here as being equality of concern for the wellbeing and dignity of all people. It is a theory of social and moral obligation that is applicable in any nation state or other form of society that has a working social contract—and such a contract must exist in any society that is governed by consent. The form of government need not be democratic, as 'democracy' is normally understood. But it must be a form of government wherein the laws and customary ways of doing things are widely accepted and complied with. In every society with such a government, there must be a social regulatory structure that is in principle discoverable and describable by anthropologists. This structure would necessarily be recorded in the society's social contract and is the key to understanding the required meta-theory for moral philosophy.

Embedded within the social contract of a society, there must be many principles of social behaviour, and recorded decisions that have been made, about which classes of individuals or other social agents have what social rights, obligations, responsibilities, or powers. They are to be found in the laws of the land, the constitutions of the governments, the conventions of social interaction, the case laws of the civil and criminal courts, and so on. Statements of these social rights, obligations, responsibilities, and powers must all be contained in the social contract, and those individuals and organisations that are members of the relevant classes will normally be well informed about the most important of them. One's moral position may then be defined with respect to this basic structure as the system of rights, obligations, responsibilities, and powers that one would ideally like to see permanently established in the society's social contract.

The resulting definitions of moral principles are all highly subjective. Nevertheless, it should be possible, given these definitions, to determine the moral outlook of a society. Specifically, we may define the set of moral principles accepted by a given society as those social principles that would receive overwhelming assent from its members. The concept of

Conclusion 205

'overwhelming assent' is, of course, vague. Hence, the distinction between the established principles of social interaction in a society, and those whose statements are accepted as moral principles, must also be vague. But nothing much hinges on this vagueness.

Given the concept of an actual or a working social contract, it is easy enough to define a form of utilitarianism that should be applicable in most parts of the world, viz. that of social contractual utilitarianism. This form of utilitarianism is different from both act- and rule-utilitarianism. The concept of utility that is required for it should presumably be a whole-of-life and whole-of-society kind of good, such as that of a maximally satisfying the desires of all people in the relevant community for a good and fulfilling life. Such is the kind of utility that social humanists believe in, although I would extend it to include the wellbeing of other sentient creatures, in so far as this is possible consistently with the humanistic principle. There is, therefore, a close bond between social humanism and social idealism, and also between social humanism and the political aim to construct some form of welfare state. They are moral and social projects that depend on a common ideological base.

It was demonstrated in Chapter 1 that the humanistic demand for social equality is best understood as a form of social contractual egalitarianism. That is, for social equality, we require not only equality *before* the law and equality *in* law, i.e. a non-discriminatory system of law, but also equality *before and in* the social contract. The concept of a socially ideal social contract can thus be adapted to fit neatly with the requirements of a socially humanistic moral philosophy.

The required humanistic social and moral philosophy was developed in Chapters 1 and 2, where the doctrines of social contractual egalitarianism and the associated doctrine of equality of opportunity were defined and argued for. Specifically, the program of equality of opportunity that was proposed is closely related to the original one of 'equality at the starting line' advocated by Michael Savage in New Zealand in the 1930s, when he established what is widely regarded as the world's first welfare state. His idea was that all young people should be provided with the best education and training that the society can afford, so that, by the time they are ready to begin their lives as independent adults, they are able to compete for jobs and careers on a more or less equal footing with other young people. Of course, this cannot be achieved unless the society itself approaches the condition of being socially egalitarian. So it is not a cure-all. But it is the kind of equality of opportunity that is needed if we are to have much hope of flourishing as human beings.

In the course of developing this humanistic social philosophy, the concept of practical freedom was developed. The concept of practical liberty stands to that of liberty in roughly the way that disposable income stands to income. This is an important concept of liberty, which has been neglected in political philosophy. Martha Nussbaum and Amartya Sen (Nussbaum

206 *Social Humanism*

and Sen eds. 1993) and Sen (1992 and 1996) argue that people need to have certain basic capabilities if they are to escape from endemic poverty, and that those who are concerned for their welfare must take appropriate steps to ensure that they can develop these capabilities. This is true. If people have no property, no resources, and no family support, and their incomes and capacities for work are fully committed to servicing their daily needs, then they are trapped by lack of practical liberty. People are not free to choose the kind of life they want to lead if they have no practical freedom to do anything more, or other than, what they are doing already. A humanitarian must therefore try to ensure that people are not trapped in this way. As Sen has frequently stressed, people need practical and realistic opportunities that they can choose between if they are to live well.

The final chapter was concerned with the global relevance of social humanism. In this chapter, it was argued that there are at least three major issues to which these philosophies are relevant. The first is the issue of global harmony. Currently, we live in a culturally and morally divided world. And this fact is surely a danger to world peace. Social humanism is plausibly relevant to solving this problem. It is a secular theory that is essentially culturally relative, and so it is able to accommodate a wide range of different cultural traditions. But it is not so culturally relative that it is vacuous. For, the axioms of this form of secular humanism are the foundations of all sound theories of human and animal rights, and these rights, in so far as they are genuinely human or animal rights, must be demanded of all cultures. Where humanism is flexible is in the area of social moral rights, i.e. rights that derive from social solutions to social problems. These principles of social interaction have become so deeply entrenched in particular cultures that they have taken on the characteristics of moral rights. But they are not moral rights that must command universal assent. Hence, they are not necessarily human rights, although they might just happen to be universally acceptable. The reason why there could be a degree of cultural relativity is that cultures with different traditions may have solved these, or at least some very closely related, problems in different ways, and feel no less committed than we do to defending their own solutions.

The second is the issue of corporate control. Social idealism is the only metaphysics of morals that argues for the existence of collective agents in society as well as individual ones. These collective agents do not, of course, make choices independently of the individuals that run them. But then individuals do not make choices independently of the cultures and social milieus in which they grew up and were educated. It may be harder to pinpoint the effects of social causes on individuals than conversely. But they are no less real. Indeed, by any reckoning, the decisions and actions of corporations, governments, police, universities, schools, and hospitals have far greater effects on human lives and their cultural freedoms than things done by individuals. But this whole issue of individualism, and the alleged one-way

Conclusion 207

dependence of social choices on individual ones, has not been neglected here. It was the subject of a thorough investigation in Chapter 5.

Given this perspective on social agency, and the theory of agency developed in Chapters 3 and 5, it should be clear that corporate boards should be regarded as social agents, just as individuals are. However, they are much more powerful. It is therefore imperative that societies should move to control them directly. Corporations ought not to be regarded as the playthings of the directors. Boards of directors are active and powerful agents that can make or break governments, destroy natural environments, and create financial crises that can bring untold harm and misery to the world. They can also do an enormous amount of good. They can bring wealth and happiness to people living in poverty and hopelessness, and they can create the tools necessary for the kind of world in which most of us would ideally want to live. Therefore, if we are social contractual utilitarians, we must legislate to control the activities of these monster organisations and make them work for the good of humankind. We cannot let them go on thinking that their sole responsibility is to make as much money as possible for themselves and for their shareholders. To do this, I suggest (in Chapter 7) that we must use the criminal law, as well as all existing approaches, and legislate to criminalise corporate activities that are agreed to be contrary, or a grave danger, to the common wealth.

Obviously, corporations cannot be put in prison. But their directors can be, and so can auditors, accountants, or other partners in crime. And it should not be beyond the wit of legislators to dream up appropriate punishments for corporate criminal offences. Nor should it be impossible for nations to settle on a Charter of Corporate Social Responsibilities that every member of every corporate board of directors must be bound by law to uphold. I believe that criminal laws of some kind must be used to control corporate boards, since the shareholders to whom they are currently responsible are not sufficiently representative of the general public and are, in any case, normally too dispersed to exercise this responsibility effectively. Corporate agents have big social responsibilities, and there is no sufficient reason why the full force of the law should not be used to hold them to account. Similar views have been expressed by Paul Johnson (2010) in his book on the origins of the market, where he speculates on measures that might have been, but were not, taken in the nineteenth century to combat some of the dangers to the national or global economies that were then foreseen. I quote:

> Imagine that instead of being repealed in 1868, Barnard's Act, which rendered illegal the 'mischievous practice' of dealing in 'time bargains', had been rigorously enforced, and then strengthened over time. The entire business of option contracts in commodity and stock markets would have been terminated. . . .Imagine that the critique made almost two centuries ago, in 1811, of the payment by insurance companies of

208 *Social Humanism*

up-front commissions to agents who sold their products had led to the same punitive legislative response that the 1906 Prevention of Corruption Act served up to small businessmen and traders who offered secret commissions. . . . Imagine that corporations formed with limited liability for shareholders and unlimited liability for directors—an almost entirely neglected element of the 1867 Joint Stock Companies Act—had become the norm through legislative fiat. This might, at first, have led to massive flight from directorial positions, but in due course an insurance market for directors' liability would have emerged. In order to evaluate the risk of insolvency, insurers would have needed to audit rigorously each company, and through the insurance contract could have placed prudential requirements on directors far in excess of those imposed by company legislations. (Johnson, 2010: 232–233)

These are just some of the measures that might once have been, and could yet be, perhaps, taken in response to the GFC to regulate corporations. But my concerns are much wider than Johnson's. The social and moral responsibilities of these powerful organisations must be regulated more generally if we are to deal with issues like climate change. It is not enough to appeal to the moral consciences of corporate directors to do the right thing by the societies they serve. Corporate culture is, and always has been, considered to be amoral. The corporate consciences of directors therefore have to be educated, just as those of individuals have to be, by the civil and criminal law. But the civil law is a very inadequate weapon for disciplining corporate directors. Firstly, few individuals can afford to sue a corporation, and secondly, by the time a class action can be brought against a corporation, a great deal of harm may already have been done, and the real culprits may well, by then, have moved on or overseas. The criminal law would seem to be a much more appropriate instrument if our aim is to prevent criminal activity.

Notes

NOTES TO THE INTRODUCTION

1. Lord Beveridge was appointed by the Conservatives before the war to write his famous report, and John Maynard Keynes provided the economic theory that was needed to implement Beveridge's proposals.
2. Of course, there was abject poverty in the world. But it was not so obvious that this was due to the kind of crisis in capitalism that led to the Great Depression.
3. These ideals have been most clearly articulated by R. M. Titmuss (1976). The theoretical commitment to welfare in the UK in the long boom from the end of World War II to the mid-seventies was based straightforwardly on the values of social humanism—equal concern for the dignity and wellbeing of all, and the construction of social systems that are at once socially egalitarian and fully adequate. Titmuss argues that efforts should be made to avoid the creation of two streams of welfare services—one for the rich and middle class, and a second, but much inferior service, for the poor—on the ground that universalist welfare services, (perhaps with levies or higher charges for people on high incomes, if the costs of providing such services are too high), were generally to be preferred to selective ones requiring means testing, because of the intrusiveness and generally offensive nature of such testing.
4. In my case Australian, but what I have to say here should apply in almost any modern democratic society.
5. My preferred biological analogy for a society is that of a tribe. The individual members of a society, like the members of a tribe, all have their own genetic endowments and may therefore have some basic character traits that others lack.
6. I am indebted to Will Hutton (1996) for the concept of social contract employed here. It will be developed fully in Chapter 2.
7. These laws and conventions are always class specific. Therefore, as Strawson (1961) points out, the fact that we are all bound by them does not imply that all individuals are subject to the same demands.
8. Such as the right to equality of opportunity; the right of every person to a decent home; the right to adequate medical care, protection from the economic fears of old age, sickness, accident, and unemployment; and the right to a good education.
9. This qualification is necessary, because liberal humanists around the world are evidently much more concerned about restrictions on freedoms of speech than they are about homelessness, chronic poverty, unemployment, or the lack of adequate health-care provisions. Social humanism presents a much more balanced view of human rights.

210　*Notes*

NOTES TO THE PART I INTRODUCTION

1. Rights, such as those included in Franklin Delano Roosevelt's Second Bill of Rights, announced in his State of the Union Address in January 1944.
2. Peter Singer sees this as a difficulty for act-utilitarianism, and Garrett Cullity (2003) as a practical refutation of it. I agree with Cullity.

NOTES TO CHAPTER 1

1. I do not mean the Tobin tax on all spot currency conversions that was proposed by Nobel Laureate James Tobin in 1972, although this is sometimes referred to as the 'Robin Hood' tax.
2. An argument to this effect was developed in Ellis (1981, 2009: 156–159). However, these arguments were not as strong as they should have been. For, the actions A and B were not assumed, as they should have been in this context, to be independent of one another, i.e. the prior probabilities of A, B and AB were not assume to be such that $P(A) \times P(B) = P(AB)$.
3. The only constraint imposed by this condition on actions and outcomes is that the prior probability of AB + BC should be more than twice the prior probability of ABC.
4. To derive the table, one should first derive the prior probabilities of A~B, ~AB, and ~A~B from the assumptions (a). Then, given the assumptions (b), one should proceed to derive the prior probabilities of AB~C, ~ABC, A~BC, ~AB~C, A~B~C, ~A~BC, and ~A~B~C, and hence all of the conditional probabilities (c) and (d), and finally the utilities (e).
5. However, my conception of *eudaimonia* is not the same as Aristotle's. His concept of the virtues in *Nichomachean Ethics* and *Politics* (Aristotle, 1941) may have been appropriate for the burghers of a Greek city state in 300 BE, but not for the citizens of any advanced society today.

NOTES TO CHAPTER 2

1. These circumstantial constraints, and what to do about them, will be discussed under the heading of 'Equality of Opportunity' in the latter half of this chapter.
2. I suppose this puts me in the camp of the internationalists in moral philosophy (Van Hooft, 2007: 307). However, international efforts to achieve a global social contract would be greatly preferable to Van Hooft's more ambitious project of developing the required human attitudes ahead of such an agreement. If morals are social ideals, then global moral principles must ultimately depend on global agreements between societies about which social ideals they have in common, which are different but tolerable, and which are different but intolerable.
3. The position was defended by L. T. Hobhouse in his Home University Library book on liberalism, first published in 1911, which was reprinted a number of times in the 1920s and 1930s. For a historical account of social liberalism in Australia, see Sawer (2003).
4. There is in fact a formal connection between them. The measure of one's practical economic liberty is simply proportional to one's disposable income.
5. There has indeed been a good deal of resistance to any serious discussion of such a concept. H. Steiner (1983: 74), for example, argues that this concept confuses liberty with ability. 'If this is a proper conception of liberty at

Notes 211

all', he says, 'it is certainly not the one that concerns us as political philosophers. Liberty is a social relation . . . a relation between persons.' F. Hayek (1960) argues that the identification of liberty with what is here being called 'practical liberty' confuses liberty with power. Naturally, he does not argue that power is not a concern of political philosophers. But he does think that power and liberty are essentially different concepts. I agree with Steiner and Hayek that practical liberty is not an ideal of liberty, as negative and republican liberty are. But it is, nevertheless, a conception of liberty that is just as closely related to the ideal of liberty as disposable income is to income, and therefore just as important.

6. 'Social liberalism' and 'social humanism' are two very closely related positions. In my view, they are the same. But, I use the term 'social liberalism' here, and throughout the next few sections, to refer to the position that I wish primarily to develop while the various concepts of liberty are being discussed.

7. This is my term, not Raz's. Nevertheless, I think the phrase 'socially autonomous' helps to clarify Raz's position. It explains why he thinks of autonomy as a social capacity that needs to be socially provided for, rather than as a metaphysical one that we all have necessarily as human beings.

8. The importance of practical rights was recognised early in the history of liberalism. As Baron de Condorcet (1795/1955: 125) remarked, 'It would be vain to look, in those countries which we call free, for that liberty which infringes none of the natural rights of man; a liberty which not only allows man to possess these rights but allows him to exercise them.'

9. Robert Young (1989) distinguishes between the formal and the substantive requirements of the principle of equality of opportunity. The conditions (c) and (d) restate his formal requirement. The condition (b) is a background requirement, which is neither substantive nor formal. But it is, nevertheless, essential to any programme to establish equality of opportunity.

NOTES TO THE PART II INTRODUCTION

1. Hume did not believe that there was any such thing as agency.

2. The exceptions in Western philosophy are mainly the utilitarians, who do not believe in moral principles.

NOTES TO CHAPTER 3

1. I wish to acknowledge that parts of this section, and of the following one, were based on a paper of mine that is to be included in Greco and Groff (2012) and to thank the editors and the publisher for their permission to include this material here.

2. As Philip Pettit (2001) would say, the disposition to act must be 'under discursive control'.

3. The lens of rational insight would seem to be preferable to the veil of ignorance, for the purposes of constructing a moral theory for S, because I do not imagine that Rawls would be willing to sacrifice the interests of the mentally handicapped people in S by requiring them to agree rationally to the principles of social behaviour that are about to be imposed on them. Yet they are not supposed to know that they are mentally handicapped. No. The principles have to be the ones that they would agree to if they were genuinely capable of judging what is really in their self-interest.

212 Notes

4. David Gauthier (1986) is an egoistic rational idealist, and Scanlon (1998), as I understand him, is an idealistic one.
5. In Chapter 4, I develop Smith's concept of a belief and desire set, which I use here for convenience, a little further by including social attitudes (of approval or disapproval). I wish to allow that social agents can do what is right, just because they think it is right, and for no other reason. Also, I wish to allow that they can avoid doing what is wrong, not because they don't want to do it, but just because they think it is wrong. I will argue that Kant was absolutely right to make this a central plank of his metaphysics of morals.
6. I have argued at length elsewhere (Ellis, 2001, 2002a, 2002b) that there is an important distinction between analytic and metaphysical necessity. In my view, 'Water is H_2O' is not analytic, but metaphysically necessary.

NOTES TO THE PART III INTRODUCTION

1. The other question, which must also be asked when constructing a moral theory, is: What social characteristics would you expect all, or nearly all, people in your ideal society of ordinary human beings to have? This question is concerned with the ideals of character that are required for civilised societies. They are related to the ideals of society. But they are not the same. Yet they are no less important. These ideals have been described here in general terms. We require people to be compassionate, honest and fair in their dealings with others. But I have nothing much to add to the general philosophical literature on what this involves. The question of how specifically ordinary individuals should be disposed to act in civilised society has been a primary focus of moral theory for a very long time.

NOTES TO CHAPTER 4

1. Will Hutton (1996: 71–78, 257–285) made use of a similar concept to contrast the British, European, and American social systems, arguing that the Americans are at the far *laissez faire* end of the social spectrum. Anthropologists have long used much more fully articulated concepts to describe the societies they are studying. I am indebted to Hutton, however, for drawing my attention to this way of describing societies.
2. This passage was written in late 2010. Political attitudes since then have changed considerably, and as of July 2011, most Australian voters seem to be against putting a price on carbon.
3. Harman (2000: 13) distinguishes between agreements of intentions and ritual agreements. A ritual agreement can lead to an agreement of intentions only if the participants intend to abide by it.
4. However, it makes no difference to the viability of social idealism if 'moral duties to oneself' are accepted as legitimate, provided that one is also prepared to allow that people may have the corresponding social obligations to themselves.
5. It may be objected here that 'this makes morality too much like legality—for many moral circumstances there will be no such framework within which the agent is to operate', as my colleague Robert Young has said. But there is always a framework. The ordinary citizen in ordinary circumstances is a member of this class of citizens, and so has the moral responsibilities of any member of this class. If there are no specific rules that are applicable in these circumstances, then the individual will be required to obey the non-specific

Notes 213

injunction to do what he or she thinks will do the most good or the least harm, which is the default moral response.

6. It is important to understand that I am talking here only of social moral obligations or moral obligations of social origin. I am not talking generally about moral obligations.

7. This concept of moral responsibility is essentially different from that of being an agent responsible for having brought something about. The sense in which a caregiver is morally responsible for her charges is obviously very different from that in which it might be true to say that the man with the gun was morally responsible for the death of the vicar.

8. The final clause of this definition is included for the following reason: There could be a principle that nearly everyone would accept as a principle of individual moral behaviour, but reject as a social one. For example, the vast majority of Australians are compassionate and would always behave considerately and with kindness towards refugees. But Australians have long feared that one day they will be swamped by people from the overcrowded countries to Australia's north, and the fear of this happening is easily whipped up by a political party striving to hold on to or achieve power, especially when supported by ruthless media propaganda. Consequently, most Australians appear to be afraid to sanction a humane refugee policy. They are disposed, as individuals, to be kind and considerate to asylum seekers. But, collectively, they are disposed to treat them badly and to vote for the political party, whichever it may be, whose attitudes to asylum seekers are the most hostile. Psychologically, this two-faced attitude allows Australians to continue to treat individual asylum seekers with the kindness and consideration they think they deserve, while simultaneously rewarding a political party that will promise to do just the opposite, if this is what they think they have to do to stop the perception of large numbers of 'boat people' arriving. Therefore, the principle of behaving with kindness and consideration towards refugees is individually sanctioned as a moral principle in Australia, but it is not held by the Australian society as a moral principle. This kind of situation may be fairly commonplace in totalitarian societies. But, thankfully, it is fairly rare in democracies.

9. As was demonstrated in Chapter 1.

NOTES TO CHAPTER 5

1. According to S. Lukes (1973: 110), methodological individualism is the thesis that 'all attempts to explain social (or individual) phenomena are to be rejected (or, according to a current, more sophisticated version, rejected as "rock-bottom" explanations) unless they are couched wholly in terms of facts about individuals'. This is precisely the thesis that I am calling the epistemological one.

2. I am told that this is too swift. Economists allow for what they call 'psychic income'. But this move should also be open to a defender of social intervention in the market. Why not object to those critical of such intervention that it produces 'increases the psychic incomes of everyone whose social security is affected'.

3. $pV \alpha T$, where p = pressure, V = volume, T is temperature in degrees absolute.

4. The concept of an individual's ideal society was defined in Chapter 4 as the projected limit of possible improvements to the social contract of the individual's own society, according to that individual's own values and social attitudes.

214 *Notes*

NOTES TO CHAPTER 6

1. I am told that Kuhn has since revised his position on this. Scientists working within different paradigms may understand each other, even though they have different conceptual frameworks. Nevertheless, the point remains that a bona fide research worker in a given field must be committed to a particular research program and be disposed to see the problems of the area in much the same way as his or her co-workers do. Alternative points of view are therefore unlikely to be seriously entertained if the research in question seems to be progressing nicely.
2. This appears to be fairly standard practice. But I am concerned that human rights criticism is much too selective. Failure to allow freedom of speech is widely regarded as a gross violation of human rights. But failure to respect the prima facie moral obligations of governments to provide access to good education, good health services, and adequate protection from the economic fears of old age, sickness, accident, and unemployment is seldom regarded as a violation of human rights. In my view, all these things should be.
3. The tradition of moral objectivism dates back at least to the early Renaissance, when it took the form of Natural Law theory.
4. There is some dispute about the status of synderesis. The term used to describe it suggests that it was thought of as a habit of mind. But this is an issue of scholarship to which I am unable to contribute.

NOTES TO CHAPTER 7

1. There is a tradition that goes back at least as far as 1955 that freedom of choice is the only basic human right, and that all others depend upon it. 'Unless it is recognized', H. L. A. Hart (1955) says, 'that interference with another's freedom requires a moral justification the notion of right could have no place in morals; for to assert a right is to assert that there is such a justification'. But according to the main thesis of this book, a moral justification is nothing other than a good social justification, which is normally not hard to find, because there are plenty of ways of harming people other than by restricting their freedom of choice.
2. Newsreel footage of this part of his address, which was recorded after he had finished his audio address to the nation, was not given much publicity. In fact, it was buried in an archive at the University of Maryland and did not resurface until Michael Moore unearthed it for his documentary 'Capitalism, A Love Affair', screened internationally in 2009.
3. I have numbered the clauses in this document for easy reference.
4. I say 'prima facie duties', because it may well be beyond the resources of poor countries to provide everyone in need with these guarantees.
5. 'The metaphysicians of Tlön do not seek for the truth or even for verisimilitude, but rather for the astounding' (Borges, 1964: 34).
6. If one wished to strengthen this, then one could also require every such body, as a matter of routine, to submit sealed copies of the minutes of its meetings, the decisions it takes, and the members votes on these decisions, to some kind of Corporate Crimes Commission—which documents could, and could only, be opened in the presence of witnesses in the event of a criminal trial involving that corporation or company. For, with such material on file, the directors or managers of businesses that are charged with criminal offences could not so easily escape justice, and individual

members of these teams could more reasonably be expected to get their just deserts. However, for social reasons having nothing to do with the business community, I should be very reluctant to introduce such a draconian measure. For it would, almost certainly, have serious consequences for non-business organisations as well.

7. For a list of the crimes committed by General Electric from 1990 to 2001, and the billions of dollars in total fines imposed on them, see Bakan (2004: 75–79).

References

Appiah, K. A. (2006): *Cosmopolitanism: Ethics in a World of Strangers*. New York; W. W. Norton and Co.

Argy, F. (2006): *Equality of Opportunity in Australia: Myth and Reality*. Discussion Paper No. 85. Canberra; The Australia Institute.

Aristotle (1941): *Nichomachean Ethics* and *Politics*. In *The Basic Works of Aristotle*, edited by Richard Mckeon. New York; Random House.

Bakan, J. (2004): *The Corporation: The Pathological Pursuit of Profit and Power*. London; Constable.

Bentham, J. (1795/2002): 'Anarchical Fallacies' in *Rights, Representation and Reform: Nonsense upon Stilts and other writings on the French Revolution*, in P. Schofield, C. Pease-Watkin and C. Blamires eds. Oxford; Clarendon Press.

Berlin, I. (1969): 'Two Concepts of Liberty', in *Four Essays on Liberty*, edited by I Berlin. London, Oxford, New York; Oxford University Press, pp. 118–172.

Borges, G. (1964): 'Tlön, Uqbar, Orbis Tertius', in *Labyrinths: Selected Stories and Other Writings*, edited by D. A. Yates and J. E. Irby. New York; New Directions.

Bradley, F. H. (1876/1959): 'My Station and Its Duties', in *Ethical Studies*, Second Edition, 1927. Oxford; Clarendon Press, pp. 160–213.

Bunge, M. (1979): 'A Systems Concept of Society: Beyond Individualism and Holism', *Theory and Decision* 10: 13–30.

Burke, E. (1953): *Reflections on the French Revolution*. Introduction by A. J. Grieve. Everyman's Library, London; J. M. Dent, 1910.

Carruthers, P. and James, S. M. (2008): 'Evolution and the Possibility of Moral Realism', *Philosophy and Phenomenological Research* 78: 237–44.

Cavanagh, M. (2002): *Against Equal Opportunity*. Oxford; Clarendon Press.

Condorcet, Baron A.-N. de (1795/1955): *Sketch for a Historical Picture of the Progress of the Human Mind*. Translated by June Barraclough. New York; The Noonday Press.

Cullity, G. (2003): 'Asking Too Much', *The Monist* 86: 402–18.

D'Arcy, E. (1961): *Conscience and Its Right to Freedom*. New York; Sheed and Ward.

Davis, W. C. (2006): *Thomas Reid's Ethics: Moral Epistemology on Legal Foundations*. London; Continuum International Publishing Group.

Dworkin, R. (2000): *Sovereign Virtue: The Theory and Practice of Equality*. Cambridge, Mass.; Harvard University Press.

Ellis, B. D. (1981): 'Retrospective and Prospective Utilitarianism', *Nous* 15: 325–339.

Ellis, B. D. (1990): *Truth and Objectivity*. Oxford; Basil Blackwell.

Ellis, B. D. (2001): *Scientific Essentialism*. Cambridge; Cambridge University Press.

218 *References*

Ellis, B. D. (2002a): *The Philosophy of Nature: A Guide to the New Essentialism.* Chesham; Acumen Publishing.

Ellis, B. D. (2002b): 'Human Agency, Realism and the New Essentialism', in *Recent Themes in the Philosophy of Science*, edited by S. Clarke and T. D. Lyons. Dordrecht; Kluwer Academic Publishers, pp. 193–208.

Ellis, B. D. (2005): 'Physical Realism', *Ratio* 18: 371–384.

Ellis, B. D. (2009): *The Metaphysics of Scientific Realism.* Durham, UK; Acumen Publishing.

Feldman, F. (1974): 'World Utilitarianism', in *Analysis and Metaphysics*, edited by K. Lehrer. Dordrecht, Holland; Kluwer Academic Publishers, p. 1951.

Flannery, T. (2010): *Here on Earth.* Melbourne; Text Publishing Company.

Gauthier, D. (1977): 'The Social Contract as Ideology', *Philosophy and Public Affairs* 6: 130–164.

Gauthier, D. (1986): *Morals by Agreement.* Oxford; Oxford University Press.

Gauthier, D. (1991): 'Why Contractarianism?', in *Contractarianism and Rational Choice*, edited by P. Vallentyne. Cambridge; Cambridge University Press, pp. 15–30.

Greco, J. and Groff, R. eds. (2012): *Guide to Powers and Capacities in Philosophy.* New York; Routledge

Harman, G. (1977): *The Nature of Morality.* Oxford; Oxford University Press.

Harman, G. (2000): *Explaining Value and Other Essays in Moral Philosophy.* Oxford; Clarendon Press.

Harris, S. (2010): *The End of Faith.* New York; The Free Press.

Hart, H. L. A. (1955): 'Are There Any Natural Rights?', *Philosophical Review* 64: 175–191.

Hayek, F. A. (1960): *The Constitution of Liberty.* London; Routledge and Kegan Paul.

Hayek, F. A. (1976): *The Road to Serfdom.* London; Routledge and Kegan Paul.

Hobbes, T. (1651/1914): *Leviathan.* London; J. Dent and Sons, Everyman's Library No. 691.

Hobhouse, L. T. (1911): *Liberalism.* London; Oxford University Press.

Hume, D. (1777/1975): *Enquiry Concerning Human Understanding*, edited by P. H. Nidditch. Oxford; Clarendon Press.

Hutton, W. (1996): *The State We're In.* London; Vintage Books.

Jackson, F. C. (1998): *From Metaphysics to Ethics*: *A Defence of Conceptual Analysis.* Oxford; Clarendon Press.

James, S. M. (2009): 'The Caveman's Conscience: Evolution and Moral Realism', *Australasian Journal of Philosophy* 87: 215–233.

Johnson, P. (2010): *Making the Market: Victorian Origins of Corporate Capitalism.* Cambridge; Cambridge University Press.

Judt, T. (2010): *Ill Fares the Land.* London; Allen Lane.

Kant, I. (1785/1946): *Grundlegung zur Mataphysik der Sitten.* Translated by T. K. Abbott as *Fundamental Principles of the Metaphysic of Ethics* Tenth edition. London, New York, Toronto; Longmans Green.

Kuhn, T. S. (1962): *The Structure of Scientific Revolutions.* Chicago and London; University of Chicago Press.

Leonard, M. (2008): *What Does China Think?* Sydney; HarperCollins, Fourth Estate imprint.

Lukes, S. (1973): *Individualism.* Oxford; Blackwell.

Mill, J. S. (1861/1971): 'Utilitarianism', in *Utilitarianism: with Critical Essays*, edited by S. Gorovitz. Indianapolis, New York; Bobbs Merrill.

Miller, D. (2009): 'A Spoonful of Sugar Helps the Medicine Go Down: Gillian Brock on Global Justice', *Journal of Global Ethics* 5: 253–259.

Monro, D. H. (1967): *Empiricism and Ethics.* Cambridge; Cambridge University Press.

References 219

Moore, G. E. (1903): *Principia Ethica*. Cambridge; Cambridge University Press.

Nagel, T. (1986): *The View from Nowhere*. New York; Oxford University Press.

Newton, I. (1687/1964): *The Mathematical Principles of Natural Philosophy*, with Introduction by Alfred del Vecchio. New York; Citadel Press.

Nozick, R. (1974): *Anarchy, State and Utopia*. Oxford; Basil Blackwell.

Nussbaum, M. and Sen, A. eds. (1993): *The Quality of Life*. Oxford; Clarendon Press.

O'Neill, J. ed. (1973): *Modes of Individualism and Collectivism*. London; Heinemann.

Paine, T. (1791–1792/1996): *Rights of Man*. Ware, Hertfordshire; Wordsworth Classics of World Literature.

Pettit, P. (1997): *Republicanism: A Theory of Freedom and Government*. Oxford; Clarendon Press.

Pettit, P. (2001): *A Theory of Freedom: From the Psychology to the Politics of Agency*. Oxford and New York; Oxford University Press.

Pogge, T. (1992): 'Cosmopolitanism and Sovereignty', *Ethics* 103: 48–75.

Popper, K. R. (1973): Excerpt from 'The Poverty of Historicism', *Modes of Individualism and Collectivism*, edited by J. O'Neill. London; Heinemann, pp. 68–87.

Prichard, H. A. (1937/1949): 'Moral Obligation', in *Moral Obligation: Essays and Lectures*. Oxford; Clarendon Press, pp. 87–163.

Rawls, J. (1971): *A Theory of Justice*. London; Oxford University Press.

Rawls, J. (1993/1996): *Political Liberalism*. New York, Chichester; Columbia University Press.

Raz, J. (1986): *The Morality of Freedom*. Oxford; Clarendon Press.

Rousseau, J.-J. (1968/1762): *The Social Contract*. Penguin Classics Translated by M. Cranston from Rousseau's original.

Salmond, J. (1996): *Michael Joseph Savage: 'His Life and His Legacy'*. Memorial Lecture, La Trobe University.

Sawer, M. (2003): *The Ethical State? Social Liberalism in Australia*. Melbourne; Melbourne University Press.

Scanlon, T. M. (1982): 'Contractualism and Utilitarianism', in *Utilitarianism and Beyond*, edited by A. Sen and B. Williams. Cambridge; Cambridge University Press, pp. 103–128.

Scanlon, T. M. (1998): *What We Owe to Each Other*. Cambridge, Mass. and London; Belknap Press of Harvard University Press.

Scott, K. J. (1973): 'Methodological and Epistemological Individualism', in *Modes of Individualism and Collectivism*, edited by J. O'Neill. London; Heinemann, pp. 215–220.

Sen, A. (1992): *Inequality Re-examined*. New York; Russell Sage Foundation.

Sen, A. (1993): 'Capability and Well-Being', in *The Quality of Life*, edited by M. Nussbaum and A. Sen. Oxford; Clarendon Press, pp. 30–53.

Sen, A. (2000): *Development as Freedom*. New York; Random House, Anchor Books.

Sen, A. (2009): *The Idea of Justice*. London, New York; Allan Lane.

Singer, P. (1972): 'Famine, Affluence and Morality', *Philosophy and Public Affairs* 1: 229–243.

Smart, J. J. C. (1959): 'Sensations and Brain Processes', *Philosophical Review* 68: 141–156.

Smart, J. J. C. (1963): *Philosophy and Scientific Realism*. London; Routledge and Kegan Paul.

Smart, J. J. C. and Williams, B. (1973): *Utilitarianism: For and Against*. Cambridge; Cambridge University Press.

Smith, H. (1991): 'Deriving Morality from Rationality', in *Contractarianism and Rational Choice*, edited by P. Vallentyne. Cambridge; Cambridge University Press, pp. 229–253.

220 References

Smith, M. (1994): *The Moral Problem*. Oxford; Basil Blackwell.

Smith, M. (2004): *Ethics and the A Priori: Selected Essays on Moral Psychology and Meta-ethics*. Cambridge; Cambridge University Press.

Steiner, H. (1983): 'How Free? Computing Personal Liberty', in *Of Liberty*, edited by A. Philips Griffiths Cambridge; Cambridge University Press, pp. 73–89.

Strawson, P. F. (1961): 'Social Morality and Individual Ideal', *Philosophy* 36. Reprinted in *Freedom and Resentment and Other Essays*, London; Methuen, 1974, pp. 26–44.

Tännsjö, T. (1990a): 'Methodological Individualism', *Inquiry* 33: 69–80.

Tännsjö, T. (1990b): *Moral Realism*. Savage, Md; Rowman & Littlefield Publishers.

Tännsjö, T. (1998): 'Metaphysics of Morality', *Inquiry* 41: 355–359.

Thayer, H. S. (1953): *Newton's Philosophy of Nature*. New York; Hafner.

Titmuss, R. M. (1976): *Commitment to Welfare*. Second Edition, with Introduction by Brian Abel-Smith. London; Allen and Unwin.

United Nations (1948): *The Universal Declaration of Human Rights*

Van Hooft, S. (2007): 'Cosmopolitanism as Virtue', *Journal of Global Ethics* 5: 303–315.

Van Hooft, S. (2009): *Cosmopolitanism: A Philosophy for Global Ethics*. Stocksfield, U.K; Acumen Publishing.

Victorian Government (2006): *Charter of Human Rights and Responsibilities Act*.

Wong, D. (1991): 'Relativism', in *A Companion to Ethics*, edited by P. Singer. Oxford; Blackwell, pp. 442–450.

Young, R. (1989): 'Equality of Opportunity', *Pacific Philosophical Quarterly* 70: pp. 261–280.

Index

A
Abortion, 153, 191–192, 203,
agency
  animal, 72
  autonomous, 50–51
  causal realist theory of, 76–78
  collective, 5, 33
  divine, 71
  fixed, 5, 72–73, 143
  human, 6, 61, 71–73, 98, 128
    Kant's theory of, 77–80
    meta-causal theory of, 76–78
    Malebranche's theory of, 71
    Newtonian theory of, 66
    power of, 5, 77–78, 83, 141–147
    primary causal, 61, 66, 98, 119, 128
    rational, 5, 6, 61, 77–80, 83
    secondary causal, 66, 98
    variable, 72–73, 143
agents
  collective, 5, 61, 64, 76, 104, 108,
    116–117, 123, 129, 147–148,
    186, 200, 206
    corporations, x, 5, 104, 108, 124,
      129, 177, 179–183, 206–208
      charters for, 11, 125–126
      regulation of, 11, 182–183,
        196–200
    governments, ix, 5, 44, 57,
      64, 97, 105, 126, 162. 169,
      192–197, 200
    universities, 125–126
  individual, 34, 76,
    the normal class N, 123–124
    specialised (e.g. doctors, plumbers,
      MPs), 5, 105,
  morally responsible, 5, 64, 76, 84,
    119, 123, 142, 147, 148, 200
  rational, 5, 34–37, 79–80, 83–86

  social, ix, 8, 61, 108,
  social and moral obligations of,
    111–116
  social and moral powers of, 116–119
  social and moral responsibilities of,
    116–119
  social and moral rights of, 111–116
Albert the Great, 159
animals, 3, 17–18, 24, 72–76,
  capacities of, 72–76, 143–146
  compassion for, 3, 202
  moral principles applicable to,
    17–18, 24
  social, 135
  uniqueness of human, 144, 145–146
Appiah, K. A., 44
a priority
  in moral theory, x, 2, 5, 10, 64, 134,
    158, 168, 203
  synthetic, 64, 158, 168
Aquinas, St. T., 159–160
Argy, F., 49, 55
Aristotle, 5, 38, 63, 120, 210
autonomy, 16, 50, 51, 61, 74–76, 211
  condition for social responsibility, 51
  metaphysical theory of, 74–76

B
Bakan, J., 181, 197, 199–200, 215
Barnard's Act (1868), 207
belief and desire sets, 26, 77–78,
  83–86, 88, 96–98, 127,
  129–130, 141, 202
  in Smith's causal realism, 83–86, 88,
    212
Bentham, J., 32, 111
Berlin, I., 50, 74
  on positive and negative liberty, 50
Beveridge, W., 209

222 Index

Borges, G., 194, 214
Bradley, F. H., 7–8, 132, 184
  two kinds of social ideals, 7–8, 184
bribery, 182, 185–186, 202
  a social moral prohibition, 182,
    185–186, 202
Broad, C. D., 168
Bunge, M., 128
  systemism, 128

C

Calvinism, 6
capabilities, 206
capitalism, ix, 1, 2, 9, 16, 113, 209
  laissez faire, 2, 16
  metaphysical individualism in,
    97–98, 127–129
Carnot, S., 137
Carruthers, P., 90
causal powers
  fixed, 72, 143
  meta-, 73–74, 76, 143–147
  variable, 72–73, 135, 143
causation
  agency theory of (*see*: agency)
  causal realist theory of (*see*: agency)
  regularity theory of, 67, 71,
    social, 98, 129, 135–141, 150
Cavanagh, M., 47–48, 57
C_{IDEAL}, 112–113, 118
compassion, 3, 17, 21–22, 24–25, 202
  principles of, 24–25, 202
communism, ix, 9, 113,
Condorcet, Baron de, 211
conscience, x, 2, 198
  collective, 132, 208
  moral, 198, 208
  right of, 99, 157, 160, 171
  social, 15, 83,
consequentialism (*see*: utilitarianism)
containment
  principle of, 161–162
contracts (*see*: social contracts)
corporations (*see*: collective agents)
corporatocracy, 199–200
cosmopolitanism, 20, 42–44
  internationalism, 44
  stepping stones to, 20
  universalism, 25
crime and punishment, 26, 30, 119,
    165, 166, 197, 200
Cullity, G., 210
cultural relativity (*see*: moral
    principles)

D

D'Arcy, E., 160
Davis, W. C., 165
death with dignity, 190
debate, 194–195
  failings of, 194–195
decision-making, 10, 30, 38, 77, 86,
    110, 116, 117, 141, 144–151,
    197
  collective, 10, 30, 76, 86, 104, 169,
  Kant's theory of, 77
  theory of, 73–76, 150
Descartes, R., 65–66
democratic
  rights, 189, 192–193
  socialism, 2, 47, 132
democracy
  adversarial, 45–46, 193, 195
  collaborative, 45, 193
determinism, 144, 146
dominance principle, 31–32, 80, 110,
    126
  limitations of, 157, 169–173
Durkheim, E., 132
duties (*see also*: obligations)
  of care, 116
  to act ideally rationally, 63
  of directors, 124
  of honesty, 26
Dworkin, R., 171

E

Egalitarianism
  social contractual, 3–4, 17–20, 23,
    40–46, 58
    cosmopolitan implications of, 187,
      192–193,
    legal, 39–40
equality
  in and before the law (*see*:
    egalitarianism)
  in and before the social contract (*see*:
    egalitarianism)
  of concern for wellbeing and dignity,
    15, 19, 21–22, 27, 43–44, 169,
    204, 209
  of opportunity, 3–4, 18–19, 39, 45,
    47–49, 51–58
  Cavanagh's conception of, 47–48, 57
  formal and substantive require-
    ments on, 211
  real, 3–4, 18, 45, 47–49, 51–58
  Savage's conception of, 47, 54, 56,
    91, 205

Index   223

equation of state, 137
essences, 50, 70, 142, 183
ethics (*see also* moral theories)
  pure and applied, 64, 82–83, 123–124,
  professional and institutional,
    123–126
eudaimonia, 38, 210
euthanasia, 115, 190
Euthyphro argument, 170
explanation in social science, 132–141
  covering law theory of, 142
  epistemic location theory of, 133, 135
  kinds of
    historical, 138–9
    historicist, 98, 128
    holistic, 133, 136–139, 141
    individualistic, 133, 139–141
    mixed, 133, 140–141

F

Fairness principles
  of no unjustified advantage, 27
  of no unjustified disadvantage, 27
Feldman, F., 37
Flannery, T., 44
freedom (*see also*: liberty)
  of choice, 40, 50–55
  of speech, 18, 193–195, 203, 209, 214

G

Gauthier, D., 63, 106, 212
Global Ethical Project, 11, 182
global financial crisis, 125, 180
goods and harms, 17–18
  principle of greatest good, 17–18, 23,
    24–25
  principle of least harm, 17–18, 23,
    24–25
  trade-offs between, 22, 26, 30, 32,
    42, 156, 166, 169
governments, 5, 57

H

Harman, G., 92, 101, 103, 212
Harris, S., 64–65, 91
Hart, H. L. A., 111, 214
Hempel, C. G., 142
happiness (*see*: utilitarianism)
Hayek, F., 1, 50, 132, 136, 151, 211
historicism (*see*: explanation in social
    science)
Hobbes, T., 10, 106
  state of nature, 24, 106, 156, 166,
    172

Hobhouse, L. T., 48–49, 210
holism
  in thermodynamics, 137
  in macro-economics, 137–138
Holocaust, 21
honesty
  duty of, 26
human rights, (*see also*: freedom,
    liberty)
  of children, 189, 191
  Declaration of the Rights of Man,
    22
  of life, 190–192
  positive, 9, 10, 15, 22, 111
  Roosevelt's second bill of, 188–189
  theory of, 186–96
  Universal Declaration of, 21–23,
    27–28, 156–157, 177
  Victorian Charter of, 22, 27
humanism
  global, 4, 20, 25, 42, 44, 46, 160,
    169, 177–206
  liberal, 10, 15–16, 39, 41, 57
  perspective of, 17, 23, 84, 161–162
  social inclusiveness of, 161–162
  principles of
    concern for human dignity and
      wellbeing, 15, 19, 21–22,
      43–44, 169, 204, 209
    duty of honesty (*see*: honesty)
    greatest good, 17–18, 23–25, 31,
      33, 164, 184, 186, 202
    least harm, 17–18, 23–26, 31–33,
      157, 163–164, 184, 190–191,
      202
    real equality of opportunity, 3, 4,
      39, 45, 55–57
    respect for persons, 40, 58, 104,
      187–188, 195, 204
    social contractual egalitarianism,
      3, 4, 17,-18, 20, 23, 40–43, 46,
      58, 201, 205
    social contractual utilitarianism,
      3, 4, 18, 34, 38–40, 113, 122,
      150, 205, 207
  social (*see also*: liberalism, social)
    characteristic theses of, 3, 31, 40,
      99, 201
humanity
  classical essence of, 5, 63,
  social humanist essence of, 183–184
Hume, D., 5–6, 61, 64, 67–68, 70, 71,
    76, 77, 108–109, 211
  regularity theory of, 67, 71

224 *Index*

Hutton, W., 105, 107, 209, 212

I

Idealism
  rational
    Kant's original version, x, 1, 6–7,
      61, 63–64, 77–80
      consequentialist, 82
      egoistic, 81
    idealistic, 81
    neo-Kantian versions of, 80–83
    Parfit's version of, 82
    Rawls's version of , 80–81
    Scanlon's version of, 81
  social (*see also*: social idealism)
    basic theory of, 6–10, 95–100
    P. F. Strawson's theory of, 96,
      101–102, 209
ideals (*see also*: C_{IDEAL} and S_{IDEAL})
  of character, 1, 3, 7, 82–83, 202–
    203, 212
  of society, 1, 3–4, 7, 15, 26, 82–83,
    95–99, 115, 202–203, 212
imperatives
  moral, ix
  categorical and hypothetical, 78–80,
    158
individuals
  mind-sets of, 130–131, 133, 135,
    138
  normal, ix, 16, 64, 80, 82, 99, 112,
    123
  the class N of 112, 123
individualism, 127–151
  metaphysical, 97–98, 127–129, 150
    epistemological thesis of (ETI), 97,
      132–141
    methodological thesis of, 43,
      132–141, 213
    ontological thesis of, 97, 127,
      129–132
    primary agency thesis of, 61, 98,
      119, 128
  political, 9, 16, 41, 127, 130
intentions, 75–76
  agreements of, 212

J

Jackson, F. C., 64, 96
  on physical realism in moral theory,
    88–89
James, S. M., 90
Johnson, P., 207–208
Joint Stock Companies Act (1867), 208

Judt, T., v, x, 1, 2
justice
  corporate, 200, 214
  Rawls's theory of, 104, 163
  Sen's theory of, 163
  social, 43, 47, 50, 172,
    principles of, 27, 43, 48, 51, 57

K

Kant, I.
  a priorism, 64, 134, 158, 168
  categorical imperative, 78, 79, 80,
    158
  metaphysics of morals, x, 1, 6–7, 64,
    77–80, 95, 111, 119, 212
  Newtonian theory of causation, 64
  rational idealism, 1, 6–7, 61,
    63–64, 77–80, 82, 95–96, 170,
    201–202
  theory of the rational will, 63, 74,
    77, 78
Korsgaard, C., x
Kuhn, T. S., 154–155, 214

L

Laws
  civil, 8, 26, 126, 181, 185, 199–200,
    204, 208
  corporate, 11, 181, 196–200,
    207–208, 214
  criminal, 181, 196–200, 207–208,
    214
  moral (*see also*: moral principles),
    79–80
  of nature, 66–67, 144
lens of rational insight, 211
Leonard, M., 193
liability (*see also*: responsibility)
  limited, 181–183, 198, 208
  personal, 11, 181
liberalism
  forms of, 48–52
  social, 49–51
  neo-, ix, 2, 9, 48–50, 96–98,
    126–128, 134–135, 151
liberty
  ideal of, 4, 5, 15, 19, 22, 33, 48–51,
    107, 195
  negative, 19, 41
  positive, 41
    Berlin's conception of, 50
    Raz's conception of, 50–51
  practical, 4, 48, 52–58
    as capability, 48, 205–206

Index 225

cf. disposable income, 48, 205
Sen's domains of choice for, 53
objections to concept of, 210
republican theory of, 51
Lukes, S., 132, 213

M

Malebranche, N., 71
market fundamentalism, 31, 50, 127
Marx, K., 2, 4, 98, 106–107, 128, 132, 151, 155
mechanism
Cartesian, 5, 63, 65–66,
passivity in, 5, 66, 77–78
metaphysics
of morals, x, 1, 6, 61, 63, 77–91
Kantian, 6, 61, 63, 77–80
neo-Kantian, 80–82
realistic theories of, 83–91
socially idealistic theory of, (*see*: social idealism)
of scientific realism, 63, 68, 70, 77–78, 142
methodology of morals
aims of, 153–154
Socratic, x, 10–11, 98–9, 121–122, 152–155, 158–159, 163–164, 166–167
Mill, J. S., 32, 193–195
mind-body dualism, 77–78, 118–119, 202
mind-sets, 130, 131, 133, 135, 138
Monro, D. H., 171
Moore, G. E., 167
moral motivation, 110, 134, 163–164, 173
moral objectivism, 10–11, 88, 99, 126, 155, 157–160, 168, 171–173
moral principles
epistemology of, x, 10, 159, 163
as black and white laws, 23, 29,
as culturally evolving, x, 23, 29, 30, 105, 113
as culturally relative, x, 10, 30, 42, 112, 155–157, 159, 168–169, 186, 206
defined as
ideals of good character, 1, 3, 82–83, 159, 202
the limits of tolerable behaviour, 27, 82, 159
ideals social behaviour for S_{IDEAL} (*see*: social idealism)

evolution of, x, 23, 29–31, 42, 65, 82, 90–91, 99, 104–105, 113, 158, 192, 204
by case law, 23, 29–30, 108, 115, 119, 126, 204
kinds of
egalitarian, 3–4, 17–20, 23, 41–46, 58, 201, 205
essentially universal, 27, 42, 183–184, 186, 190
humanistic, 6, 21, 23, 27–29, 39, 45, 58, 99, 156–157, 161–162
individualistic, 16–17, 22–23, 24, 27, 29, 58, 96, 112–113, 121, 156, 183–184, 202–203
'Robin Hood', 30, 210
social, x, 16–17, 18, 19, 22–23, 26–27, 29–31, 39, 42, 83, 99, 113, 121, 155–157, 162, 169, 172–173, 177, 183–186, 188–189, 202–206
sub-act-utilitarian
principle of greatest good, 23–25
principle of least harm, 23–25, 182–183
moral reconciliation, 182–183
moral theories
broad reflective equilibrium, 10, 11, 83, 121–122, 152–153, 155
cultural relativity of, 157–159, 168–169, 186, 206
intuitionist, 158, 164, 168,
moral sense, 158, 164–165, 167
objectivist, 126, 155, 157–161, 171–173
rationalist (*see*: rational idealism)
realist (*see*: moral realism)
social idealist *see*: social idealism)
utilitarian (*see*: utilitarianism)

N

Nagel, T., 160
native, 28, 41, 187, 191–193
definition of, 28
natural kinds (*see*: metaphysics of scientific realism)
Natural Law, 159–160, 169
neo-liberalism (*see*: liberalism)
Newton, I., 64–67, 71, 139–140
nihilism, 155, 156
Nozick, R., 97, 107
Nussbaum, M., 205,

226 *Index*

O

Obligations (*see also*: duties)
    bearers of, 112
    social idealist theory of, 101, 104,
        106–116

P

Paine, T., 16, 22
Parfit, D., 63, 80–82
    triple theory of, 81
Parliament of the World's Religions,
    182
passivism, 78
Pettit, P., 51, 211
Pogge, T., 42–43
Popper, K., 1, 68, 136, 151
positivism, 67–69
powers
    causal, 5, 6, 61, 63–78, 82, 141–147,
        150
    formal, 8–9, 96, 117–118
    social and moral, 117–118
pragmatic contradictions, 85, 87
Prevention of Corruption Act (1906), 208
prisoners' dilemma, 37
Prichard, H. A., 110
profiles
    action 75–76, 165
        modification of, 75, 150
        monitoring of, 76
    causal power, 73–76
    qualifications and experience, 46
    social, 46, 86
properties (*see also*: causal powers)
    dispositonal, 70–72, 74, 101, 137, 144
    innate, 7, 66, 136, 167

Q

Qualities
    intellectual, 165–166
    non-natural, 164, 167, 168
    of sense, 165, 167

R

Rawls, J., 63, 80, 81, 104, 106, 160,
    163, 211
Raz, J., 50, 51, 211
rational idealism (*see*: idealism)
rational insight
    lens of, 81, 211
realism
    causal power, 5–6, 63–65, 70–74,
        76–78, 96, 141–146, 150
    dispositional, 70–71

moral
    Smith's internalist theory of,
        83–84, 87–88
        non-relativistic form of, 84, 86
        relativistic form of, 84–85
    Tännsjö's theory of, 64, 90–92,
        96, 152
    physical, 64, 88–90
    scientific, 63, 68, 70, 78, 90, 142,
        144, 146, 201
    metaphysics of, 6, 63, 88
    value, 64, 65, 90–91
Reid, T., (*see also*: moral sense theory),
    165–167
relativism (*see*: moral relativism)
responsibilities (*see*: social moral
    concepts)
responsibility
    collective, 11, 64, 76, 116–117, 119,
        147–149, 196, 200
    legal, 29,147–148, 181, 198
    personal or individual, 11, 119, 142,
        147, 181, 183, 200
    traditional concept of, 118–119
rightness (moral), 33, 84, 86–89, 121,
    134, 165, 167, 212
    internalist theories of, 84, 87–88
    Smith's definitions of, 84–88,
rightness-makers, 88
rights (*see also*: human rights)
    animal, 3, 10, 16, 22, 84, 104, 116,
        186, 204, 206
    bearers of, 112
    definitions of, 111–115, 201, 204
    moral
        to death with dignity, 190
        to liberty, 4, 5, 15, 22, 41, 49, 52,
            54, 56–57, 107, 195, 211
        to life, 97, 190–192,
    political, 22, 41, 47, 97, 113, 121,
        127, 151, 182, 186, 190,
        192–196
    practically available, 41, 55
    property, 5, 15, 22, 27, 97, 111, 186,
        189, 203,
    social
        definition of, 108, 111–115, 201, 204
Roosevelt, F. D.
    Second Bill of Rights, 188–189, 210
Ross, W. D., 168
Rousseau, J-J., 106, 107

S

Salmond, J., 47

Index 227

Savage, M.
equality at the starting line, 47, 54, 56, 205
Sawer, M., 210
Scanlon, T. M., 63, 81, 82, 212
Searle, J., 144
Secular Moral Project (SMP), 182, 192, 195–196
Sellars, W., 69
Sen, A., 53, 163, 205–206
S_{IDEAL}, 112–114, 117–118
Singer, P., 210
Smart, J. J. C., 34, 68, 69
Smith, H.
Smith, M., x, 64, 83–88, 96, 121, 158, 212
social
contracts
ideal (*see also*: C_{IDEAL}), 99, 113–114, 156, 158
real, 3, 82, 98, 105, 106–107, 113, 128, 150, 151
anthropological model of, 3, 107, 204, 212
as historical settlements, 18, 106–107
evolution of, 104–105, 113, 122, 128
global, 4, 11, 20, 42–43, 101, 125, 160–161, 177, 183, 185, 192, 200, 210
facts, 129, 134, 139, 140–142, 155
forces, 9, 98, 128, 140–141
idealism, 95–126
as a metaphysics of morals, ix, x, 1, 6, 9, 82, 88, 96, 111, 206, 212
cf. rational idealism, 61
Kantian form of, 77–80, 212
neo-Kantian forms of, 80–88
mobility, 55–56
perspectives, 101, 161–162, 177, 180
socialism, ix, 1, 2, 47, 132, 151
societies
as social organisms, 8, 23, 128, 135, 141, 147
state (nation)
minimal, 4, 22, 97, 107
welfare, ix, x, 1–4, 9–10, 16, 46–47, 95, 113, 201, 205
Steiner, H., 210–211
Strawson, P. F., 92, 96, 101–102, 209
supervenience
global ethical thesis of, 89

synderesis, 76, 159–160

T
Tännsjö, T, 64, 90–92, 96, 152
Thomism, 160–161, 163
Titmuss, R. M., 209
Tobin, J., 210
truthmakers, 88, 91

U
Universalisability (*see also*: dominance principle), 99, 156–157
utilitarianism
act-utilitarianism, 23, 33–38, 92, 121, 201, 202, 210
incoherence of, 33–38
social contractual, 3–4, 38, 40, 113, 122, 150, 205, 207
utilities
no linear scale of goods and harms, 22, 26, 30, 42, 44, 92, 156, 166, 169, 184
utopianism, 56, 107

V
Values
natural, 65, 90–91, 152, 156, 183–186, 202
humanistic, 4, 44, 65, 90–92, 156, 183–186, 189, 202
Van Hooft, S.
on cosmopolitanism, 42–43, 210
veil of ignorance (*see also*: lens of rational insight), 81, 104, 106, 160, 211
virtues, 1, 10, 17, 21–24, 29, 31, 97, 120, 153, 172, 177, 210
the prima facie duty to act virtuously, 17
Von Mises, L., 1

W
Watkins, J., 132, 136, 151
welfare states (*see*: state, welfare)
will
autonomous (*see also*: autonomy), 74–76
deliberative, 51, 211
rational
Kant's theory of, 6, 74, 77–79
Wong, D., 156

Y
Young, R., 211, 212